Building a Christian World View

Volume 1
God, Man,
and Knowledge

W. Andrew Hoffecker
Editor
Gary Scott Smith
Associate Editor

PUBLISHING
P.O. BOX 817 • PHILLIPSBURG • NEW JERSEY 08865-0817

Unless otherwise indicated, all Scripture quotations are from the Revised ⁓
Standard Version.

Printed in the United States of America

Library of Congress Cataloging-in-Publication-Data

Building a Christian world view.

  Includes bibliographies.
  Contents: v. 1. God, man, and knowledge.
  1. Theology—History. 2. Knowledge, Theory of—
History. 3. Bible—Criticism, interpretation, etc.—
History. I. Hoffecker, W. Andrew, 1941–
II. Smith, Gary Scott, 1950–
BR123.B77 1986   230'.044   86-91437
ISBN 1-59638-060-8

ISBN-13: 978-1-59638-060-8

Contents

Acknowledgments

"Acknowledgment" seems too formal and inadequate to convey my thoughts to those who have contributed to publishing this volume. Yet since Webster defines *acknowledgment* as "the owning of a benefit received, accompanied with gratitude," I would be remiss if I did not express my thanks for their help.

I acknowledge first my colleagues, past and present, at Grove City College, whose teaching and writing have made both our course in Christian world view and this book possible. Their words of encouragement gently prodded me to see the project to its completion. Their patience in enduring requests for rewriting lightened my task as editor. Original impetus for such an undertaking was given by our President, Charles S. MacKenzie, who wrote a syllabus for his class in the late 1970s. During early stages of this work John Timmerman helped shorten many a walk home to Craig Street as we discussed plans for the chapters. Even after he left our campus he helped edit some of the material. Special thanks to Gary Scott Smith for his efficient and skillful editorial assistance over the last six months. His red pencil gave a unified voice to the manuscript, and his advice on structure and details of the chapters was indispensable. Thom Notaro, editor at Presbyterian and Reformed Publishing Company, has been very helpful in the final stages of manuscript preparation by his attention to detail and suggestions for rephrasing throughout the work. I would also like to thank Valerie Vouga, who not only sat through Rel/Phil 161–162 but then typed and retyped the manuscript until I finally got it right. Lastly, heartfelt thanks to my wife, Pam, whose commitment to excellence in writing has been an inspiration. May *your* next manuscript be accepted!

My hope is that this book will contribute to the growing interest among Christians in articulating a distinctive witness to our world in the closing years of the twentieth century. May it provide a sound foundation for all who would build their lives on the Christian world view.

Thanksgiving, 1985
Grove City, Pennsylvania

Contributors

G. K. Beale, Ph.D., Associate Professor of New Testament, Gordon-Conwell Theological Seminary, South Hamilton, Massachusetts.

James Bibza, Ph.D., Assistant Professor of Religion, Grove City College, Grove City, Pennsylvania.

John D. Currid, Ph.D., Assistant Professor of Religion, Grove City College, Grove City, Pennsylvania.

W. Andrew Hoffecker, Ph.D., Professor of Religion, Grove City College, Grove City, Pennsylvania.

Charles S. MacKenzie, Ph.D., President, Grove City College, Grove City, Pennsylvania.

V. James Mannoia, Ph.D., Associate Professor of Philosophy, Westmont College, Santa Barbara, California.

Gary Scott Smith, Ph.D., Associate Professor of Sociology, Grove City College, Grove City, Pennsylvania.

Robert P. Vande Kappelle, Ph.D., Associate Professor of Religion, Washington and Jefferson College, Washington, Pennsylvania.

Preface: Perspective and Method in Building a World View

W. Andrew Hoffecker

Perspective of This Study

Faced with the myriad of facts, experiences, ideas, and feelings that make up our awareness of reality, how do we make sense out of the world in which we live? That question has occupied the minds of thinking people since the beginning of history.

Attempts to discern order among the seeming chaos of our experience reflect a yearning to understand the world and man's place in it. Not surprisingly, some have spent their entire lives searching for the meaning of life.

Today more people than ever before are spending four or more years in formal study grappling with humanity's basic questions. Confronting these issues is more than a curriculum require-ment—it is a prerequisite to consciously living out one's faith both privately and publicly. At stake is the survival of individual and social values that have given meaning and purpose to Western culture for centuries.

Underlying all that we think, say, or do are basic assumptions that form what we call a "world view." A person's world view is the collection of his presuppositions or convictions about reality, which represent his total outlook on life. Nobody is without such fundamental beliefs, and yet many people go through life unaware of their presuppositions. Operating at the unconscious level, their presuppositions remain unidentified and unexamined. The result is that people generally fail to recognize how their world views govern every dimension of their lives: *the intellectual* (what they believe is true about themselves and their place in history); *the physical* (how they treat or mistreat their bodies by eating, sleeping, and exercising); *the social* (how they interact with friends and enemies, the rich and the poor, the strong and the weak); *the economic* (why they work and how they spend their wages); and *the moral* (what ethical guidelines and obligations direct their thinking about justice and issues such as abortion and euthanasia).

Because a person's world view holds so much influence over him, examining it can prove difficult. Much as one cannot literally step outside himself in order to look himself in the eye or hear himself speak, critically analyzing notions that have become intimately a part of us can push us to the limits of our objectivity. And yet, the process by which we think about our ideas is a unique human capacity given us by God. One of the biblical writers likens our capacity for self-transcendence to seeing ourselves in a mirror that enables us to evaluate and change ourselves based on what we see (James 1:22–25; see also II Cor. 13:5; I Cor. 11:28). Evaluating our world view entails discovering the underlying roots of what we say, think, and do. We can consciously change our basic values only after we understand what they are.

In this book we seek to explain several basic world views and to help students formulate their own presuppositions about life. This basic concern is an unavoidable part of education, though it may lie below the surface in the day-to-day development of courses. Instructors in every academic discipline base their classroom lectures and discussions upon assumptions about the nature of reality. Their presuppositions affect their choice of material, how they arrange their arguments, and how they evaluate various ideas.

For example, statements in physics about "physical laws" assume the constancy or stability of the universe. Scientists also assume the reliability of the scientific method and the trustworthiness of their senses in gathering and analyzing data. Chemists depend upon the constant relationship between the elements they use. They trust that they will not get sulphur by mixing nitrates and oxygen. And in economics, the assessed value of gold as money rests upon the belief that people will always consider this mineral to be precious.

World views or perspectives also direct the study of the humanities. Historians bring to their study of human events a conception that history is either meaningful or meaningless. They disagree over whether transcendent powers influence the course of events and over whether human actions or natural and social forces are the more significant in shaping human destiny. Good teachers of literature help their students learn how to interpret novels, poetry, and short stories. They seek to equip students with the critical powers necessary to perceive an author's vision of reality and to evaluate whether he or she has chosen the best means of expressing that vision.

In the social sciences, as well, world views play an often unrecognized yet vital role. Most sociologists, for example, accept several major assumptions: empirical methods can be used to study human behavior; human behavior can be measured statistically and categorized into "laws"; social structures are more significant in influencing cultural development than are individuals; the social environment plays a greater role in shaping a person's life than his biological inheritance; and morality arises from social convention, not from divine absolutes.

Of course, there is more to identifying and articulating world views than this brief summary. But you can begin to see that all people hold world views. That is why it is important for students to investigate their own presuppositions, as well as to uncover and analyze the premises underlying the material they see, read, and hear. The cost of not doing so is to be captive to a mind-set, your own or another's, that does not afford the liberty to learn, grow, and exchange error for truth.

The authors of this book are all committed to the biblical world view. We believe that the Bible clearly presents a unified view of reality, consistent and coherent, that accurately describes the human situation. Recognizing that truth cannot be poured into readers like cement into a mold, our purpose is to challenge students to consider biblically grounded truth in relation to the history of philosophical and religious thought. More specifically, we describe a Reformed and evangelical exposition of the biblical world view and compare and contrast it with other Christian and prominent non-Christian perspectives in the history of Western thought.

Many will disagree with our views. The relationship between authors and readers, however, implies certain responsibilities. Authors should express their own ideas as clearly and compellingly as possible, and the ideas of others as comprehensively and fairly as possible. Readers should strive to understand each author's argument, to question it, and to compare it with other perspectives of life and the world. We state our basic commitments forthrightly because we are convinced that it is impossible to approach subjects from a neutral or uncommitted viewpoint. Undoubtedly many believe that scholars ought to treat the history of ideas with greater objectivity and a more detached perspective. But as we have already argued, all people are attached to their presuppositions. Here we want to lay open our own assumptions, which invariably influence our starting point, the methods we use, the goals we seek, the materials we examine, and the results we obtain.

An example of how people differ on an important world-view question may help to clarify our point. One of the questions we will face in this study is "How do you know you know?" You can place the emphasis of that question in several places. Our goal, however, is to probe deeply and ask, "How do you know that your criterion for knowing really gives knowledge?" Prominent thinkers throughout history have answered in many different ways. Some argue that we know by the use of reason: human beings possess a rational faculty, which supposedly enables them to know certain things. Yet do we know *everything* through this capacity? Others contend that we know by experience. But, again, does that account for everything we know? Still others claim that we know by intuition—an immediate, subjective awareness.

Proponents of reason, experience, or intuition as the basis for knowing often fail to examine and evaluate those unproven assumptions. Very often those three ways of knowing degenerate into the "isms" of rationalism, existentialism, and intuitionism.

Each view reduces our knowledge in all its diversity to merely one method, thus denying any validity to the other means of knowing. In our study we will attempt to identify and evaluate from a Christian viewpoint many different kinds of assumptions people bring to the problem of knowledge. Because *what* we can know, *how* we know, the *limits* of our knowledge, and how we *verify* our knowledge are vital to our world view, one purpose of this book is to enable you to answer each of these questions.

Method of This Study: Examining World Views From a Historical Perspective

The themes of this volume are theology (study of God), anthropology (study of humanity), and epistemology (study of knowledge). While we can learn much about these themes by examining what people believe today, a clear and comprehensive understanding of world views and their implications must also include what past thinkers have believed. Our biblical perspective leads us to value historical study, especially the history of ideas.

While adopting a historical approach, we readily recognize that other methods could be and have been used effectively to understand our subject. Since our primary purpose is to explain the Christian viewpoint, we could limit our investigation to biblical materials. Such a study would help us to understand the Bible's teachings, especially as we confront the diverse ideas of our secular society. That approach, however, would not enable us to compare and contrast biblical ideas with others that confronted Christians in earlier times and that directly affected the development of contemporary viewpoints. Limiting our analysis to biblical materials would also prohibit us from seeing how Christians have both defended their ideas and criticized alternative views. Since Christianity has never existed in a vacuum, its followers have always had to express and implement their faith in particular cultural environments.

A second possible approach is the strictly topical. We could simply analyze our three topics without considering the historical context in which they arose and the historical processes that affected their development. But that approach would render us guilty of "chronological snobbery," the assumption that views held today are better simply because they are modern. Furthermore we cannot properly understand ideas if we divorce them from their historical origins and development.

Many today deprecate history and avoid studying it because they consider it "impractical." Such pragmatic belittling of history is mainly a twentieth-century invention. It is a product of the beguiling modern assumption that all things, including academic studies, are to be judged by their immediate usefulness. While Christians appreciate the principle of utility, it is neither the only nor even the most important criterion for evaluating an idea or method. Contemporary views have developed only by virtue of the efforts of those who preceded us. If we see things more clearly than they, that is because we sit on the shoulders of giants of the past. Historical overviews expand our horizons. We may react to, alter, accept, or even reject outright yesterday's ideas. But we inherit the ideas as much as the monetary wealth and property of our predecessors. Not to assess the value of such an inheritance may result in our bypassing a fortune of intellectual legacies that would enrich our lives.

We believe, then, that combining historical and topical approaches will enable us to evaluate the interplay between ideas in their social settings and subsequent development. This method seems best suited to our study of God, humanity, and knowledge.

This broad approach, as opposed to a narrow focus on biblical material or topics apart from historical considerations, is most consistent with the Christian world view itself. Space and time form the setting in which the human drama is enacted. History is not "bunk" as Henry Ford so rashly claimed. It is the arena in which God works out His purposes within His creation. Therefore, our study rests on the presupposition that revelation and redemption are tied to events that are more than archaic trivia, but are historical realities with present-day significance. Mere intellectual comprehension of a series of ideas as abstract entities is insufficient. Our goal is to help students apprehend God's redemptive activity, including His purposes for the entire created order, and embrace and promote the Christian world view. We seek to challenge your minds, engage your hearts, and motivate your wills.

Directly tied to one's understanding of history is his view of man. Are humans significant actors in history? Can people make unique contributions to history?

According to the Bible, people build and direct culture because they are created in the image of God. God gave our first parents authority to exercise dominion over all the rest of creation. Men and women are free to shape the world within the boundaries God has provided. Our cultural activity is far from perfect; indeed, all too often it expresses selfishness and perversion. Witness the many political, social, economic, and even religious evils, both private and public, that plague Western civilization. Many of these problems spring from human greed, laziness, and ignorance. Man's imperfect and evil deeds are due ultimately to sin.

Our ability to shape events may be called *historical power*.[1] Everyone possesses some historical power, though not all have it to the same degree. People have greater or lesser roles in cultural formation. Some have great impact in shaping economics, while others make their mark in politics, religion, art, or some other dimension of human activity. But all people influence the lives of their families, their friends, and their associates in the working world.

In our survey we will meet persons who exercised great historical power. Some were people of action, but most were men of ideas. There is more to history than great individuals and their thoughts, but those with a vision and the courage to act on it have powerfully influenced the course of history.

Our method, then, will be to examine how both Christians and non-Christians have shaped history by their ideas. History is dynamic; ideas, events, and gifted individuals interact with each other. The influence of a Plato reaches beyond Ancient Greece as his ideas live on through history, shaping the contributions of intellectual leaders such as Augustine or Calvin. The time line

---

1. This material was originally developed by John Van Til, Professor of History Grove City College.

discussed in the introduction to part one will help students to trace such developments and transitions.

Because history is shaped and guided by a force much larger than man, all events testify to the revelation of God, written on the pages of time.

PART ONE:
THEOLOGY AND
ANTHROPOLOGY

Introduction

W. Andrew Hoffecker

Two subjects have dominated Western world views. One is theology, the study of God. Included under this topic have been debates over God's existence, discussion of God's attributes or characteristics and His relationship to the created order, and consideration of God's relation to human beings. The second subject is anthropology, the study of man. Questions about this topic have focused on human nature and its effect on man's actions, human and social perfectibility, man's relationship with his physical and social environment, the causes of evil and suffering, and whether human history has any transcendent meaning. As can be seen, theological and anthropological discussions are intimately related.

Two basic understandings of these issues have persisted in Western civilization. At various times human thought and activity have been anthropocentric, or man-centered. During such periods individuals or groups have argued that experience, reason, or some other human faculty is the ultimate arbiter of all ideas and values. The classical Greek and modern eras are excellent examples of periods when belief in human autonomy has dominated and directed all thought. At other times, however, human thought and behavior have been theocentric, affirming that God provides through revelation or some other supernatural activity an absolute or transcendent standard for human ideas, values, and behavior. The biblical, medieval, and Reformation periods are prominent eras when philosophy and theology were God-centered.

Anthropocentric periods have been characterized by cultural

3

fragmentation and decline. During times when no transcendent ideal has dominated culture, individual thinkers and schools of thought have vied for public recognition and acceptance. More often than not, Western civilization has declined during such periods because societies have lacked a unified and coherent foundation. People have failed to achieve an ethical consensus because they have not believed that absolute standards of think-ing or behavior exist. The inevitable result has been that both public and private morality have degenerated.

Such states of cultural declension have continued until a strong unified perspective has gained widespread acceptance. Then a renewed vision of God and His transcendent values has inspired hope and directed conduct. A theocentric perspective has tended historically to provide a cultural unity resting upon belief that all of life is subject to God, the only sure and ultimate basis of certainty. Commitment to God and His self-revelation offers people a means of redemption from sin, a standard for behavior, and a foundation for certainty for both individuals and social institutions. Intellectual, political, social, economic, scientific, and artistic activities depend on divine norms to give structure and purpose to human existence.

Our survey of Western thought about God and humanity can be divided into three major periods, which illustrate our conten-tion. In the ancient period (2000 B.C.–A.D. 400) biblical ideas contrasted sharply with Greek world views. The Middle Ages (A.D. 400–1500) introduced a period of synthesis in which Christians deliberately attempted to harmonize or unify Christian and Greek ideas. During the modern era (1500–present) post-synthetic approaches have developed. New systems of thought have prolif-erated that differ radically from the revival of biblical views sparked by the Protestant Reformation.

In chapters 1 and 3 of this part we explore the theocentric biblical perspective. The Old and New Testaments alike describe a sovereign God, who is transcendent yet personal and reveals Himself in history through covenants with human beings. Man, unique among all creatures because he bears God's image, is finite and fallen in sin yet capable of being redeemed by God's sovereign grace. All human activity—man's ideas, values, vocation, actions in history, and ultimate destiny—lies under the effect of sin, a rebelliousness that requires grace for the relationship with God to be healed.

Chapter 2, by contrast, includes a discussion of the anthropocentric Greek perspective. According to major Greek thinkers, the divine was either an impersonal, aloof Demiurge (a la Plato) or an *unmoved mover* (a la Aristotle). Portraying their gods as personally unconcerned with human beings, Plato and Aristotle viewed man as autonomous and self-sufficient. Thus the biblical and Greek world views were radically different, which is to say, they disagreed sharply at their roots (since *radix* means root in Latin), at the basic assumptions of their perspectives. Western thought thus began with a sharp antithesis between these two viewpoints.

In the Middle Ages (chapters 4, 5, 6), commonly referred to as the Christian era, prominent theologians attempted to synthesize, or combine, biblical and Greek ideas. Many Christian thinkers believed that Greek philosophy could be used to support the Christian faith. In trying to construct this synthesis, however, theologians altered elements of the biblical world view. Although much good was accomplished during this period—such as the rebuilding of Western culture after barbarian invasions, the establishment of universities in Europe, and the spread of the gospel to previously pagan nations—synthesis frequently compromised and diluted the Christian world view. In the beginning of the medieval period the Arian heresy depreciated God's sovereignty, and the Pelagian heresy exalted human autonomy. Later, in the thirteenth century, Thomas Aquinas used Aristotle's ideas to reinterpret Christianity to his generation. Although the medievalists sought to construct a world view that would advance Christianity in their cultural context, only Augustine in his great works *The City of God* and *On the Trinity* retained a sharp distinction between biblical ideas and their Greek counterparts.

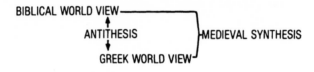

2000 B.C.	1000 B.C.	500 B.C.	0		1000
Patriarchs	David	Plato	Christ	Nicaea	Aquinas
		Aristotle		Augustine	

Many scholars include the Protestant Reformation as part of the Christian era. In so doing they make the Reformation only the beginning of the end of Christianity's impact on the rest of the world. Some even dub the modern period the "post-Christian era." We believe, however, that this period is better labeled the post-synthesis era because, from the sixteenth century to the present day, both consistently biblical and predominantly or completely naturalistic movements have vied for supremacy. Two spiritual revivals—in northern Europe, a Reformation, and in southern Europe, a Renaissance—gave birth to the modern period. This era began, then, with two world views, both of which found inspiration in earlier historical periods.

Martin Luther and John Calvin attempted to return Christian thought to its biblical moorings by reforming the doctrine, worship, and spirituality of the church. They criticized the medieval church for forming a synthesis between biblical and pagan ideas and urged Christians to rediscover the sovereignty of God, the sinfulness of man, and the supreme authority of the Bible. Reformation leaders attempted to reestablish the biblical perspective as a basis for Western thinking (see chapter 7).

But not all agreed that the foundation for civilization should be the Christian world view. Many intellectuals believed that the breakdown of medieval culture symbolized not simply the inadequacy of the church and its institutions but the inability of Christians to use the biblical world-and-life view to provide cultural leadership. Renaissance thinkers, therefore, broke from centuries of tradition and boldly chose Greek ideas over Christian ideas. In declaring man to be the measure of all things (*homo mensura*) they not only revived an important Greek theme but also set the tone for all subsequent modern thought. Renaissance leaders did not reject the biblical God outright. But as time progressed, ideas of God departed more and more from the biblical view. As the Renaissance gave way to Enlightenment rationalism, which in turn yielded to romanticism, and finally to naturalism, God became functionally irrelevant. Most thinkers during these years did not reject belief in God; they simply concluded that the supernatural is unknowable and therefore cannot serve as a basis for human thought and activity. Eventually, of course, naturalists flatly denied God's existence. At the same time, philosophers living during the fifteenth to nineteenth centuries assigned increasing importance to man and his place in nature. Human autonomy replaced divine authority. The idea that human limitations can be successfully overcome by purely natural means such as reason and the scientific method began to replace the biblical view that man is a sinner and can be saved only by the grace of God. Chapter 8 describes this major transition from a theocentric to an anthropocentric world view. Ultimately this shift involved a radical return to the naturalistic humanism of ancient Greek philosophers.

The final chapter (9) of this first part examines the varieties, sources, and basic principles of twentieth-century humanism. Humanist thinkers make denial of the supernatural and affirmation of human potential the new dogmas. The chapter distinguishes between humanism (or secularism) as a world view and secularization as a process that has influenced every area of life. We conclude that secular humanism is as much a religious world view as any perspective we have studied. Comprehensive in scope, it demands total obedience in every area of life.

To fill out our diagram of Western ideas, we may add the various post-synthesis positions as follows:

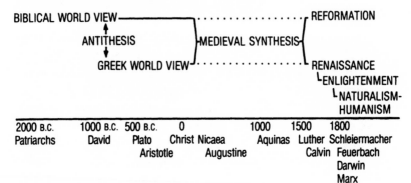

I.
BIBLICAL AND CLASSICAL
WORLD VIEWS

1

The Old Testament: The Covenant Between God and Man

Robert P. Vande Kappelle and John D. Currid

Introduction

The Old Testament is history. As the narrative of ancient Israel's long and varied existence, the Old Testament describes the founding of that great nation, its establishment in Palestine, its succession of kings, and finally its national destruction through a period of conquest and exile. Described also is the institution of a covenant between God and the Jews, specifying a code of laws to direct the nation Israel and the lives of individual Jews. All of these natural, historical events are recorded in the Old Testament in a more or less chronological fashion.

But the Old Testament is much more than a mere historical account of the Israelite people. The ancient bibical writers were aware that the history they recounted of this people was moreover "His-story," an account of God's revelation of Himself to man in time and space. Israel's development and history depended on the course God had chosen. Thus the Old Testament comprises not just natural events, a chronicle of a nation, but more importantly God's supernatural activity through which He determined Israel's destiny by initiating His covenant, revealing His law, and guiding the nation through His chosen leaders.

God's centrality to the meaning and purpose of the Old Testament is emphasized by the opening words of Genesis: "In the beginning God created . . . " (Gen. 1:1). God, the supreme Creator, is immediately introduced in His majestic uniqueness and His all-powerful autonomy. Readers are brought at once to God in order that they might recognize that all things depend on Him for their existence. This unique feature of the Old Testament, that it is the revelation of God, sets it apart from all other works describing origins and the development of the human race. The Bible *is sacred literature,* and only as sacred and Holy Writ can the Old Testament be understood properly.

The Old Testament, in fact, professes not only to be the words about God and His work but to be the words of God. By inspiration of the Holy Spirit, human authors produced an inerrant collection of historical, literary, and theological writings (see II Pet. 1:20–21). (For further discussion of this issue see chapter 10, "Biblical Epistemology.")

Furthermore, the Old Testament recorded not only what God has done in the past but also what He will do in the future. Its pages reveal the history of mankind from creation to consummation at the end of the ages. Specifically, it foretells the ministry and sacrificial death of a Messiah, whom the New Testament identifies as Jesus Christ. This chapter focuses upon Old Testament views of God and man (theology and anthropology) based upon the above considerations.

If the soul of a people is revealed by its literature, an examination of the Hebrew Scriptures reveals an intense interest in historical, human, and religious issues. Biblical thought is not abstract or even philosophical, as were the writings of Plato and many other Greek philosophers. Ancient Hebrew people did not even have a word that could be translated as "philosophy." They lived in a world of particulars, of concrete earthiness.

The Old Testament Scriptures begin with a majestic creation narrative. Whereas prominent Greek thinkers such as Plato and Aristotle virtually ignored origins, the Old Testament writers describe God's creation of the world and chronicle history in the making. Their writings cover a vast period of time—approximately one thousand years if one begins with Moses. The Israelites view their history as a relationship between God and themselves—a dynamic history. History is crucial to the Jews because they defined their existence as a nation and their self-understanding as a people in response to God's activity in history. God's calling of the patriarchs, His leading in the Exodus, His giving of the law at Mount Sinai, His speaking through appointed leaders, and His establishment of the Promised Land provide the basis for Israel's life.

The Bible teaches that history is linear, that historical events are unique, and that God is guiding history toward a consummation. Because history is the arena of God's activity and because He controls all events, history has unity and meaning.

In contrast, the early Greeks, who worshipped the forces of nature, had a pessimistic view of history. The mythical accounts of the lives of the gods and the regularity of nature's seasons taught the Greeks that history was cyclical. Both human beings and the gods were enmeshed in this cyclical series of events. Like a dog chasing its own tail, history was going nowhere. Belief that human life was destined only to repeat itself and never to achieve any unique purpose led to a sense of futility.[1] Whereas Greek thought is basically abstract and static, dealing with universal concepts and forms such as "the Good," beauty, and truth, Hebrew thought is active and dynamic, symbolic and intuitive, tied to individual things and events. Greek thinkers were concerned with essences. While Greek philosophers asked abstract questions such as "What is justice?" Hebrew writers were concerned with concrete situations and relations. They asked, "What is a just man?" or "Is this action righteous?" When Israel did at times seek security in static, abstract religious institutions and beliefs, God chastised them and broke Israel of her easy but unreal security. God was trying to teach His people that their only security was in Him. He was ever present and ever moving, yet ever faithful and trustworthy.

God was the ultimate presupposition for the Hebrew understanding of reality. The Jews never attempted to prove philosophically that God exists. Genesis begins with the essential presupposition: "In the beginning God. . . . " For the Hebrew people

---

1. In the fifth century B.C. an interest in history began to grow among the Greeks, as depicted in the efforts of Herodotus and Thucydides, who recorded history. But theirs was the old cyclical view behind a new face, for although history now had movement and meaning, it was history going nowhere as evidenced by Plato's "Myth of Er," in which time is but a cosmic "recycling machine," and life but a seemingly endless series of reincarnations.

the starting point was always God the Creator, who personally chose to reveal Himself and to reveal truth about Himself and about man through concrete historical events. As we will see in the next chapter, the Greek thinkers had no such starting point. For them there was no personal, caring, infinite God.

To understand the contrast between the Greek and Hebrew worlds, imagine two figures: the thinking Socrates and the pious, praying Jew. When grappling with a problem, Socrates remained fixed for an indefinite period of time in deep thought. His reason was active, but his body was inactive. By contrast, when the Hebrew Scriptures were read aloud in the synagogue, the pious Jew would move his whole body ceaselessly in deep devotion and adoration. In worship he would lift his arms in praise and supplication. And when he would repent, he would tear his clothes, put ashes upon his head, and moan with his whole being.

Several different aspects in their world views distinguish Greek and Hebrew thought. These differences are born out in their views of God and man.

Hebrew Theology

Above all else Hebrew theology emphasizes the *sovereignty* of God. God is the Creator and sustainer of the universe and the source of all knowledge and wisdom. God created the world, He created man, He called Israel into existence, He initiated a relationship with mankind, and He controls history.

Because God is sovereign, He demands that His people reject all rival gods. The first commandment God gave the Hebrew people (Exod. 20) is that they give exclusive allegiance to Him. All other gods are idols, and as Jeremiah stated (Jer. 2:5; 10:8; 14:22), all gods but Yahweh are mere "breath, nothingness."

A primary example of Israel's refusal to recognize rival gods is narrated in I Kings 18. In this story, Elijah, the prophet of Yahweh, confronts the prophets of Baal on the top of Mount Carmel and calls on Israel to decide which deity is the true one, Yahweh or Baal. Whoever answers by sending fire on a sacrifice is truly God. Baal's prophets call on their god all day to answer. They plead for him to hear their cries and finally resort to mutilating their bodies to get Baal's attention. But no fire appears. Finally, Elijah rebuilds the altar demolished by the prophets' anguished antics, thoroughly soaks the sacrifice with gallons of water, and calls on Yahweh. Yahweh dramatically answers by consuming with fire not only the sacrifice but also the wood, the stones, and all the water in the trench surrounding the altar.

When one reads the chapter, it is easy to see only a story of strife or competition between two rival deities, but the narrative is more than that. When the Hebrews who had witnessed the confrontation saw the outcome, they all bowed to the ground and confessed that "Yahweh is God"—that Yahweh is the only true God, and Baal does not even exist. The true religion of the Hebrews was fiercely monotheistic.

Monotheism is basic to Hebrew religion and makes Judaism unique among the religions of the entire ancient Near Eastern world. Deuteronomy 6:4–5 expresses the essence of Old Testament faith:

> Hear, O Israel: The Lord our God is *one* Lord; and you shall love the Lord your God with all your heart, and with all your soul, and with all your might.

God is seen to be related to creation in a twofold manner. (1) God is *transcendent*, that is, He is above and beyond the limits of what He has made. God stands over against all that is. This emphasis is in sharp contrast to the Greek Demiurge, Plato's weak and undeveloped craftsman figure. (2) God is also *immanent*, that is, He works within His creation. He calls His people out of Egypt, reveals His law, and leads them into the Promised Land. Yahweh is not an impersonal and abstract unmoved mover.

These two ideas form the boundary of Hebrew thought regarding God: He is greater than what He has made and is not to be identified with creation; yet He constantly works within it.

Deism, the view that God made the world but then stepped aside from it and remained uninvolved, is inconsistent with the Bible. Pantheism, the view that God and the world are so intertwined that God has no separate existence or personality, also does not square with biblical teaching.

The Hebrew conception of God is that He is dynamic and active and yet personal and intimate. Many Old Testament passages stress God's dynamic relationship in nature and history. Psalm 18:7 declares, "Then the earth reeled and rocked; The foundations also of the mountains trembled and quaked, Because He was angry." Psalm 114:4 reads, "The mountains skipped like rams, The hills like lambs," and the prophecy of Nahum 1:5a, "The mountains quake before him [God], The hills melt." These images are not references to natural phenomena such as earthquakes. Through poetic imagery the Hebrew worshipping community affirmed that the earth's stability and even its very foundations are nothing at all in comparison with the power, majesty, and holiness of God. Such hyperbole emphasizes that the Hebrew people believed in the omnipotence, greatness, and glory of God.

The Old Testament also underscores the personal nature of God by depicting Him as a shepherd who guides His people along a sure path, as a husband who loves His wife, and as a Lord who cares for His servants. The marvelous passage in Exodus 3, where God discloses His name to Moses, and consequently to the people of Israel, as the eternal "I am," also reveals God's personal nature. To the Hebrew people one's name characterized one's essential character. When God revealed Himself to Moses at the burning bush as "I am who I am" (Exod. 3:14), God revealed Himself as the eternally existing one, self-contained and self-sufficient. *Yahweh*, the Hebrew name of God, an archaic imperfect form of the verb "to be," also stresses the dynamic, continual presence of God with His people.

The ancient Hebrew people believed that if you knew someone's name you could exercise influence over that person. When God revealed His name, however, it must be understood that, although He placed Himself at the disposal of His people, He did not thereby come under their control. God can never be manipulated or controlled. Later God's personal name, Yahweh, became so sacred to the Jewish people that they dared not say it or even write it. Instead they came to call God *Adonai*, meaning "my Lord."

Another important name for God in the Old Testament is *Elohim* (or *El*), a term indicating power and might. Thus God is called *Elohim* in passages, such as in Genesis 1, that describe His creative activity and might. The names of God reflect the Hebrew understanding of a God who is a person, present with His people, who is eternally self-sufficient, who is the all-powerful Creator, and who rules mankind.[2]

The emphasis upon God's activity and personality is captured in the Old Testament by the use of anthropomorphic language, terms that ascribe human forms or attributes to God. For instance, we read of smoke coming from the nostrils of God, of darkness being under His feet, and so on. Whenever bodily parts are attributed to God, what is being described is God's personhood, especially His spiritual qualities, and not physical qualities. The Jews would never picture God in terms of the Homeric gods: as literally having hands, eyes, wings, or a nose. Instead "arm" is used to represent God's might, the assistance God gives to man; "ear" or "eye" represents God's awareness of His creation, that He is alert to the needs of His people and involved with creation.

Hebrew Scripture, then, uses striking imagery depicting God as available and accessible to man, imagery that strikes our senses, while always affirming His majesty and sovereignty.

Hebrew Anthropology

The Bible's fundamental assertion about human beings is that they are created by God, not by blind, purposeless forces of nature. Mankind's creation is a supernatural act of God. God personally chose to create, and that makes man a unique creature, loved by His personal Maker. The biblical account emphasizes that human creation is a direct act of God: "God created man." God is the ultimate presupposition underlying biblical anthropology. Although Christians disagree as to *how* God created, they

2. In the Old Testament, God holds back from fully giving His name, but in Jesus Christ, the incarnate Son of God, the name of God is finally given in its fulness, and thus the confession of the early church becomes, "Jesus Christ is Lord," Jesus Christ is *Adonai.*

affirm that man's existence is due to the personal and purposeful involvement of God (cf. Gen. 2:7).

The context for the anthropological question, "What is man?" is the worship and praise of God. In Psalm 8, for example, that very question is asked, but the Psalmist asks it in the course of thinking about God: "What is man, that Thou art mindful of him?" (v.4). In the Old Testament the meaning of man is never considered apart from his relation to God, and always in the context of worship and praise. The psalmist's answer is that "thou hast made him [man] little less than God" (Ps. 8:5). In other words, human beings have been given an exalted position in the universe, and their exalted position leads the psalmist to revert back to his initial point, an outburst of praise to God (see also Ps. 104).

In the first chapter of Genesis God concludes His creative activity by creating man. In Genesis 1:27 we read the familiar words that "God created man in his own image." Although the meaning of the phrase "image of God" (often referred to by the Latin words *Imago Dei*) is never systematically explained in any one place in the Bible, the idea presents man as "the crown of creation" who reflects God's glory. He is in harmony with the cosmos, and, as image bearer, man can know God, be in constant relationship with Him, and respond to His Word.

Although the words *image* and *likeness* occur in only three Old Testament passages, all of them in the first nine chapters of Genesis, the concept itself is integral to the whole thought-world of the Old Testament. The following four meanings help us to understand the phrase *Imago Dei:*

1. *Man's nature:* Mankind's moral and spiritual nature, the dignity of man, is implicit in the idea of the *Imago Dei*. Genesis 9:6 emphasizes human dignity by underscoring the severity of taking another person's life: "Whoever sheds the blood of man, by man shall his blood be shed, for God made man in his own image."

Because we are created in the image of God, human beings are not morally and spiritually neutral. The Bible clearly denies any form of human autonomy that claims human nature is determined wholly by individual choices. Instead it states that man was created morally and spiritually good. From the beginning human nature was positively directed to the right and opposed to the wrong. Goodness was not something extrinsic or accidental that came upon man after creation. Rather man was created good. Genesis 1:31 affirms of the entire creation, "And God saw every-thing that he had made, and behold, it was very good."

2. *Man's position:* Being made in the image of God implies personhood and attributes to human beings a unique relationship with God. Man and God are capable of intimate personal fellowship because man shares in God's image. As persons we are related to God in a manner different from anything else in the created order.

3. *Man's function:* Since human beings are uniquely related to God by creation, the Old Testament states that their primary function is to worship and serve the Creator in every aspect of life. God alone is to have first priority in human existence, a requirement underscored by the first four commandments in the Decalogue (Exod. 20:3-11): not to have any other gods, not to make images of God, not to take God's name in vain, and to worship God on the Sabbath. (See Deut. 6:4-5; also Matt. 22:36-38.)

Furthermore, mankind is in a unique relation to creation in that he is appointed caretaker or vice regent (serving God as His appointed ruler) and is given the responsibility of establishing dominion over plants and animals. His duty in naming the animals (Gen. 2:19f.) is a symbolic way of showing that man is given authority and control over them. This aspect underscores man's ecological responsibilities.

4. *The universality of the image:* We are told in Genesis 1:27 that both male and female were created in God's image. In the creation account Adam stands as the representative of all mankind, and the very name "Adam" is the generic word for man. The *Imago Dei* is not the sole possession of one tribe or race or nation. Its potential applies to all mankind since all are understood to be descendants of Adam.

Genesis 1 presents an exalted view of man as the climax of creation, standing in unique relationship to God. But Genesis 2:7 gives a different perspective, declaring that God formed man from the dust of the ground. (The Hebrew name for man, *Adam,* is a pun on the word for ground, *adamah.*) Here the connection of man with creation is being stressed—his littleness, finiteness, and limitations—over and against the greatness and the sovereignty of God.

Genesis 2:7 also states that God breathed into man the breath of life, and man became alive and is totally dependent upon God for his existence. God's breath within him made him a living being. Death is depicted as God's removing His breath from man. The absence of God's breath is viewed as nonexistence. The Hebrew mind cannot conceive of human life apart from God.

By looking at the anthropological views given in Genesis 1:27 and 2:7 we arrive at a twofold way of relating God and man. On the one hand, human beings are related to God in a way that the animals and the rest of creation are not (see *view A* below). According to this view there is a gap between God and His image bearers on the one side, and the rest of creation on the other. But insofar as man is made from dust, the gap is between God and man (see *view B* below). God is absolutely sovereign. Here man is identified as creature, as a part of God's creation.[3]

VIEW A	VIEW B
God	God
man	———
———	
	man
animals	animals
plants	plants
machines	machines

The two perspectives are not contradictory but only two ways

3. This illustration is taken from Francis A. Schaeffer, *The God Who Is There* (Downer's Grove, Ill.: Inter-Varsity Press, 1968), p. 94.

of emphasizing God's uniqueness. On the one hand, man is set apart from the rest of creation and is uniquely related to the transcendent, personal God because he is made in the image of God (Gen. 1:26–28 represented by *view A*). From another perspective God is set apart from all that He has created, and man, even though still God's image bearer, is more related to the rest of the created order (Gen. 2:7 represented by *view B*). There is a unity in man both of God-likeness and creatureliness, in which he remains a finite and dependent creature even in the highest spiritual dimension of his existence and may reveal elements of the image of God even in the lowliest aspects of his nature. In the heights of human achievement—the magnificent works of art by Rembrandt and Michelangelo, the genius of Einstein's theories, or the courageous leadership of Luther, Lincoln, or Churchill—there exist clear evidences of human limitations and weaknesses. At the same time in the tragic figures of history—the poor, outcast, deformed, and the powerless—the spiritual image is also present, which gives dignity and value to every human life no matter what its outward appearance or circumstance.

Finally, to say that man is formed from the dust of the earth is not a slur on the human body as if it were somehow intrinsically evil or the source of evil, as opposed to the soul, which is seen as good. The Old Testament does not propose that man is a dualism. The body is not bad in and of itself, but is a part of a good creation of God. Everything about man, as God created him, is good. The body is not the tomb or the prison house of the soul, as it is seen to be in Platonic thought.

Hebrew anthropology does not divide human nature into mutually exclusive parts. Rather, the Bible describes man as a unity. When soul or spirit or mind or heart is spoken of in the Old Testament, the whole person is described, with varying terms emphasizing the various aspects of human life. For instance, when the word often translated as "soul" (*nephesh*) is used, it is the life, or the individuality, or one's strong desire that is being emphasized.[4] When "heart" is mentioned, biblical writers are pointing to the will, or the conscience, or the intellect, and so on. But in all contexts the whole person is represented as acting, not merely a part of man. There is no dualism to speak of in Hebrew anthropology, though one can perhaps speak of a twofold nature, in which the links between soul and body are extremely intimate.

The Relationship Between God and Man: The Covenant

For many decades, theologians have believed that the covenant spoken of in the Bible provides the structural unity that integrates all of God's dealings with man. Indeed the Bible repeatedly testifies to the centrality of the covenant. Detailed references are found in the covenants established by God with Noah (Gen. 6), with Abraham (Gen. 15), with Moses (Exod. 20), and with David (II Sam. 7:14ff.). Because of this emphasis we need to ask, What is a covenant?

In its most basic form, a covenant (Hebrew: *berith*) is a binding relationship between God and man that has been sovereignly initiated and administered by God. A covenant demands total commitment by both parties. God never enters into an informal relationship with man, but requires an ultimate commitment extending to the extremes of life and death. A covenant would thus best be defined as "a bond in blood sovereignly administered."[5] In the Old Testament, the divine covenant may be structurally divided into two parts having much in common: the "covenant of creation" and the "covenant of redemption." The phrase "covenant of creation" is applied to God's relationship with man prior to the fall, and the "covenant of redemption" is used to describe the post-fall relationship.

The Covenant of Creation

According to the Bible, mankind was created in the image of God and was free from sin. Through this event and by speaking

---

4. In the King James Version of Genesis 2:7 the translation "a living soul" is misleading. A more accurate translation would be "a living being," thereby reflecting more clearly the unity of man.

5. O. P. Robertson, *The Christ of the Covenants* (Phillipsburg, N.J.: Presbyterian and Reformed, 1980), p.4.

directly to man, God established a unique relationship between Himself and man. This original bond between God and man is designated the "covenant of creation" by which man was created to be a caretaker or trustee over the entire creation, an exalted position even above that of the angels (Ps. 8:5; Heb. 1:14). He was to be protector and steward of God's kingdom. This authority was firmly established in what is called the cultural mandate, God's command for His creatures to fulfill certain cultural duties. In Genesis 1:28 God commands, "Be fruitful and multiply, and fill the earth and subdue it; and have dominion over the fish of the sea and over the birds of the air and over every living thing that moves upon the earth." All of life was placed under the dominion of man who was to rule under God's authority.

Although mankind was assigned an exalted position in the original covenant relationship, human beings were not created to be autonomous monarchs with absolute freedom and control. In reality the Bible defines man's office of stewardship at creation as that of a ruler and a servant who performs these roles in religious devotion to God. Because God is the Creator and sustainer of the universe, all people are accountable to Him in all things. God is the great King, whereas man is a mere prince and servant. Everything belongs to God; we are the caretakers, not the owners, of the created order. The psalmist explains that, although we rule over the garden, we remain only trustees of the garden: "The earth is the Lord's and the fulness thereof; the world and those who dwell therein" (Ps. 24:1).

As God's image bearing stewards His creatures were thus given great responsibilities in administering God's kingdom. But in order to fulfill these duties mankind was required to obey the laws or ordinances established by God at the creation. The covenant relationship demanded obedience to God's revealed will. First, it demands *vocation*. Because all are created in the image of God, we have a unique responsibility to "subdue" and "fill the earth." Human labor reflects God's work in creation (Gen. 1:28; 2:15). We are to unfold the full potential of the earth in ways that bring glory to God. Second, the covenant demands *devotion*. Man is consciously to act out religious devotion in all things; that is, he is to be committed totally to God. Everything a person does in each area of life (family, vocation, leisure, etc.) is to be devoted to God. A person is accountable to God not simply in private and public worship but in every activity of life. Each of these creational demands helps define human existence and provides human life with meaning.

In addition to these broad responsibilities, however, man was responsible to obey a specific law prohibiting eating from the tree of the knowledge of good and evil (Gen. 2:15-17). The command to man was clearly stated: (1) he could eat to his heart's content from any tree of the garden; but (2) he must not eat from the tree of the knowledge of good and evil; (3) if he ate of that particular tree, he would surely die.[6] This restriction was to test man's willingness to remain morally and spiritually faithful to God and to depend on God's word. Genesis 3:1-19 narrates what happened to God's original covenant of creation. Adam and Eve deliberately disobeyed what God commanded. Instead of following God's word and thereby doing what is implied by "the tree of knowledge of good and evil," they willfully refused to discern good and evil by eating the fruit. They ate in response to the temptation that in so doing they would "be like God." Thus the root of human sinfulness is a rebellious refusal to live according to the word of a sovereign God. Man "fell," therefore, from a condition of original righteousness and immediately shattered the covenant existing between God and His creatures.

The consequences of man's sinful action appear in the succeeding verses: (1) the man and woman were afraid of God and hid themselves, indicating their alienation from Him (3:8); (2) they were alienated from one another in their shame of nakedness (3:7); (3) they were alienated from the garden (3:24); (4) they were alienated from life eternal (3:19). Indeed the covenant of creation, with its major emphasis upon administering God's lordship over creation, had ended. These conditions are echoed in

---

6. A direct translation of the Hebrew literally says, " . . . in the day you eat of it you shall die die." Repetition of words in biblical Hebrew is for the purpose of emphasis. There was no question, then, what the consequence would be if man disobeyed the commandment.

the rest of the Old Testament as describing human sinfulness (see, for example, Ps. 14:1–3; 32:1–4; Isa. 44:21, 22; Jer. 33:8).

The Covenant of Redemption

Man's sin destroyed the creation covenant and fractured his relationship with the Creator. Because God loved man, however, He provided a means by which man could be restored to a right relationship: the covenant of redemption. In the ancient world there were two types of redemptive covenants—those governing relationships between *equal* parties and those specifying relationships between *unequal* parties. The second type of covenant, such as between an overlord (the superior, also known as the "suzerain") and the vassal (the inferior) forms the basis for the covenant of redemption. Within this form, the suzerain, as the more powerful party, takes on most of the responsibility for the stipulations of the covenant. Although the vassal also has obligations, because of limited capabilities and resources he is not held accountable to the extent the suzerain is.

The suzerain-vassal treaty is the covenant form used by God to redeem man in the Bible because God is the great suzerain King and man is a mere royal vassal. Two forms of the suzerain-vassal treaty are found in the Bible: (1) In the *promise covenant* God took on all the responsibility and obligations set down in the agreement. A prime example of this is found in Genesis 15, where God promised Abraham descendants that would possess much of the land of Canaan. In the account Abraham prepared the ritual seal of the covenant. He divided a few animals into two pieces with the intention of walking through them to consummate the treaty. A deep sleep, however, overcame Abraham and God alone passed between the parts. God thus assumed full responsibility for the covenant and the promise that He had declared.

(2) A *law covenant* is an agreement between God and man consisting of responsibilities and obligations for both parties to the treaty. It is built upon four basic and essential parts:

1. The majority of the covenant states the duties of the vassal. God established the laws by which man was to live.

In the redemptive covenantal relationship the law has a threefold purpose: it designates what is sinful by forbidding certain behavior; it convicts man by pointing out sins; and it promotes righteousness by revealing God's will so that man can live accordingly. Although the law established in the covenant relationship is concerned with human behavior, God, the suzerain, also has demands to meet. His obligations, however, are often more implied than stated.

2. Because both God and man are required to fulfill certain covenantal demands, they both stand under what is known as the "sanction," which describes the results of obedience or disobedience to the stipulations. Sanctions were both positive (a reward or blessing) and negative (a punishment or curse).

3. The vassal was to pledge allegiance to the overlord. Vassals did so verbally in conjunction with an overt ritual act.

4. A seal or ritual sign of blood confirmed the agreement. The significance of using blood in the ritual is important, for the Hebrews believed that blood was the key to life. To seal a covenant with blood expressed the ultimacy of the commitment between God and man: it implied blessing and curse, a matter of life and death. In fact, the terminology used in the Old Testament for sealing a covenant agreement between God and man is "to cut a covenant." The idea of cutting, of course, implies blood. The rituals themselves entailed a cutting process. The best known examples are the "cutting" of the animals by Abraham in Genesis 15 and the "cutting" of circumcision in Genesis 17 ("You shall be circumcised in the flesh of your foreskins, and it shall be a sign of the covenant between me and you").

In the Old Testament, the purpose of God's establishing the covenant with man was twofold. First and foremost, the law and promise covenant was *revelation*. God disclosed Himself to a particular people (Israel) in a concrete historical framework. The divine revelation was thus not speculative or subjective, but factual and objective. The true God broke into history and granted man true knowledge of His being and what He requires of His people. The second major purpose of the covenant was *redemption.* God was attempting to restore man to a correct relationship with Himself. In a sense the covenant and its laws, no matter how minor, were redemptive in their purpose. During the Exodus from Egypt—the most significant event and certainly the most formative event in Israel's experience—the Hebrew people came to understand, through revelation, the meaning of animal sacrifices to God. No other event so strongly prefigures the redemptive event of the cross in the New Testament as the institution of the Passover (see Exod. 12:1–13:16), which reveals the significance of the shedding of blood for sin.[7] Sacrificing a lamb became an act of deliverance and atonement.

The main principle in the sacrificial system of the Old Testament is that of substitution. In animal sacrifices, the sins of men were symbolically placed on an undefiled, unblemished sacrificial lamb, which would then be offered up to God through the mediatorial work of a priest. By means of this sacrifice, God's righteousness would be imputed to the repentant person. God's people learned that because of His love for them He had set up this institution whereby sinful people could receive God's perfection and experience His forgiveness.[8] Substitution as a means of redemption is profoundly displayed in one of the most deeply moving passages of the Old Testament, Isaiah 53. Isaiah speaks of the vicarious work of a coming suffering servant who would make Himself an offering for sin (v. 10). He would bear our griefs and carry our sorrow, being wounded for our transgressions and bruised for our iniquities (vv. 4–5). God would lay upon Him "the iniquity of us all" (v. 6). Through His suffering, believers would be restored and healed (v. 5), and His righteousness would "make many to be accounted righteous" (v. 11).

Despite elaborate provisions for a mediatorial priesthood and a

---

7. The key to blood atonement is found in Lev. 17:11, "for the life of the flesh is in the blood. . . ."
8. Cf. the various kinds of offerings described in Lev. 1–7, and especially the meaning of the Day of Atonement and the events related to it as found in Lev. 16.

system of animal sacrifices, the Old Testament remained incomplete in terms of providing a lasting and decisive cure for sin. Only the New Testament unveiled the historical fulfillment and consummation of the sacrifices of the Old Testament and of the prophecy of Isaiah 53 in the once-and-for-all sacrifice of Jesus, God's Son incarnate, who died that faithful people everywhere might be forgiven, reconciled, and renewed (see Heb. 9:26; 10:10; also II Cor. 5:21; Rom. 5:18–19; Gal. 2:20).

The Old Testament describes how God has worked to redeem rebellious human beings and to reestablish a covenant relationship with them. God initiated His covenant with Abraham by making him an unconditional promise of future blessedness. This promise was not only to his posterity, Israel, but through Israel and later through the Jew, Jesus of Nazareth, to all the world. At first it seemed almost impossible for Israel to hold these two truths together, the reality of the covenant (that they were God's chosen people), and the universality of the image of God in man. They had to understand, first, that there was but one God and that the gods of the other nations were mere idols. And they had to learn their own weakness and their basic need to remain dependent on and faithful to their God.

In the latter years of Israel's history the prophets repeatedly called the Jews to faithfulness once again, and they promised that God would do something new in the future.[9]

Summary

The general intent of this chapter has been to highlight the distinctive presuppositions and unique approaches to God and man as found in the Old Testament Scriptures. The Hebrew people expressed their world view through worship and work, in response to the initiative taken by a personal yet sovereign God.

9. Cf. the promise of a new covenant, to be written on tablets of the heart instead of on stone, found in Jer. 31:31–34. This hope became associated with the idea of a coming Messiah, who would restore faithful Israel to God and with this remnant restore hope for a lost mankind that had long before, in Adam and thereafter, forsaken God. In the New Testament, through Jesus of Nazareth, God extends His covenant to man once again.

Hebrew thought, as revealed in the thirty-nine books of the Old Testament, displays a concern with an immanent God, who works in the time and space of history. Through His self-revealing acts in history God is known to be personal, holy, loving, self-sufficient, and all-powerful. Man is created in the image of God, as the "crown of creation." Hence he is in a position of unique and intimate fellowship with God. Because God is sovereign, man's primary function is to worship God and obey His will. God, the Creator of all reality, initiated a relationship with mankind, and later with an elect people, under the terms of a covenant, a binding agreement involving promises and obligations. But man selfishly disobeyed God, misused his freedom, and fell from grace. Even the Israelites, God's chosen people, failed to be faithful in their covenant relationship.

The Old Testament reveals that God is merciful. He moves to restore a remnant of Israel to covenant faithfulness by instituting the sacrificial system. But Old Testament Israel looked forward to the coming of a Messiah who would accomplish God's ultimate redeeming work. At a unique point in history, which the apostle Paul called "the fulness of the time" (Gal. 4:4, NASB), God sent His own Son, Jesus, to flesh out the meaning of His eternal covenant, as shown in the name Emmanuel, "God with us" (cf. Matt. 1:23), and to display His universal intention (cf. Rom. 5:1f.) by dying on behalf of His people.

For Further Reading

Archer, Gleason L. *A Survey of Old Testament Introduction.* Chicago: Moody, 1964.

Bright, John. *A History of Israel.* 3rd ed. Philadelphia: Westminster Press, 1981.

Geisler, Norman L. *A Popular Survey of the Old Testament.* Grand Rapids: Baker, 1977.

Harrison, R. K. *Old Testament Times.* Grand Rapids: Eerdmans, 1970.

Kaiser, Walter C. *Toward an Old Testament Theology.* Grand Rapids: Zondervan, 1978.

Kline, Meredith G. *The Structure of Biblical Authority*. Grand Rapids: Eerdmans, 1972.

McComiskey, Thomas. *The Covenants of Promise*. Grand Rapids: Baker, 1985.

Pfeiffer, Charles F. *Old Testament History*. Washington: Canon, 1973.

Robertson, O. Palmer. *The Christ of the Covenants*. Phillipsburg, N.J.: Presbyterian and Reformed, 1980.

Schultz, Samuel. *The Old Testament Speaks*. New York: Harper and Row, 1960.

Vos, Geerhardus. *Biblical Theology: Old and New Testaments*. Grand Rapids: Eerdmans, 1969.

2
Classical Greek Humanism
Charles S. MacKenzie

Introduction
The small country of Greece has made a lasting mark on Western civilization. Its great thinkers discovered, discussed, and debated theological and anthropological ideas the impact of which remains with us today.

Greeks who lived in the ten centuries prior to Christ's birth thought about the gods much as other ancient peoples did. They worshipped the nature gods Demeter (goddess of corn), Poseidon Phytalmos (god of the growth of plants), and the Charities (givers of all increase). They revered deities that were partially or entirely animal-like representations of brute natural forces. Believing their lives were affected by such forces of nature, the Greeks sought their aid by conceiving of them as gods whose favor could be won. By the sixth century B.C. the Greeks tended to picture the gods in human form. Xenophanes, for example, declared that God is "without body, parts or passions," but he acknowledged that man, until he became a philosopher, would endow his gods with human form:

> One God there is greatest of gods and mortals;
> Not like to man is he mind or body.
> . . . .
> But mortal man made gods in his own image.[1]

Homeric Religion
In the ninth century B.C. the Greeks recognized many gods with

---

1. Xenophanes, fragments 1, 2, 5, 6. See also Rom. 1:23.

human characteristics and form. In his *Iliad* and *Odyssey*, Homer described the polytheism of ancient Greece by narrating the lives of the Olympian deities. Essentially Homer's gods and goddesses were personifications of nature. Collectively, they represented a universal, overarching plan that affected the lives of men. In the beginning of the *Iliad* we read, "and the will of Zeus was fulfilled." A little further we discover the words, "strength, I suppose, is a gift from god?" The influence of the Olympian gods over men is a major theme of Homeric religion, which dominated Greece from the ninth century B.C. to the time of Plato.

Olympian gods, containing characteristics of both local Greek nature deities and the gods brought by peoples who migrated into Greece from the north and east, came to symbolize power. Zeus was the "Father of gods and men." Because Zeus ruled among all immortals, before him man stood helpless, a creature of a lower order. The distinction between the gods and men was one of power, not of morality; the Olympian gods were vengeful, licentious, quarrelsome embodiments of power, not virtue. They connived, cheated, and lied to help themselves and their favored patrons among men.

Human creatureliness and finitude stand out in early Greek religion. Anthropomorphic Olympian gods (gods conceived as having human characteristics), who drank excessively and loved passionately, shared the moral weaknesses of men, and therefore they usually did not judge men on the basis of morality. Instead they affected human existence by demanding personal loyalty and punishing personal offenses so that man was at the mercy and the whim of the gods. Zeus condemned Ixion to eternal torment for assaulting Hera, Zeus's wife. Sisyphos was punished for having told the secret of one of Zeus's intrigues. Prometheus's great sin was his attempt to place in human hands powers that belonged to the gods. Unlike the gods, which had considerable power, people were weak, subject to forces beyond their control. Each was destined to live within his own order, to acknowledge his own limitations.

Yet even the Olympian gods of Homer were subordinate to an older moral power or order called *Moira*, or Destiny.[2] Zeus and his fellow deities were not omnipotent, but were limited by this overarching Destiny.[3] Herodotus remarked, "It is impossible even for a god to avoid the fate that is ordained" (1. 91). Destiny in Homer's writings was essentially impersonal and amoral: she was a blind, automatic fate, which wrought vengeance on all who challenged her decrees. Each man and each god had his own appointed province, realm, or sphere within which he was free to act, but his place was appointed by a powerful, though purposeless, Destiny.

Hesiod (c. 800 b.c.) wrote his Theogony, which was a genealogy of the Olympian gods. He described the world as divided into three portions (*moirai*), which were then assigned to Zeus, Poseidon, and Hades. While the starry heavens belonged to Zeus, Poseidon ruled over the sea, and the air or the earth was the realm of Hades. Associating powers in the cosmos with diverse gods reflected the earlier periods when gods were viewed as personifications of nature.

Since Destiny appointed the bounds of men and of gods, the Greeks considered challenging the fates to be immoral. Hubris, pride that challenges Destiny's decree, is the epitome of immorality and brings forth her wrath and retribution.

In Homer's works, destiny had decreed that gods hold power over mortal men. Yet these gods mated with women, had mortal offspring, shared human frailties, and were, along with man, punished by Moira. Although the gods had an element of the

2. As Greek thought developed, Zeus came to be regarded as the supreme deity who dispenses and upholds Moira. Zeus appeared to take the place of Moira even as Plato later depicted reason as taking the place of Zeus. The Greeks were seeking order in the universe.

3. Moira, because of its limiting power, is generally viewed as a negative force, though its negative aspect may be the recoil of a positive, dynamic impulse toward order.

human in them, there was no hint of the divine in man. Rather, they were helpless in the face of Moira and the gods. Despite the distinction between the human and divine, the gods interacted with people. For example, in the Iliad we read, "So he prayed, and Phoebus Apollo heard him. He came down from the summits of Olympus. . . . " Again we read, "It is Zeus who sends dreams. . . ." Thus, we are not surprised to find that individuals promised devotion to the gods in exchange for favors. Yet Destiny had fixed an impassable gulf between man and the gods. Gods inspired, guided, and communicated with man as they descended to men and women, but people did not ascend to them. The Greek view of man as described by Homer was pessimistic. He saw human life as meaningless. Humanity was to be annihilated finally by death, which was a weak and miserable existence. Thus Achilles could say that he would rather be a laborer toiling for a poor man on earth than a king among the dead (Odyssey 11, 489ff.).

While Olympian religion described by Homer and Hesiod was most significant, it was not the only form religion took in ancient Greece. Dionysian[4] rites were known to Homer, but their orgiastic frenzies, which usually took place at night, contradicted the sense of order he saw existing among the gods. Participants were mostly women, some of whom carried snakes wreathed about them or entwined in their hair. Music, frantic dancing, wine, and sexual license whipped them into a wild state of emotion in which they would see visions, tear live animals apart, and play with fire. Such rituals produced states of *ecstasy* (literally "standing outside oneself") and *enthusiasm* ("possession by the god").

Worship of Dionysius met with stiff resistance in Greece because the rational Greeks were reluctant to allow their reason to be overwhelmed by passionate desires. Yet Dionysian religion spread because, unlike Homeric religion, which kept human beings

---

4. Dionysius was the god of creative nature. The Dionysian cult came to be associated with the name of the Thracian bard Orpheus. Dionysian Orphism believed in the transmigration of the soul, a belief that probably came from India and that invaded Greece at some unknown time in antiquity.

at a distance from the gods, it offered the worshipper *unity with the gods*. At the height of ecstasy, he became one with his god and thus became immortal.

Contrasts between Homeric and Dionysian religion could hardly be more pronounced. On the one hand, Homeric deities were materialistic, immortal, and aloof, distinguished from human beings primarily by their power. They ruled a cosmos ultimately governed by Destiny and affected human existence on the basis not of morality but of personal patronage. On the other hand, Dionysian gods were spiritual and intimate. They desired to be worshipped through wild, enthusiastic experiences, and they dwelt in men to thrill and inspire them. Homer was pessimistic about immortality and maintained a sharp division between humanity and deity, while Dionysian gods boldly promised worshippers that they would receive immortality by being exalted to the divine state.

Ionian Philosophy

A third strand of early Greek life was Ionian philosophy. Naturalistic philosophy was born in the great commercial seaports of Ionia, Miletus, Ephesus, and Samos, where affluence allowed the upper class time to think. Three Milesian thinkers sought to find the basic substance underlying all things. Thales (c. 610–545 B.C.) proposed water as the substance out of which everything is made. Anaximander, his younger contemporary, argued that an unoriginated, indestructible, infinite "boundless" is the indefinable, primary substance underlying reality. Anaximenes, also of Miletus, believed air to be the cause and source of all things. Repudiating the mythical views of Homeric and Dionysian religions, these three philosophers adopted a naturalistic or scientific view of reality.

The questions they raised were discussed extensively. How do multiplicity and change arise from *the one*, which is the basis of everything? Heraclitus (c. 504 B.C.), who taught that fire is the basic stuff of reality, declared "all things are in a state of flux." Everything changes! He said, "You cannot step twice into the same river, for fresh waters are ever flowing in upon you." Reality is one, but change and the conflict of opposites are essential to the existence of *the one*. Paradoxically, *the one* is simultaneously singular and plural. As the basic stuff of reality, fire underlies all things, yet it is constantly changing. It condenses into moisture and compresses into water, which congeals into earth. Fire is in constant motion, underlying tension and strife, consuming, kindling, and going out. All things change—that is, they are in the process of becoming. Therefore, knowledge of the world is impossible since the world is different from one instant to another.

Parmenides (sixth century B.C.) of Elea, in southern Italy, sharply disagreed with Heraclitus. He declared that change is an illusion and that there is one primary force that forms our reality. This *one* is unchangeable, sensual, material being. Being, whatever its nature, cannot *not* be. It is the source of all that is, and unlike Heraclitus, who trusted the senses to apprehend what is in constant flux, Parmenides asserted that only reason can perceive what eternally remains in the state of being.

In later Greek thought, Heraclitus's emphasis on becoming and Parmenides' emphasis on being developed into a dualism, a sharp division between physical, temporal reality, which constantly changes, and a spiritual world, which is eternally unchanging. In the fourth century B.C. two of the world's great philosophers, Plato and Aristotle, attempted to synthesize being and becoming.

Ionian and Eleatic philosophers seemed to believe that the riddle of the universe would be solved if they could discover the underlying identity, the basic "stuff" of reality. They all believed that this basic substance contained within itself the principle of change and motion, which suggested it was alive. That stuff, which was intimately related to the gods and, therefore, divine, could be discovered by reason. Unbounded faith in the powers of human reason was expressed in man's capacity to understand the divine. Yet these Greeks also recognized human limitations. According to both Heraclitus and Parmenides sense impressions could lead to skepticism and illusions.

Plato's Theology and Anthropology

The grand synthesis of Plato wove the various theological and anthropological strands of earlier Greek thought into a pattern that would influence human thought throughout the centuries. Plato (427–347 B.C.) came from an aristocratic Athenian family. Having been given the name Aristocles, he was later nicknamed Plato because of the breadth of his chest. At the age of twenty, after studying under the Heraclitan philosopher Cratylus, Plato met Socrates. As a young man he travelled extensively and finally settled in Athens. There he opened his school called the Academy where he taught and wrote until his death at eighty years of age.

Plato was deeply influenced by the Orphic-Pythagorean dualism.[5] In his dialogues the *Phaedo* and the *Symposium*, Plato developed his own dualism in which he differentiated between the changing material world, which, as Heraclitus had taught, is constantly becoming (in motion), and the transcendent, unchanging world, which Parmenides had described as being. He postulated an unchanging transcendent world of being inhabited by a host of unchanging *ideas* or *forms*, which influence the material world. For example, in the transcendent, supersensible world of eternal, unchanging ideas there exists the universal *ideal* of "treeness." In our material, changing world of physical things we find pine, oak, and maple trees, each of which is different and subject to constant change or becoming. Yet each particular tree shares or copies the eternal ideal and exists as a "tree" because of its relationship to the universal idea or form. Individual trees exist because they imitate or participate in the essence of the eternal ideal. Imitation and participation bridge the gap between the transcendent world of essences and the material world of particular things.

Thus Plato constructed a dualism in response to the problem

5. Pythagoras, nearly a hundred years earlier, had espoused a doctrine of the transmigration of the soul. The basic nature of things is numerical and transcendent. He also taught a cosmic dualism in which matter and form were two equal and independent ultimate principles.

of "the one and the many," being and becoming, discussed earlier by Heraclitus and Parmenides. Because only stable objects can be known, Plato argued that the essential and unchanging exist in the transcendent world of ideas. Plato taught that this world contains not only ideals or forms corresponding to objects in our material world. Also present are forms of beauty, justice, and truth, which he believed are absolute and objects of rational reflection. This world of transcendent ideas is the basis of all true knowledge. For educated Greeks these ideals replaced the immoral Homeric deities and served as a new foundation for theology. Highest in the hierarchy of forms was the idea of the Good, which gave being and reality to all subordinate forms.

In contrast, the material world, which consists of numerous tangible particulars, was to Plato merely appearances and illusion. His sharp dualism between spiritual ideas and physical particulars was also reflected in his anthropology. A human being, in Plato's view, is a dualism of mind and body. The mind or soul is of supreme importance, while the body exists merely as a vehicle to serve the soul. The soul's rational part is eternal; it inhabits the world of ideas prior to and after this life. When a person is born, the soul is united for a lifetime to a body. But at death the soul flees as a bird out of its cage. The soul will be judged according to its moral conduct on earth and then reborn into life in either a higher or a lower form to live another existence on earth.

As man transmigrates from one existence on earth to another, he passes through the "River of Forgetfulness." When reborn into earthly existence, he retains memories of the universal ideas he previously knew. A person returns to this life purified and essentially good, though he then may become polluted and corrupted largely through the influence of the sensual body in which his soul is imprisoned. Plato explained this cyclical view of human existence in his famous myth of Er in the closing pages of his *Republic*.

The *Phaedo*, another of his famous dialogues, illustrates his exaltation of the soul and denigration of the body:

Socrates: And does not the purification consist, as we have said, in separating the soul from the body, as far as possible, and in accustoming her to collect and rally herself from the body on every side, and to dwell alone by herself as much as she can both now and hereafter, released from the bondage of the body?

Simias: Yes, certainly.

Socrates: Is not what we call death a release and separation of the soul from the body?

Simias: Undoubtedly.[6]

The human soul, therefore, is a virtual prisoner within the body, and a true philosopher lives to die. Death is not an enemy, but a friend because it releases man to inhabit the eternal world of ideas. Socrates lived this philosophy to his very dying day. When his followers mourned his death sentence for corrupting the youth of Athens with his new philosophy, the great teacher rebuked them for not rejoicing that his soul would soon be released from the body. Then he would return to the eternal realm from which he originated, where he could blissfully meditate on the transcendent forms.

In addition to his sharp distinction between body and soul, Plato articulated a threefold division in the human soul: the rational, spirited, and appetitive parts. In the *Republic* he asserts that reason's task is to reflect on the eternal forms. Appropriately lodged in our heads, reason should rule over the soul's spirited and appetitive parts. Reason's function is to contemplate the Good, thus enabling a person to know goodness wherever it may be found. Man's highest task, therefore, is to know the Good and pattern his life after it.

The soul's appetitive part corresponds to human passions associated with sensuous desires for pleasure, food, and sex and is located in the belly. Such desires, while natural, often pull an individual in directions that conflict with reason, tempting him

6. *Phaedo* 676-d, trans. F. J. Church.

to give free rein to pleasure and to dissipate his life in sensual gratification. Natural impulses, therefore, distract the soul by demanding freedom from reasonable restraints. These impulses are correctly represented as irrational appetites, which require the rational part of man's soul to restrain or control them. Plato's vivid analogy in the *Republic* is that reason restrains the passions as a master calls off his dog from following its animal instinct to attack.

The spirited part of the soul is more difficult to describe. Residing in the chest it can ally itself either with reason or with sensual desires. Ideally it convicts us to love what reason rightly tells us to love and to conform our lives to noble ideals, which lead to virtuous living. But the spirited part can instead incline us not to Goodness but to baser impulses associated with the appetitive part of the soul. Therefore, it plays a pivotal role in the formation of human character and should ally itself with reason, enabling men to govern (restrain) bodily impulses. Plato's goal for human life, therefore, is that the head (reason) should rule the belly (appetites) through the chest (feelings).

Plato wished to order all of life according to reason. Rationality was central to his vision of man as a moral being. Unfortunately, Plato did not presuppose a personal deity as a foundation for his view of morality. Moral life receives its sanctions from an impersonal, abstract ideal rather than from a personal sovereign God who defines moral goodness, promulgates it in a covenant, and holds people responsible for fulfilling it in everyday life.

Though he showed no interest in deciding whether there is one god or many, Plato came close to describing a god in his description of the Demiurge. According to his dialogue *Timaeus*, the Demiurge shaped and fashioned the universe using transcendent ideals as models. At best the Demiurge was a craftsman, an impersonal, abstract force that, like the Moira of Homeric religion, destined things to be as they are. Plato probably used the Demiurge to symbolize the operation and function of reason as it orders the universe.

In Plato then we see the emergence of an intellectual system that would profoundly influence Western thinking. Seeking to answer questions raised by earlier thinkers, it affirmed man's essential goodness and his ability to perfect himself and his world. Plato believed people to be capable of achieving true knowledge through self-sufficient, autonomous reason. Plato recognized the existence and the ultimate reality of the transcendent forms and considered the physical world in general and the body in particular of little value. He left little room for deities as they had been conceived by the Greeks of earlier times.

Aristotle's Views of God and Man

Plato's most famous pupil was Aristotle (384–322 B.C.). His friendship with Plato began when Aristotle was seventeen, and for twenty years thereafter he studied at Plato's Academy. As a youth Aristotle accepted the entire Platonic philosophy, but as time passed, Aristotle deviated from his teacher's philosophy. By the time he founded his own Peripatetic School on the Lyceum of Athens, Aristotle had altered his thinking significantly. He rejected belief in a transcendent world of changeless principles or forms and emphasized instead the empirical world of concrete particulars.

For example, he said that the changeless form of treeness is *in* the tree itself, not out there in some otherworldly realm of existence. Thus he solved Plato's most difficult problem of explaining how transcendent forms are related to particular objects in our material world. He gave priority to the existence of the individual, sensible, material object. A philosopher, by rational thought, analyzes and abstracts from each physical object the principles or forms that give rise to particular objects. Aristotle saw reason as powerful, autonomous, and capable of discerning the forms in things.

Aristotle's anthropology described human beings, like all other things, as a mixture of form and matter. Reason, as the highest and best part of human nature, makes people unique, enabling them to identify with God. Through the power of reason, human beings can attain union with the divine.

Aristotle did not seem particularly interested in the question of human immortality. He explicitly rejected Plato's view of the transmigration of the soul and did not seem to believe that the soul could survive without the body. He maintained, however, that man's noblest function, the capacity for thought, might survive death and be absorbed into the one eternal mind. In *De Anima* he said:

> Concerning nous, or the faculty of active thought, we have as yet no evidence. It appears to be a generically different manifestation of soul, which alone is capable of separation, as the eternal from the perishable. The other parts of soul have been clearly demonstrated not to be capable of separate existence. . . . [7]

His view of man's final destiny was vastly different from that of Plato.

In the opinion of many of his critics Aristotle's "God" is the epitome of a "philosopher's god." In keeping with his description of reality as filled with objects composed of form and matter, he conceived of God as the only pure form existing totally without matter. God is engaged in the highest of all activities—eternal thought—contemplating in a single instant the whole realm of being. Because Aristotle's "God" is not material, it cannot change; it is eternal, immovable, and separate from all sensible things.

However, Aristotle thought that all things in the world, by realizing and fulfilling their own forms, are related to the pure form of God. Everything moves from potentiality to actuality. Since all things develop, progressing toward actuality, God must be the eternal, incorporeal (existing without a body) *unmoved mover*, which moves or influences all things not by "pushing" but by "pulling." Just as a magnet attracts iron filings, so God draws out actuality from the potentiality of all objects within the world. God does not, however, "interfere" or exercise a positive influence in human affairs in the manner of a personal being. Rather the unmoved mover simply draws out potential human abilities or character traits to a state of actuality.

7. *De Anima* 412. 6. 4.

Aristotle's "God," however, is not a personal being who hears and answers prayer. Such activity requires a personal God—unlike the unmoved mover, which is indifferent to the world, occupied by eternal self-contemplation.

In the world views of Plato and Aristotle, Greek views of theology and anthropology reached a high-water mark. The way Plato and Aristotle conceptualized and synthesized the questions and issues raised by earlier generations of Greek thinkers has fascinated succeeding generations.

Both philosophers exalted autonomous, self-sufficient reason. They declared that, since man is essentially good, human reason also is good and capable of bringing people into union with the ultimately real. Reason is able to reach true and certain knowledge by discovering unchanging forms or ideas. Crucial to their optimistic views of human nature was their belief that the human will is not in any way evil or corrupted by sin. Wrong behavior is due not to any flaw in human nature but to ignorance. They implied by their confidence in reason that once people are taught what is right they will be virtuous. Belief in people's potential to perfect themselves characterizes Plato's and Aristotle's world views as idealistic.

Plato and Aristotle also assumed that a divine being exists. Their notions of God were abstract, coldly intellectual, impersonal, detached, and unconcerned about the world. Though much different from the Olympian gods of Homer, Plato's Demiurge and Aristotle's unmoved mover were philosophical attempts to reconcile the conflict of permanence and motion between being and becoming. Plato's ideas and Aristotle's forms sought to explain how knowledge is possible in a world where the tension between oneness and many-ness makes knowledge difficult to obtain. In later centuries, the Neoplatonists, the young Augustine, Thomas Aquinas, and many others found their insights helpful, even as do many today.

Yet for all the intellectual rigor of Plato's and Aristotle's theological and anthropological speculations, their ideas lack qualities stressed in Hebrew religion. Their views of Goodness and the unmoved mover challenge human reason, but they do not propose a uniquely transcendent personal God who sovereignly reigns over history yet also immanently hears and answers prayer and fulfills His will in human events. In human reason Plato and Aristotle attributed a greatness to man, challenging him to affirm virtue and to repudiate vices. But the ancient Hebrews more accurately described human nature when they said that although man still reflects the image of God, the fall brought sin, which perverts the human heart, making God's grace and forgiveness the precondition to virtuous living.

Later Greek Thought

The spiritual bankruptcy of Greek culture and the inadequacy of Greek conceptions of man and God became evident in the years following Plato and Aristotle. A failure of nerve set in. Reason was not saving men and society. People did not seem to be essentially rational and good as Plato and Aristotle had taught, and society was not being perfected. To the contrary, a state of confusion prevailed in Greek society after Alexander the Great (356–323 B.C.) spread Greek philosophy throughout the ancient world. Meanwhile, new centers of education in other parts of the ancient world were challenging Greek intellectual leadership.

Greece's population and prosperity were both declining as Greek philosophers proved impotent to inspire the masses and to enable individuals to overcome their petty, selfish interests. Devoid of a relevant and convincing vision of reality, their endless speculations in philosophy served simply as a refuge from the miseries of life. Those who studied the world scientifically began to separate themselves from philosophers, who seemed powerless to provide a unified picture of reality. Greek society decayed as Platonic and Aristotelian ideas were unable to save men and nations from the problems of life.

Among the movements of the period following Plato and Aristotle were Stoicism, Cynicism, Epicureanism, and skepticism. Zeno of Cyprus (334/333–262/261 B.C.) was the founder of Stoicism. His students were called Stoics from their meeting place, the Stoa (the Porch).

In the midst of confusing and changing times, the Stoics looked to scientific research to find a firm philosophic support for the moral life. Zeno, relying on Heraclitus's teaching that all individual things in the world are manifestations of one primary substance, rejected any tendency toward dualism, and he argued that only physical objects were real. The most perfect substance, permeating all things like a warm breath (fire), was perfect reason, which was, in effect, God. The Stoics tolerated worship of popular Greek religious gods, although later Stoics condemned the mythical, anthropomorphic tales of Homer's gods. The Stoics conceived God to be the soul, the supreme reason imparting divinity and reason to the cosmos. This God could be worshipped through the gods of mythology. Because God is the soul of nature and the world is founded on reason (God), people should live in harmony with nature. The world in effect is God's body, and God inhabits the universe as its soul.

Man's soul is corporeal, the noblest and purest form of matter. Because all men possess reason, a spark of the divine, they are equal. Stoics professed no particular belief in personal immortality. Rather, after death, all souls, as indeed all reality, returned to God, as waves return to the sea. The early Stoics believed most men are fools because they fail to live harmoniously with nature. Stoics were convinced that reason would enable people to achieve this goal if they would boldly accept things as they are (fatalism). Such an attitude became known as stoic resignation.

Though Stoicism would eventually become a potent force in history, its influence was not sufficient to revive Greek culture. Its goals of virtue and perfection were too lofty for people to achieve by their own strength and reason. By appealing only to the morally and intellectually strong, Stoics ignored the masses, who often live by emotions. Stoic philosophy appealed to intellectuals who already accepted a correspondence between the soul of man and the external world. It could not, however, win the allegiance of either tough-minded skeptics or the morally unconcerned and confused.

A second school that aspired to fill the vacuum after Plato and Aristotle was the Cynics. While earlier Cynics emphasized the suppression of desire, later ones criticized belief in the gods, as well as science and traditional culture. They offered the ancient world little beyond their advice to adapt and to surrender to life.

A third attempt to provide answers during this time of cultural declension was Epicureanism. Epicurus (341–270 b.c.) taught in Colophon, in Mitylene, in Lampsacus, and finally in the Garden in Athens. He wrote some two hundred volumes, but little has been preserved.

Epicurus rejected many traditional Greek notions about the gods. While he assumed many gods exist who have human form, distinctions, and activity, he argued that they are not involved in human affairs. Their preoccupation with their own happiness and immortality has made them uninterested in human lives. The gods play no causative role in the universe. Instead reality consists of atoms and empty space and functions in a mechanistic manner. Epicurus believed that such an explanation freed men from fear of divine intervention into human affairs.

Individual man was seen as having primary significance. His greatest good is pleasure and his greatest evil is pain. Epicurus stressed that the mind has power over bodily suffering. The wise person is so free of external constraints that he is devoid of pain, contented, and self-sufficient. Epicurus assumed that people would be happy if they would "live hidden," that is, withdrawn from and independent of the world. He saw the human soul as composed of fire, air, spirit, and an unnameable substance. At death the soul's atoms are scattered so that men cease to exist. Epicurus argued, however, that while men live, they have a freedom of will, a view in sharp contrast with the determinism of Stoic fatalism. According to Epicurus, men are free to follow the self-centered pleasure principle.

It is not surprising then that skepticism revived in such an atmosphere. Pyrrho (d. 275 b.c.), Timon (d. 230 b.c.), and Arcesilaus (315/314–241/240 b.c.) sparked that revival. They declared that people cannot know the nature of things because perception reveals things not as they are but as we subjectively experience them. Knowledge about God, the world, or ourselves is impossible.

This journey through Greek thought reveals continual skepticism. Uncertainty about God inevitably leads to uncertainty about man and knowledge, just as false judgments about God inevitably lead to false judgments about man and knowledge. These speculations of Greek thinkers have continued to influence philosophers through the ages. Yet the high-water mark of Greek thought reached in Plato and Aristotle was never again to be rivaled in ancient times. Certain knowledge about reality was the aim of Greek thought. Though the Greeks achieved many profound insights into the nature of reality, they never obtained the certainty necessary to motivate men and nations. The Greek legacy was one of uncertainty and confusion as the era of Greek intellectual dominance ended with more questions than answers.

In summary, the dominant Greek understanding of man pictures him as finite. Human beings are entirely subordinate to the transcendent realm, but they are capable of achieving a type of salvation through their unaided, autonomous, rational efforts. Human nature is essentially good, and the soul participates in eternal being. Reason and contemplation are the basis of all knowledge and the way of salvation.

The Greek understanding of God was a curious melange. While deity was perceived in many different ways, conceptions of the ultimate may be summed up in the words *aloof* and *unconcerned*. By his own efforts, man could bridge the gulf between his own finitude and the infinite. By mystic rapture (the Dionysians) or by rational contemplation (the Ionians, Plato, Aristotle), Greek thinkers believed that the infinite could be known and attained. Even though man was capable of reaching the infinite, the infinite was unconcerned about man.

Throughout the history of Western culture, the Greek view of human perfectibility has been popular. In the twentieth century the Greek ideal has reappeared with special force and appeal in secular humanism. Consequently, many argue that man can perfect not only himself but also society as a whole. We are capable of realizing the infinite in both our individual and our social life. Such is the belief of modern "Greeks." They, like the Greeks of old, are unaware of man's essential sinfulness and of any need for the infinite to be revealed to the finite. Therefore, they will experience the same frustrations and disappointments that brought Greek culture to despair and to the failure of nerve that finally destroyed it.

For Further Reading

Burnet, J. *Greek Philosophy, Part I. Thales to Plato.* London: Macmillan, 1914.

Copleston, Frederick C. *A History of Philosophy*, vol. 1. Garden City, N.Y.: Doubleday, 1962.

Cornford, Francis MacDonald. *Before and After Socrates.* Cambridge: Cambridge University Press, 1932.

———. *The Republic of Plato.* New York: Oxford University Press, 1945.

Guthrie, W. K. C. *A History of Greek Philosophy*, 6 vols. Cambridge: Cambridge University Press, 1971.

Jowett, Benjamin. *The Works of Plato.* New York: Tudor, n.d.

Kerferd, G. B. "Aristotle" in *The Encyclopedia of Philosophy*, vol. 1. New York: Macmillan, 1967.

Passmore, John. *The Perfectibility of Man.* New York: Charles Scribner's Sons, 1970.

Ryle, Gilbert. "Plato" in *The Encyclopedia of Philosophy*, vol. 6. New York: Macmillan, 1967.

Taylor, Alfred Edward. *Plato, the Man and His Work.* New York: Dial, 1929.

3
The New Testament:
The Covenant of Redemption
in Jesus Christ

G. K. Beale and James Bibza

The Old Testament Covenantal Background

The whole Bible is about a covenant that will redeem man from sin, and the New Testament describes how the coming of Christ fulfills this promised covenantal redemption. The phrase *Old Testament* actually means "Old Covenant," and *New Testament* literally means "New Covenant." In fact these names indicate that there is an essential covenantal continuity between the two basic divisions or parts of the Bible.

As mentioned in the Old Testament chapter, God established the covenant of creation with man in the Garden of Eden when He made Adam in His own image to be His ruling representative on earth. The Lord promised Adam intimate communion with Himself as long as Adam faithfully carried out his stewardship responsibilities. But Adam's disobedience shattered this perfect relationship between God and himself and ended the covenant of creation. Because God loved mankind, He established a new *covenant of redemption* through which human beings could be restored to a right relationship with God.[1]

This covenant of redemption not only provides the means of human redemption, but also clearly reveals God's nature, espe-

---

1. This covenant was actually a promise of salvation, which was intimated in Gen. 3:15, where it is predicted that one of Eve's future descendants would fatally destroy the satanic serpent, and in Gen. 2:21, where God sheds animals' blood and covers Adam and Eve with the skins, a symbolic anticipation of the shedding of the Lamb's blood at the cross for the covering of human sin. God's promise is spelled out further to Abraham in Gen. 12:1–3, 13:15, and 15:18, and developed in the remainder of the Old Testament.

cially His unchanging attributes of grace, love, and justice in space-time history. Through His covenantal dealings, God acts in the world (i.e., He is immanent), much unlike Plato's impersonal forms and Aristotle's passive unmoved mover.

The coming of Jesus Christ to earth inaugurated the New Covenant (or New Testament). By dying on the cross He ratified the promised and long-awaited covenant of redemption (see Heb. 7:21–22; 9:24–26). Christ's mission was primarily to reveal the nature of His divine Father to the world and, secondarily, to provide a means of salvation for fallen, sinful man.

New Testament Theology: The Person and Work of Christ

Having said that, however, we must raise the question of who Jesus was and what He actually did. We will discover that Christ's titles, teaching, and miracles, as well as His death and resurrection, are all integrally related to His carrying out the covenant of redemption, and they testify to both His divinity and His true humanity.

The Titles of Jesus

"Messiah"

The Old Testament speaks often about a coming messianic age in which God would deliver Israel from its oppressors and establish it as the dominant kingdom on earth.[2] The word *Messiah*, "anointed one," or *Christ* in Greek, is used twice in the Old Testament to describe the coming deliverer (Ps. 2:2; Dan. 9:25). In ancient Israel kings, priests, and prophets who were chosen by God for special purposes were anointed with oil as a symbol of their divine appointment.

During the centuries immediately preceding Christ's birth most Jews fervently believed that the coming Messiah would militarily defeat Israel's enemies and reestablish the nation as a strong

2. Isa. 26–29; Ezek. 38ff.; Dan. 2, 7, 12; Zech. 14, etc.

earthly kingdom.[3] While the Messiah was seen primarily as a political leader, He was also expected to have strong religious convictions. The New Testament offers further evidence that Jewish tradition understood the promised Messiah mainly in terms of the Old Testament office of *king* (Mark 15:26; Luke 23:2). For example, when the multitudes began to perceive Jesus' miracles as a demonstration of His messiahship, they tried to "take him by force, to make him [an earthly] king." This expectation was an erroneous one, however, since Jesus had come as a Messiah who sought primarily *spiritual* and redemptive aims. Therefore, he "withdrew" from the crowds and did not allow them to fulfill their misguided desires (John 6:6–15).

It is somewhat surprising that in the Gospels Jesus rarely refers to Himself as "Messiah." Mark 8:29–30 is especially difficult to understand. In this passage, Peter confesses that Jesus is indeed the Messiah, but Jesus instructs His disciples not to reveal His identity to the Jewish people. Why would Jesus try to hide this fact from the multitudes? Some scholars answer that He did not. They theorize that the Christian church added these words later to explain why Jesus so seldom spoke of any kind of "messianic" mission and why He was not openly recognized by all as the Messiah. That theory, however, does not seem plausible. If Jesus never claimed to be the Messiah, how can we account for the first century church's strong conviction that He was such? It is unlikely that early Christians would have invented this idea themselves, since pronouncing a crucified man blessed was blasphemous. How much worse to call such a person Messiah! (cf. Deut. 21:23; Gal. 3:13–14).

The Gospels reveal, instead, that Jesus did view Himself as Messiah, but He interpreted that role very differently from the majority of His Jewish countrymen. Since most Jews expected the Messiah to be a political military leader, Jesus did not want to make His messianic claim public *until* people clearly understood that He was not coming to set up an earthly reign. Jesus' own understanding is stated in Mark 8:31. He explains to the disciples

---

3. Cf. Pss. of Sol. 17–18; IV Ezra 12–13.

that His messiahship must be understood in the light of the fact that he "must suffer many things and be rejected . . . and be killed, and after three days rise again" (Mark 9:12, 13). He had come to inaugurate a spiritual kingdom by dying on a cross. Only after the resurrection could people—including the disciples—understand this ironic messianic mission. After His resurrection Jesus freely acknowledged His messiahship since then it was clear to all that He was not a political messiah (see Luke 24:26).

Matthew 16:16 and Luke 9:20 clearly state Jesus' messianic consciousness as He defines the spiritual nature of His mission. Jesus believed that He was fulfilling Old Testament prophecies about a Messiah who would come principally to save men from their sins in order to fulfill the promises of the covenant of redemption.

During His trial Jesus was asked of Caiaphas directly, "Are you the Christ?" (Matt. 26:63–68; Mark 14:61–65). Caiaphas's charge that Jesus' answer was blasphemy, and subsequent accusations by His prosecutors that He called Himself the Messiah indicate that Jesus answered Caiaphas's question affirmatively (Matt. 26:68; 27:17, 22; Mark 15:32). In professing to be the Messiah, Jesus was acknowledging that He held the Old Testament offices of Prophet, Priest, and King. In fact the response that Jesus' claim was blasphemous implies that His claim carried a divine connotation.

"Son of God"

Two primary ideas are associated with this title. During an enthronement ceremony in the ancient Near East a king was often referred to as a "begotten son" because he was inheriting a kingly office bequeathed to him by his father, the former ruler. The formal designation "Son," together with birth metaphors, symbolized the official transfer of authority and the beginning of the son's long-awaited rule, for which he was born. This background helps to explain the prophecy in Psalm 2:6–8, which ultimately relates to Jesus' reception of His kingship in the Gospels: "I have installed my king. . . . You are my Son, today I have become your Father. Ask of me and I will make the nations your inheritance . . . " (v.7, NIV). The Gospel writers allude to this psalm when they narrate the divine address to Jesus at His baptism at the beginning of His ministry: "This is My beloved Son . . . " (e.g., Matt. 3:17; Mark 1:11). After His resurrection this same phrase was applied to Jesus again in order to denote the beginning of His heavenly reign and inheritance of His Father's kingdom (e.g., Acts 13:33; Heb. 1:2–5).

A second idea connected with "Son of God" is Jesus' *unique* filial relationship with His Father, which directly points to Christ's having the same divine nature as His Father (John 10:30–38). Jesus refers to God as *His* Father over one hundred and fifty times throughout the four Gospels. Matthew 11:27 (cf. Luke 10:22) expresses Jesus' unique sonship. This verse declares that only Jesus is able to reveal the Father to mankind, indicating that He has an exclusive relationship with God shared by no other human being. In addition, knowledge of the Son here appears to be equivalent to knowledge of the Father, which points clearly to the Son's deity.

John's Gospel emphasizes Jesus' unique sonship more than the Synoptics. Four different times Jesus is called the "only begotten Son" (John 1:14, 18; 3:16, 18, KJV). Statements concerning Jesus' essential deity as God's Son directly teach His uniqueness. For example, after Jesus healed a lame man on the Sabbath, the Jews accused Him of breaking God's law, which required people to rest on the Sabbath. Jesus defended His action by declaring that, since His Father works on the Sabbath, He must also work, thereby "making himself equal with God" (John 5:18). In John 10 Jesus says, "I and the Father are one [in essence]" (v. 30). In response to this statement the Jews took up stones to kill Jesus because they recognized that He was making Himself equal with God (see John 10:33). It is interesting that Jesus did not deny their understanding of His claim, but rather rebuked them for their lack of faith! In fact, one of the primary purposes of Jesus' mission was "to *explain* the Father" to the world (John 1:18) through revealing His own divine nature, which He shared with His heavenly Father (John 1:1, 14).

Several other features likewise indicate Jesus' uniqueness as

God's divine Son. Jesus' repeated statements that He "had been sent by the Father" testify to His divine preexistence (John 3:34-35; 5:36, 38). In John 8 Jesus states that "before Abraham was born, I am" (NIV). Abraham lived about eighteen hundred years before Christ. In saying this Jesus identified Himself with the great "I AM"—Yahweh—the God of the Old Testament (cf. Exod. 3:14; John 8:58). Also the Son alone can reveal the Father and speak His words (e.g., John 6:46; 8:26). Furthermore, the Son's functions are identified with God's functions, such as judging and imparting eternal life (e.g., John 5:19-30).

With such a strong emphasis upon the deity of the Son of God in John's Gospel, it might be thought that John denies the true humanity of Jesus. Nothing could be further from the truth. In fact, in John 1:14 we find one of the most explicit affirmations of Jesus' humanity: "And the Word became flesh and dwelt among us."

Some of Jesus' statements do show that the Son has limitations the Father does not have (e.g., Matt. 24:36; Mark 13:32; John 5:19). Jesus' remarks should be understood, however, as His contrasting the unbounded heavenly condition of the Deity (of God the Father) with His own restricted condition as God incarnate on earth. While on earth Jesus voluntarily surrendered not His deity but the free exercise of some of His divine attributes until after the resurrection (cf. Phil. 2:5-11).

"Son of Man"

Another of the most important yet mysterious of Jesus' titles is "Son of Man." Before Christ's birth this title was used only in the Old Testament. Because Jesus took the name from this source, it is necessary to understand how this phrase is used in the Old Testament.

The phrase "son of man" occurs in Psalm 8:4-6, Psalm 80:17-19, throughout Ezekiel, and in Daniel 7:13. Daniel 7:13 especially had the greatest influence upon Jesus' use of this title. In chapter 7 Daniel reports a prophetic vision in which he saw that in the end times God would judge the evil world empires and their ultimate ruler, Satan, removing their cosmic kingship

from them (Dan. 7:1-12, 17, 19-22b, 23-26). Then Daniel saw
that

> with the clouds of heaven one like a Son of Man was coming,
> and He came up to the Ancient of Days and was presented
> before Him. And to Him was given dominion, glory and a
> kingdom. . . . His dominion is an everlasting dominion . . .
> which will not be destroyed (Dan. 7:13-14, NASB).

God revealed to Daniel that the Son of Man was given dominion over the world, which had been taken away from the evil
rulers. Believing saints will receive the same eternal kingdom and
rule with the Son of Man, but only after they first have suffered
(Dan. 7:18, 21-22, 24-25, 27).

Although some scholars argue that Christ did not actually utter
many of the Son of Man sayings, the fact that the authors of the
New Testament Epistles use this name for Jesus only three times
points in a different direction. This title is authentic with Christ
who used it frequently because it summarized very well the kind
of ministry he had *before* the crucifixion. After His death this
phrase was rarely used because His other titles better described
the nature of His post-resurrection ministry.

With this Old Testament background in mind, we find that
Jesus used the phrase "Son of Man" in two general ways. First, it
refers to the three-year period of His public ministry, during which
He assumed a life of suffering and humble servanthood. What
appeared in Daniel's prophetic vision as a Son of Man gloriously
coming before God's throne to receive heavenly kingship, began
its fulfillment on earth as the paradoxical, inglorious three-year
ministry of Jesus. Nevertheless, Christ's mission did climax in His
receiving kingship before the divine throne at His ascension.
Furthermore, Jesus also used "Son of Man" to refer to His future,
latter-day glorification as cosmic King.

Of central importance is the Son of Man's purpose to lay down
His life to pay the penalty for man's sin (e.g., Mark 8:31; 9:12;
10:45). Perhaps the most significant passage in this category is
Mark 10:45 (Matt. 20:28): "For even the Son of Man did not
come to be served, but to serve, and to give his life as a ransom

for many" (NIV). In addition, there are clear indications that the glorified Jesus will return at the close of history to judge the wicked and deliver the saints (e.g., Mark 13:24–27; 14:62).

"Suffering Servant"

Jesus' emphasis upon His suffering and sacrificial death leads us to consider the concept of the "suffering servant." While this phrase is not a formal title for Jesus, He did apply this important Old Testament concept to Himself. The primary passage from which Jesus derived the concept of a "suffering servant" is Isaiah 52:13–53:12 (cf. Isa. 42:1–9; 43:10; 49:1–6). Isaiah 53 states several features that predicted Jesus' mission. The servant would be rejected, despised, and forsaken by His own people (53:1–3). He would suffer an excruciating, undeserved penalty for the sins of this people, even though He Himself would commit no sin (53:4–12). His suffering would be vicarious (substitutionary). Through it the guilty would be released from the penalty due them (53:5, 10–12). Although He would be buried with wicked criminals, He would be buried in a rich man's grave (53:9). Through His death the servant would win a victory over death and receive a reward as well (53:10–12).

Thus Isaiah 53 is the most articulate explanation of a divine servant's substitutionary suffering. Because Jesus was about to fulfill this role, He naturally applied this passage to His mission (e.g., Mark 9:12; Luke 22:37; John 12:38). Mark 10:45 most clearly illustrates the suffering servant passages where Christ applied to Himself ideas that were distinctives of the prophesied suffering servant of Isaiah 52:13–53:12. He was "to serve" in obedience to God and for the sake of other people. He was "to give his life" "a ransom"—as a substitutionary punishment or guilt offering. This guilt offering was to be "for many" (53:11–12). The whole verse represents a good summary of the major themes of Isaiah 53. We should note that elements of Isaiah 53 point towards a truly human servant. The Gospel writers strikingly testify to the deity and humanity of Jesus. While He continued to share the nature and attributes of His Father, He also mourned, hungered, thirsted, and grew tired—all human characteristics.

Our examination of four of the seventy titles applied to Jesus in the New Testament enables us to understand who He was and what He did. What is most striking is that no one prior to Jesus applied all four titles to one person. In particular, no one had ever explained that the titles "Messiah," "Son of God," *and* "Son of Man" could ever be understood through the concept of the suffering servant of Isaiah 53. The messianic mission traditionally associated with the first three titles was now interpreted in the light of Isaiah 53, a radically new and creative departure from the traditional Jewish view. Mark 8:27–37 is a significant passage in this respect, since three of these titles are applied to Jesus in one brief conversation, and the fourth title, "Son of God," is implied in "Messiah" (cf. Mark 1:1; Matt. 16:16; 26:63).

The Coming Kingdom of God as Expressed in
The Life and Teaching of Jesus

Just as Jesus' titles anticipated the *formal* beginning of the messianic kingdom at the ascension, so also do His teachings and deeds. Both represent the breaking in of the kingdom of God into space-time history.

Describing the kingdom Jesus has inaugurated, George E. Ladd says that it is

> the redemptive reign of God dynamically active to establish his rule among men, and that this Kingdom, which will appear as an apocalyptic act at the end of the age, has already come into human history in the person and mission of Jesus to overcome evil, to deliver men from its power and to bring them into the blessings of God's reign. The kingdom of God involves two great moments: fulfillment within history, and consummation at the end of history (G. E. Ladd, *A Theology of the New Testament* [Grand Rapids: Eerdmans, 1974], p. 91).

The Jews believed that the promised kingdom would come only at the end of world history when God would openly destroy the world's wicked kingdoms. Jesus, by contrast, taught that this kingdom, which would come at the end of history, had *already* begun in a hidden, mysterious form in the *midst* of history through His own ministry. His parables especially convey this hidden, mysterious nature of the kingdom. Examining a few sample parables will make this evident.

Parables

The parable of the sower and the seeds (Mark 4:1-10) describes different responses to the announcement of the kingdom. If Jesus was the Messiah initiating the long-awaited kingdom of God, why did not everyone believe and follow Him? This parable explains that the kingdom is not forced on anyone; many will reject the invitation to enter the kingdom, and only a few will accept. The problem is not with the sower or his seed! The problem is with the soil. God's kingdom is concerned with human hearts and works actively within individuals; it is not primarily an external force involved in political action.[4]

The parable of the tares of the field (Matt. 13:36-43) further explains the mysterious activity of the kingdom in the present age. Jewish tradition asserted that at the coming of the Messiah, God would separate the wicked from the righteous in order to judge the wicked. This parable teaches, however, that the initial form of the messianic kingdom allows the wicked to continue existing alongside the righteous without suffering the full judgment due them, while the righteous already begin to enjoy their blessings. The final separation and judgment will definitely occur, not now but at the end of history, when the messianic kingdom assumes its final form.

The parables of the mustard seed (Matt. 13:31-32) and of the leaven (Matt. 13:33) stress another aspect of the kingdom's hidden activity in this world. These parables teach that although Jesus' ministry begins small and apparently insignificant, the coming kingdom is nevertheless real (albeit invisible) and present. At the end of world history it will become visibly dominant on

---

4. In the Gospels Jesus' rejection as the Messiah is due to the Jews' unwillingness to accept His claims. Yet mysteriously their refusal was part of God's plan of salvation (see Jesus' comments on the people's inability to understand the parables [Mark 4:10-13] and His parable of the wicked tenants, as well as His remark about the rejected stone [Matt. 21:33-43]).

the earth. God's growing kingdom was not transforming human societies directly and immediately as the Jews expected the Messiah to do. The kingdom Jesus brought, however, was changing spiritual life, providing the foundation for social and cultural change. Expressing this difference, Jesus says, "My kingship is not of this world. If my kingship were of this world, my servants would fight, that I might not be handed over to the Jews; but my kingship is not from the world" (John 18:36). These parables not only explain the hidden, secret form of the kingdom; they also describe the "already-and-not-yet" temporal aspect. Jesus' earthly ministry inaugurated God's kingdom, although this kingdom will not be consummated until the end of history.

Another important category of parables consists of ones in which Jesus Himself is the subject. A major example is the parable of the vineyard owner who rents out his property to some tenants and goes away for several years. At each harvest time he sends servants to collect rent, but they are beaten and sent away empty-handed. Finally he sends his son to collect rent, but the tenants kill him. In this parable the vineyard owner is God, the tenants are the Jews, the servants are the Old Testament prophets, and the son is Jesus. The parable stresses the long-suffering of God the Father, and it predicts Jesus' rejection by the Jews and His imminent death. It implies that in rejecting Jesus, the Jews were rejecting the true kingdom of God inaugurated by Jesus, God's divine Son, and consequently would receive not salvation, but judgment (Luke 20:9-19).

Miracles

Jesus' miracles further emphasize the kingdom message of the parables and reveal more about His divine-human nature. One of the most striking examples of Jesus' miracles is His casting out demons from possessed people. Jesus explicitly stated, "If I drive out demons by the Spirit of God, then the kingdom of God has come upon you" (Matt. 12:28, NIV; cf. Luke 11:20). His power over demons testifies to His present victory and rule over Satan's kingdom which were central to the present messianic kingdom (Matt. 12:25-29; Mark 3:23-27; Luke 11:19-22). Hence Christ, during His ministry, saw "Satan fall like lightning from heaven" (Luke 10:18). Jesus' power over such a supernatural satanic foe clearly indicates His deity.

Jesus also viewed His miracles of healing as indications that the coming "day of the Lord" or "kingdom of God" was already present (cf. Matt. 11:4–5 and Luke 7:22, which quote Isa. 35:5–6 and 61:1–2). These miracles, especially those which healed the blind and deaf, attest that God appointed Jesus as Messiah to establish His kingdom on earth.

Furthermore, these healings point to the theological truth that Christ came to heal man's *spiritual* disease, which resulted from sin. This is clear in Mark 2:2–12 where Jesus directly connects His power to heal the body with His ability to forgive sins: "But that you may know that the Son of man has authority on earth to forgive sins . . . I say to you, rise, take up your pallet and go home" (Mark 2:10–11). The New Testament emphasizes that the power of God's kingdom was dramatically present in such physical and spiritual healing. Also, since only God has the authority to forgive sin, it is logical to conclude that in Mark 2 Jesus is implicitly claiming to be divine.

Jesus' ability to command the forces of nature offers further evidence that God's rule was breaking into history. His calming of the stormy sea (Mark 4:35–41) and His walking on water (Mark 6:45–52) show that Jesus is more than a mere man, since in the Old Testament only Yahweh controlled nature. In addition, since the *stormy seas* in the Old Testament symbolize satanic forces, the Gospel writers portrayed Jesus as reigning over such forces, which reinforces what they said explicitly in connection with His exorcisms.

The miracles wherein Jesus multiplied bread and fish to feed the multitudes probably have a twofold significance. They identify Jesus with Yahweh, who fed Israel with bread (manna) in the wilderness (see John 6:49–50). Moreover, miraculous meals may be the beginning of the messianic banquet of the divine kingdom, which Jewish tradition expected only at the end of history. By feeding people miraculously Jesus demonstrated how God's kingdom unexpectedly infiltrates space-time history.

Nothing holds more fear and dread for humans than death. Only God has the power to bestow life. Thus, Jesus' raising the dead (e.g., Mark 5:22-43; John 11:38-46) expresses His deity and reveals His ability to give not only physical but spiritual life to men's dead souls. These resurrections foreshadow His own resurrection, as well as the future resurrection of believers at the end of time. Therefore, such miracles graphically witness to the advent of God's kingdom, which is *formally* inaugurated at Christ's resurrection and ascension and is consummated at the end of the age when Christ returns.

The Resurrection of Jesus

Jesus' resurrection is of such significance that it needs to be discussed separately. His resurrection represents His conquest over death, and His ascension highlights His glorious exaltation to the right hand of the Father as King (Mark 16:19).

In I Corinthians 15:1-19 Paul explains that the gospel of Christ is absurd without a historical resurrection, and he summarizes the evidence for the resurrection found in the four Gospels. Jesus appeared to Peter and James, to all of the apostles, to a group of five hundred people, and, last of all, to Paul. The resurrection was the final verification of Christ's divine claims (cf. Rom. 1:4) and His kingdom message of salvation.

Many have objected, however, that such a historical resurrection did *not* take place. It is generally recognized that the tomb of Jesus was empty and that His disciples thought they saw the risen Jesus. Several major theories have emerged, however, to provide alternative explanations for the evidence traditionally offered to support the resurrection. These hypotheses attempt to explain both the empty tomb, short of Jesus' actually rising from the dead, and the resurrection appearances of Jesus.

According to the "wrong tomb" theory, on the first Easter morning the disciples went to a tomb where no one was buried. As a result, they mistakenly supposed Jesus to have risen from the dead. While this simple explanation appears to eliminate a miraculous exit from the grave, it is highly implausible since the empirical data do not support it. Not only was an official Roman guard placed at Christ's tomb, but a well-known citizen and follower of Jesus (Joseph of Arimathea) provided the tomb. Such a burial site would have been easy to find. In addition, if the disciples had gone to the wrong tomb, why did not the Jewish authorities simply produce the body of Jesus? This would have put a stop to the disciples' unsettling claims that Jesus had risen bodily from the grave. Thousands of Jews were accepting the claim as true. With every reason to prove them wrong, the Jews' failure to point out the proper tomb and produce the body of Jesus implies powerfully that they were *unable* to do so. Therefore, the "wrong tomb" theory is unpersuasive.

Recognizing this fact, some scholars have proposed that the Roman authorities took Jesus off the cross *before* he was dead, and that Jesus was revived by the tomb's coolness. Returning to His followers, Jesus was somehow able to convince them that He was resurrected from the dead. Yet, how could Jesus, in His weakened condition have moved the heavy stone that sealed the tomb and avoided being seen by the posted Roman guard? In such an injured condition He could hardly have impressed His disciples as being the Lord of life. Moreover, the Gospels present compelling evidence that Christ was dead before He was removed from the cross (cf. John 19:33–34), and no one in antiquity ever disputed that Jesus was dead when He was taken from the cross.

Others suggest that the disciples stole Jesus' body and then claimed He had risen from the dead. This proposal encounters several difficulties: How could the small band of fearful disciples overcome a trained Roman guard? How could this theory account for the radical change in the disciples' attitude? They acted cowardly during the trial and crucifixion but later dedicated their lives (most as martyrs) to spread Christ's claims and message of salvation. Jesus' disciples would hardly have been willing to die for what they knew to be a fraud, especially since Jesus had demanded absolute integrity.

A variation of this theory proposes that the Jewish leaders stole the body to prevent the disciples from doing it. But, if that were so, why did they have the Roman guard posted? Moreover, they certainly would have produced the body when the disciples began claiming that Christ had risen from the grave.

Even if one of these three theories could be shown to be plausible, it would still be necessary to account for the disciples' claims to have seen the risen Jesus. Thus, some have argued that these appearances were hallucinations rather than observations of actual historical events. However, the situations in which the apostles claimed to see Christ do not fit the standard characteristics of hallucinations. Hallucinations usually happen to individuals, not groups, and are subjective in character (contrast I Cor. 15). The physical senses other than sight would tend not to corroborate an imagined "appearance" (contrast John 20:17, 27; Luke 24:39-43). Hallucinations are usually restricted to certain times and conditions (contrast Jesus' appearances at different times and places). A precondition for hallucinations seems to be a strong desire to see the person or thing that "appears." Thus, those hoping and expecting to see departed loved ones are usually the people who claim such encounters (contrast the disciples' cowardice, desertion, and loss of hope). Furthermore, hallucinations tend to occur over a long period with regularity, while Christ's appearances were within a period of forty days, and then, with the exception of one appearance to Paul, they ceased completely.

Having examined the attempted explanations for the empty tomb and the appearances of Jesus, we must conclude that the "wrong tomb" theory, the "swoon" theory, the "stolen body" theory, and the "hallucination" hypothesis are extremely implausible. Presuppositions that rule out the miraculous have yet to produce a credible explanation for the empty tomb and the resurrection appearances. The most reasonable conclusion from the historical evidence of the Gospels is that Jesus rose bodily from the grave and actually appeared to His disciples. His resurrection authenticated His claims to deity and His message of salvation. It also validated His claim to be Messiah in that it led directly to His ascension to His Father's heavenly throne, where He began His *formal* reign over God's kingdom.

Thus the parables emphasize that Jesus is the Messiah who brings a kingdom to earth, and they *imply* that He is divine (cf. the parable of the vineyard in Luke 20:9-19). Jesus' titles and miracles not only point directly to His messianic office but they bear witness to His *divine* identity.

Jesus' own teachings about Himself as God's Son in the Gospel of John perhaps offer the clearest testimony to His deity. In proclaiming Himself to be the Son of God, Jesus boldly asserted that He had the same divine nature as His heavenly Father. Because He and the Father were one, Jesus identified Himself as the preexistent Yahweh of the Old Testament. Just as Yahweh demonstrated and revealed His deity in the Old Testament by performing miracles, so Jesus did the same thing in the New Testament.

Hence, our examination of Jesus' teaching brings us to the conclusion that Jesus presented Himself as the divine King—the God-man Himself—and not merely some great moral teacher as many have argued. One might ask at this point, What other alternative exists for someone who acknowledges that there is some historical truth in the New Testament, but who rejects Jesus' claims to be the Son of God? Here two explanations are possible. (1) Jesus could have *known* His claims were false and thus deliberately misrepresented Himself and the God who "sent" Him. In this case, Jesus would clearly have been a liar and a hypocrite. Since these claims led the Jews to kill Him, Jesus would have to have been a fool. Or (2) Jesus might *not* have known that His claims to deity were false. In this case, we could say that Jesus was sincerely deluded, or a lunatic.

C. S. Lewis has summarized nicely the alternatives:

> You can shut Him up for a fool, you can spit at Him and kill Him as a demon; or you can fall at His feet and call Him Lord and God. But let us not come up with any patronizing nonsense about His being a great human teacher. He has not left that open to us. He did not intend to (*Mere Christianity*, [New York: Macmillan, 1952], pp. 40, 41).

New Testament Anthropology and Its Relation to the Redemptive Work of Christ

When Adam and Eve first sinned in the Garden of Eden and broke the covenant of creation, which God made with them, their sinless nature became a sinful one. As a result, Adam's and Eve's descendants go "astray from the womb, they err from their birth" (Ps. 58:3); "every imagination of the thoughts" of their hearts is "only evil continually" (Gen. 6:5). Jeremiah asserted that "the heart is deceitful above all things, and desperately corrupt" (Jer. 17:9). This sinfulness is universal "for there is no man who does not sin" (II Chron. 6:36), so that "surely there is not a righteous man on earth who does good and who never sins" (Eccles. 7:20). "Can the Ethiopian change his skin or the leopard his spots?" asked Jeremiah. Then neither can a man change his sinful nature (Jer. 13:23).

Building upon this Old Testament background, Jesus stated that each person "is a slave to sin" (John 8:34), whose will is dedicated to serving the desires of "your father the devil" (John 8:44). Consequently we are unable to change our desires and "come to" believe in Jesus unless "the Father draws" us through grace (John 6:44, 65).

Like Jesus, Paul also portrayed humans as inherently sinful. Romans 1–3 is Paul's most systematic presentation of our sinful condition and its harmful effects. Paul teaches there that when Adam sinned and broke his original covenant relationship with God, he became spiritually separated from God. The condemnation arising from sin also fell upon all of Adam's descendants: "As sin came into the world through one man, and death through sin, and so death spread to all men . . . " (Rom. 5:12). Adam was a *federal representative* for man, which means that Adam's sinful act and resulting condemnation were attributed to all people. His sin and its consequences were reckoned by God to be ours. Legally it was as if all people had done what Adam did and must suffer what he suffered. Both Jew and Gentile are included under this condemnation (cf. Rom. 1:18–3:18), so that there is no one righteous, not even one; there is no one who understands, no one who seeks for God . . . there is no one who does good, not even one (Rom. 3:10-12, NIV).

This means that we are "totally depraved" in that our whole being is affected by sin. While we may perform "good acts" toward our fellowman, none of our works are good enough to gain our salvation: "For no human being will be justified in His sight by works of the law" (Rom. 3:20). It is not that we are as bad as we could be. But left to ourselves, we are completely unable to overcome our spiritual separation from God and achieve the original relationship Adam had with his Creator. Being spiritually dead because of sin, we are unable to impart life to ourselves (Eph. 2:1-3). If we remain in such a condition throughout our temporal life, we will remain separated from God in our eternal life.

Paul concludes in Romans 3:23 that "all have *sinned* [broken God's moral laws] and are condemned because they "fall short of the glory of God [are spiritually separated from His presence]." The only solution to our predicament is explained in Romans 3:24ff.: Christ's death and resurrection are the exclusive means of our salvation. Paul portrays Jesus as the one who has finally come to fulfill the covenant of redemption promised to Abraham. In Galatians 3:13-14 Paul says:

> Christ redeemed us from the curse of the law, having become a curse for us . . . that in Christ Jesus the blessing of Abraham might come . . . so that we might receive the promise of the Spirit through faith.

Paul appeals to three different concepts in Romans 3:24-25 in order to explain how Christ's death accomplished our salvation and fulfilled the covenant of redemption.

The first concept is justification, which means that those who believe Christ's death was on their behalf are *declared* (not made) righteous or just. Individuals are *considered* or *accounted* to be just (cf. Rom. 4:5-9), not on the basis of their own works, but because of Christ's sinless life and substitutionary death. Righteousness is transferred to the believer, and the believer's sin and separation from God are transferred to Christ at the cross. Instead of the believer's being eternally forsaken, Jesus Himself becomes "forsaken" by the Father at the cross (Mark 15:34).

The term *justification* has a legal connotation and its verb forms in Greek were often used in judicial contexts to pronounce persons "not guilty" who had been proved innocent through trial. So Paul was saying that the believer is pronounced "not guilty"—justified—because of Christ's death. Christ's last words on the cross, "It is finished," indicate that the eternal debt for man's sin had at last been paid (cf. Rom. 3:25–26). In fact, during the first century the words "it is finished" were commonly written across bills after debts were paid. By dying on the cross, Christ accomplished the same thing for believers on an infinitely larger scale.

Justification is a gift of God's grace (Rom. 3:24a). It does not result from anything human beings do themselves. Of course, from the human perspective, people can be justified only by having *faith* in Christ's death. Yet even human faith is a result of divine grace (Eph. 2:8–9), since justification can *never* stem from any human cause (thus Rom. 3:24a and 9:16: "it [salvation] depends not upon man's will or exertion, but upon God's mercy").

In Romans 3:24b justification is accomplished "through the *redemption* which is in Christ Jesus." The word *redemption* means "release by a price or cost," and the language of redemption was often used in the slave market of the ancient world. It described how slaves could be released if someone would pay a ransom price for them. Paul views mankind then as in bondage to sin and deserving its penalty. But believers are released from this punishment by the price of Jesus' shed blood at the cross (Rom. 3:25a; Rev. 5:9). As Jesus said, the Son of man came "to give his life as a ransom *for many*" (Mark 10:45; 5:9). Thus, *release* from both the bondage and the condemnation of sin through Christ's blood is essential to accomplishing justification.

One of the least understood words used to describe salvation is the term *propitiation*. Yet propitiation is also an integral part of justification: "God displayed [Jesus] publicly as a propitiation in his blood" (Rom. 3:25a, NASB). The word translated "propitiation," literally means "mercy seat." It refers to the place in the innermost part of the temple in Jerusalem where annually a lamb's blood was shed to "cover" Israel's sins committed during the past year. The temporal penalty the Jews deserved for their sins God executed on the lamb instead. The nation Israel would have perished if this provisional substitution had not been in force.

Paul regarded these Old Testament sacrificial lambs at the "mercy seat" as foreshadowing or pointing to the ultimate penal substitutionary sacrifice of Jesus, the Lamb of God. Christ experienced the eternal wrath and condemnation from God on behalf of believers at the New Testament "mercy seat," the cross (cf. Heb. 9-10). While justification and redemption involve the idea of penal substitution, propitiation highlights this concept.

Propitiation describes the relationship between God the Father and Jesus the Son in which Jesus suffered the eternal wrath of the Father by dying on the cross. Because Christ's death satisfied divine justice, God looks upon the believer's debt as having been paid, and declares him to be just. Propitiation also enables Jesus to redeem believers from their servitude to sin and their deserved punishment. In this justifying work for the believer Christ is a Last Adam and is seen as man's *federal representative* (his spiritual "congressman"). His act of suffering eternal condemnation is viewed legally as our act—as if we had actually been there dying on the cross ourselves (cf. Rom. 5:16-19; II Cor. 5:18-21).

But the death of Jesus would have had no saving effect without His resurrection from the dead. His resurrection validated and authenticated the effectiveness of the salvation Christ wrought by His death. So Paul affirmed that Jesus was *raised* in order to accomplish our justification (cf. Rom. 5:16-19; II Cor. 5:18-21).

There are a number of other results of Jesus' redemption. When a person believes through the regenerating work of the Holy Spirit (Titus 3:5), his old sinful nature is transformed into a new, spiritual nature (i.e., he is "born again"; cf. John 3:4-9; Rom. 6), so that he begins to desire and is progressively able to obey God. Moreover, when the Holy Spirit gives new life to a person, the Spirit indwells that person from then on, inspiring him or her to do good works perpetually (cf. John 16:1-15; Rom. 8:1-17). The ultimate, long-range effect of redemption is the future resurrection of the believer's body and his entrance into the new heavens and new earth, and into God's eternal presence (cf. Dan. 12:1-2; I Cor. 15:18-23; Rev. 20-22).

Conclusion

Jesus Christ came as the God-man in order to offer Himself as a penal substitute through death for man's sin. He rose again to authenticate His divine claims and redemptive message. His saving death and resurrection were necessary to accomplish the covenant of redemption. This covenant had been promised ever since Adam's fall as a way to restore human beings into the saving presence of the Lord. Jesus' restorative work has created a new spiritual race whose members begin a spiritual transformation in this life and render service to the Lord throughout eternity.

As indicated above in our discussion about Jesus' possible identities (liar, lunatic, or Lord), the New Testament writers present a world view that involves much more than simply a set of intellectual ideas. They challenge readers from all ages and every condition in life to study the claims of Christ and to respond personally in repentance and faith. Biblical writers present not just compelling *ideas* but a spiritually moving *appeal* aimed at transforming both the minds and the hearts of their readers.

The biblical world view presents the Gospel of Jesus Christ as truly "good news" to all of us who are enslaved by our sinfulness. However, just as a person dying of cancer must personally apply a newly found cancer cure, so the good news is meaningless to people with spiritual cancer if it is not internalized by their accepting Jesus as their own Redeemer and Master. After twenty centuries Christianity still claims that Jesus is "the way, the truth, and the life" (John 14:6). People's changed lives attest to His power to motivate His followers to implement Christian values in a fallen world. The Christian world view prompts us to proclaim the gospel as God's offer of redemption to fallen human beings. In subsequent chapters we shall see that Christianity also forcefully challenges believers to practice biblical ideas in every area of life. Indeed, there is no aspect of life, private or public, that would not be revolutionized if Christians were to take seriously the practical implications of the Christian world view.

For Further Reading

Anderson, Norman. *The Teaching of Jesus.* Downers Grove, Ill.: Inter-Varsity, 1983.

Boice, James Montgomery, *Awakening to God.* Downers Grove, Ill.: Inter-Varsity, 1979.

———. *God the Redeemer.* Downers Grove, Ill.: Inter-Varsity, 1978.

———. *Our Savior.* Downers Grove, Ill.: Inter-Varsity, 1980.

Bruce, F. F. *The New Testament Documents: Are They Reliable?* Grand Rapids: Eerdmans, 1943.

Copeland, E. Clark. "The Covenant, the Key to Understanding the Bible," *The Book of Books.* Edited by John White. Phillipsburg, N.J.: Presbyterian and Reformed, 1978.

Green, Michael. *The Empty Cross of Jesus.* Downers Grove, Ill.: Inter-Varsity, 1984.

Ladd, George. *I Believe in the Resurrection of Jesus.* Grand Rapids: Eerdmans, 1975.

———. *The Presence of the Future.* Grand Rapids: Eerdmans, 1974.

McDonald, H. D. *Jesus, Human and Divine.* Grand Rapids: Zondervan, 1968.

McDowell, Josh. *The Resurrection Factor.* San Bernardino, Calif.: Here's Life, 1981.

Sproul, R. C., ed. *Soli Deo Gloria.* Phillipsburg, N.J.: Presbyterian and Reformed, 1976.

Stein, Robert. *The Method and Message of Jesus' Teachings.* Philadelphia: Westminster Press, 1978.

II.
SYNTHETIC MEDIEVAL
WORLD VIEWS

4
Christian Theology Emerges: The Council of Nicaea

W. Andrew Hoffecker

Introduction

Thus far in our study we have outlined two radically different perspectives on God and man—the pagan Greek and the Judaeo-Christian views. New Testament writers frequently contrasted biblical ideas and the emerging Christian theology with Greek philosophy and wisdom.

In some instances Christian thought is simply portrayed as opposite to the ways of "the world" (cf. I John 2:15-17; James 4:4). On other occasions the authors of the New Testament specifically refer to a clash between Christian and Greek ideas. In I Corinthians 1:18-2:13, for example, Paul contrasts "the word of the cross" with the "wisdom of the world" and "the wisdom of this age." By the "word of the cross" Paul means preaching Christ's death as the only atonement for man's sins. Only those who repent and trust Christ as Savior and Lord will be redeemed. How different from "the wisdom of the world," the vain attempts by Greek "wise men," "scribes," and "debaters," to find paths to salvation based on human wisdom. Explicitly Paul states that "Greeks seek wisdom, but we preach Christ crucified" (I Cor. 1:23). While Greek and Christian cultures often existed in close geographic proximity in the first century A.D., intellectual leaders from both sides viewed their controlling ideas as fundamentally irreconcilable. The apostles made little attempt to fuse elements from Christian and Greek world views into a larger synthesis. They did not believe that Christian thought should or could assimilate Greek ideas into its basic structure. Dominating New Testament theology is the antithesis, the emphatic contrast,

73

between Greek and Christian views. For example, John's use of the Greek *logos* ("word") for Jesus in the prologue of his Gospel (1:1–18) illustrates how Christian authors fundamentally altered Greek ideas if they used them at all. The apostle did not incorporate Greek concepts into Christianity unchanged, but *transformed* the impersonal, abstract "word" into dynamic, personal terms as the incarnate Son of God: "And the Word became flesh and dwelt among us, full of grace and truth; we have beheld his glory, glory as of the only Son from the Father" (John 1:14). Greek thinkers such as Plato and his later followers would never have conceived of the ultimate in personal terms, and still less would they have proposed that ideals could be incarnated in the sense that Christ was truly the Son of God manifested in human flesh.

Second- and Third-Century Christianity

Whereas first-century Christians perceived a sharp contrast between New Testament theology and Greek philosophy, in the second and third centuries some Christians came to believe that great insights from other cultures and world views could be used to support and advance biblical ideas. We now turn our attention to those who deliberately attempted to construct such syntheses. Beginning in the second century and continuing through the Middle Ages, the Renaissance, and beyond, certain Christian theologians sought to weave biblical and Greek ideas together. Leading Christian thinkers manipulated previously separate traditions in a multitude of ways to render biblical and Greek ideas more compatible.

In this chapter we consider the first of four ecumenical councils convened to discuss the person of Christ. They were called ecumenical (from the Greek word *oikomene*, meaning "world") because participating delegates represented churches located throughout the Roman Empire, and their decisions were considered binding on the whole church. Councils were held at Nicaea (A.D. 325), Constantinople (A.D. 381), Ephesus (A.D. 431), and

Chalcedon (A.D. 451). All dealt with issues in what we now call the christological controversy.

Each council was charged with formulating a definitive position regarding Jesus Christ, the Son of God. Was He God in the same way as the Father is God, or was He merely the first created being? Did Christ have both a divine and a human nature, and, if so, were they separate and distinct or mixed together in a confused fashion? Such questions were discussed in great detail, and answers to them were formulated in creeds (from the Latin *credo*, "I believe") as statements of doctrine for all Christians to affirm.

These profound theological questions required the church to publish authoritative answers. Any Christian who reflects on the person of Christ as He is presented in the pages of Scripture is likely to think of these issues. Until Nicaea, church leaders gave no definitive explanation of the nature of Christ other than by appealing to certain Scripture passages. Even in apostolic times Christians struggled to express in words who Christ was. Leaders of the early church strongly opposed views of Christ that were not in keeping with apostolic teaching. Some members of churches founded by Paul denied Christ's *deity* and transformed the gospel into a system of laws (Col. 2:8ff.) that required obedience to numerous rituals and food regulations (Col. 2:16ff.). By contrast, John contended with others who denied Jesus' true *humanity*, inasmuch as they believed that a true incarnation was impossible (I John 4:1ff.). The apostles penned strong letters to combat such heretical ideas and to affirm both Christ's deity and His humanity.

By the third century, however, various parties had emerged whose leaders offered conflicting explanations of how the title "Son of God" was to be understood. How was "the Son of God" related to the one God, Yahweh, whom Jews professed? Should the church simply recite various scriptural passages to settle such an issue? Or should the church seek to establish a systematic biblical statement, a standard such as a creed, to judge conflicting ideas?

The Nicene Controversy

Initially, two schools, one in Alexandria, Egypt, and the other in Antioch in what is now southern Turkey, offered different interpretations of the person of Christ. Each school charged that the other distorted what Scripture teaches. The dispute came to a head in A.D. 318 when the Bishop of Alexandria took offense to a letter from one of his presbyters, Arius. Arius held that since there is but one God, the Father, who alone is Creator, all other beings must be creatures, an order of being distinct from God. God the Father is unique. Therefore the Son *is* a creature, albeit the first and perfect creature. The Son came into being, out of nothing, through an act of creation. Arius achieved infamy with the phrase, "There was when he was not," that is, there was once a time when the Son did not exist. In short, Arius denied that the Son is God.

Athanasius, secretary of the bishop, championed the cause of those who found Arius's views at odds with the New Testament. He carefully pointed out that Arius's view of Christ contradicted the Bible's clear teaching in two important respects. First, Arius ignored or rejected biblical passages that unequivocally affirm the deity of Christ. Drawing material from John's Gospel, Athanasius pointed out that the Son was "in the beginning with God" and "was God" (John 1:2, 3). Throughout that Gospel Jesus claims for Himself the prerogatives of God. He "gives life to whom he will" and has been entrusted with judgment so that "all may honor the Son even as they honor the Father" (5:21–23). In John 10:38 Jesus declares, "The Father is in me and I am in the Father," and in 8:58 He even assumes the Old Testament name for God, "I AM," leading Jews to pick up stones to kill Him for blasphemy. In numerous other passages Jesus claims for Himself, and New Testament writers repeatedly ascribe to Him, full deity.

Worse yet, Arius's view of Christ's person could not explain how Jesus accomplished redemption by dying on the cross. If the Son were not God, His death on the cross could not pay for the sins of others. It would only provide an example of sacrificial love. Only a Son who was truly God could die a death that could redeem sinful men. Otherwise His death and resurrection were effective only for Himself. The necessity of Christ's full humanity and deity is evident in I Timothy 2:5, 6: "For there is one God, and there is one mediator between God and men, the man Christ Jesus, who gave himself as a ransom for all. . . . " In subsequent centuries Christian theologians further refined how Christ's full humanity and deity were necessary for salvation. Only if Christ was truly *God* could He overcome the power of sin; only if Christ was truly *man* could His death and resurrection be applied to other human beings.

Debate over Arius's and Athanasius's positions centered on which of two words correctly describes Christ's person in the New Testament. The Arians held that the Son is *homoiousios* with the Father, literally "of *a similar* substance." The Athanasian party argued instead that the Son is *homoousios* with God the Father, "of *the same* substance," and they contended that the issue was more than a theological dispute over Christ's nature. Central to the debate was whether Christ's work on the cross could save men from their sins.

The Council of Nicaea agreed with Athanasius. Delegates composed a creed to state the issues clearly. It contained the following phrases, which are incorporated in creeds still used today in church liturgies:

> We believe in one God the Father All-sovereign, maker of all things visible and invisible; And in one Lord Jesus Christ, the Son of God, begotten of the Father, only-begotten, that is of the substance [*homoousios*] of the Father, God of God, Light of Light, true God of true God, begotten not made, of one substance with the Father, through whom all things were made, things in heaven and things on earth; who for us men and our salvation came down from heaven and was made flesh, and became man. . . .

The creed explicitly affirms Athanasius's position on the deity of Christ, and just as explicitly it denies the Arian position. The creed was so worded that an Arian could not possibly subscribe to it. It affirms that the Son was "not made" (not created) but was "begotten." Thus, Christ is not merely "of a similar substance" but "of one substance with the Father." Father and Son are both

God. The Son is the "only begotten" Son of God (taken from John 1:14) and therefore is unique. No other sons are of the same substance with the Father. (By contrast Paul states, in Gal. 4:5, that Christians are sons of God by "adoption.")

Having stated belief in the Son's deity, the creed briefly mentions a second crucial issue, what the Son did. By being God and then subsequently becoming flesh, the Son was able to save. But unless the Son was God, His incarnation, death, and resurrection were impossible.

The Nicene Creed became the definitive statement for Christians on the deity of Christ. Other ecumenical councils built on its foundation in their attempts to clarify biblical teachings on the Trinity, the divine and human natures of Christ, and the deity of the Holy Ghost. Each council drafted a creed to resolve the issues its delegates debated. Such creeds became recognized as authoritative statements of Christian faith, thereby giving the church a standard for distinguishing between orthodoxy ("right teaching") and heresy (false teaching).

Nicaea in Historical Perspective

How are we to assess Nicaea in the context of our study of perspectives on God and man? The Nicene theologians sought to explain the nature of Christ on the basis of the Scriptures. To some extent they ventured beyond Scripture by employing the language of the "substance" (*ousios*) of God, a notion somewhat foreign to the biblical writers. Unlike the pre-Socratic philosophers, who tried to explain all of reality in terms of an ultimate "substance" or "stuff," New Testament writers affirmed Jesus' deity in terms of all that He, like His Father, could *do*. He healed people's diseases, exercised authority over powers of nature, claimed the prerogative to forgive sin, and even raised the dead. The question of whether the Father and the Son are of the same "substance" or similar "substances" did not find expression until Greek Christians, confronted with Christ's unique claim to be divine, sought to explain the deity of Christ by means of a concept rooted in their own culture.

Thus Nicene orthodoxy went beyond the language of Scripture. As a response to a question growing out of the Greek cultural milieu, Athanasius's position correctly expounds the New Testament view of Christ's person and shows the unbiblical nature of Arius's position. Although, of course, the Nicene statement does not have equal authority with the Bible, its creed became the standard for the whole church, in that the Council of Nicaea was ecumenical in scope.

But as an attempt to interpret Christian doctrine in terms influenced by Greek categories as much as or more than by New Testament ones, the Nicene teaching prepared the way for the subsequent synthesis of Greek and Christian thought in the Middle Ages. Athanasius and his followers could have achieved more of a balance by emphasizing that a better way to understand Christ's deity was in terms of His office or function. He came to save men from their sins. The Bible thus understands God and man in dynamic terms rather than in the more static Greek ontological terms of "substance." Theology that is most akin to biblical thinking constantly relates Christ's person and work to each other and resists viewing them in abstraction from each other.

To illustrate the point, consider that in contemporary society we understand people from two points of view: who they are and what they do. Someone may *be* your friend, brother, or enemy. You would expect that person to *act* in a friendly, brotherly, or hostile manner toward you depending on how you view him or her as a person. If what an individual claims to be does not coincide with how he acts, you immediately note the disparity. Therefore, you constantly relate to people on these two levels. Sometimes you consider the ontological (who or what one *is*), and on other occasions you look to the functional (how a person *behaves*). The two views are complementary and should not be isolated from each other. The Council of Nicaea tended to be more concerned about the ontological than the functional. In that respect it dealt with the person of Christ more from a Greek than from a biblical perspective.

While elements of synthetic thinking are present in the Nicene Creed, its message is overwhelmingly biblical. In comparison with synthetic theologies developed in the later Middle Ages, the theology of Nicaea contains only a trace of synthesis. Positively,

Nicaea was a milestone in Christianity's first three hundred years. It successfully countered one of the first heresies that threatened to gain widespread support in the church. By stating its findings in creedal form, it affirmed what all Christians were to believe. The creed reiterated the New Testament truth that Jesus Christ, the Son of God, was God incarnate and not simply another creature. Throughout church history Christians have recognized the positive influence Nicaea had in determining Christian doctrine by its statement of a biblical view of Christ as God. The Nicene Creed has helped believers in every age to confess their faith in Christ. Notwithstanding its use of Greek categories, it affirmed the central truth of the New Testament, that Christ was "God of God, Light of Light, true God of true God."

For Further Reading

Elwell, Walter, ed. *Evangelical Dictionary of Theology.* Articles on "Arianism," "Athanasius," and "Nicaea, Council of." Grand Rapids: Baker, 1984.

Kelley, J. N. D. *Early Christian Creeds.* 3rd ed. New York: Harper and Row, 1972.

———. *Early Christian Doctrines.* Rev. ed. New York: Harper and Row, 1960.

Murray, John Courtney. *The Problem of God.* New Haven: Yale University Press, 1964.

Nash, Ronald H. *Christianity and the Hellenistic World.* Grand Rapids: Zondervan, 1984.

Norris, R. A. *The Christological Controversy.* Philadelphia: Fortress, 1980.

Richardson, Alan. *Creeds in the Making.* Philadelphia: Fortress, 1935.

Schaff, Philip. *A History of the Christian Church.* New York: Charles Scribner's, 1910.

5
Biblical Interlude:
Augustine's Trinitarianism

Charles S. MacKenzie

Augustine's Career

Intellectual leaders have deeply influenced both the form and substance of Western civilization. In numerous ways their ideas have filtered down to the masses, sometimes creating movements and forces that have profoundly shaped Western history. Most important among Christian leaders who have significantly affected the course of Western society are Augustine, Aquinas, Luther, and Calvin. Their interpretations and commentaries on Judeo-Christian theology and history established major patterns for Western thought and culture. This chapter and the following two will explore similarities and differences among the teachings of these prominent theologians.

Augustine was a colossus who gave Christian thought much of its formative character. He was Catholic and yet evangelical, a sophisticated citizen of the world and yet a humble, devout Christian. He was born in 354 in Tagaste, Algeria, a town the Romans had built. Surrounded by high whitewashed walls, it boasted a forum, a theatre, baths, and a marketplace. Augustine's father, Patricius, owned a small farm and a few slaves. Although he was harsh and uncompromising, Patricius was unconcerned about morality and allowed his son to do whatever he wished. Augustine's mother, Monica, in contrast to her husband, was a devout Christian who dearly loved Augustine, as well as his brother and sister.

An African by birth, the young Augustine had dark bronze skin, was tall and long-limbed, and had magnificent eyes. He loved athletics, was highly competitive, and was a crack shot slinging stones. His love for gambling once led to his being thrashed for rolling dice in school. As a boy he quarreled, fought, lied, stole, and was quite rambunctious.

When he was twelve years old, his parents sent him to Madaura to attend a school for intellectually gifted children. There Augustine began his education by reading Vergil and other Greek and Roman poets. In his early teens his lust and sensuality also blossomed. He later wrote, "I dared to roam the woods and pursue my vagrant loves. . . . the torrent of my fornications tossed and swelled and boiled and ran over."

When he was sixteen years old, his father died, and being without funds Augustine would have been forced to return home had it not been for a wealthy man named Romanian who paid for his further schooling in Carthage. This seaport city on the Mediterranean had a reputation for being one of the most corrupt cities of the Roman Empire. While studying there Augustine was caught up in sensuality, about which he wrote later, "My mother commanded me not to commit fornication . . . this seemed to me no better than woman's counsel. . . . " His mother's advice lingered in his mind, however, for he uttered his famous prayer, "God give me chastity—but not yet." In Carthage he took a mistress and fathered a son, Adeodatus.

Meanwhile his intellectual growth continued. His study of philosophy made him disillusioned with the style and substance of the Bible, and he became involved with a cult called the Manichaeans. Their founder, Mani of Babylonia, taught a dualism wherein a cosmic kingdom of light wages war against a cosmic kingdom of darkness. While some light is confined in man, he is essentially a material, bodily prison house of evil. Salvation comes from right thinking (reason) and an ascetic rejection of physical appetites and desires. Adherents of Manichaeism were divided into two classes. The few, called the elect, practiced a strict, monastic life. The many, designated auditores or hearers, simply accepted the doctrines intellectually. Attracted to its emphasis on rational demonstration of wisdom, its rejection of the Old Testament, and the vigorous spirituality of its elect, Augustine remained a Manichaean hearer for ten years.

On one of his visits home to Tagaste, Augustine told his mother of his interest in this cosmic dualism. Upset that this abstract system made no room for Jesus' redemptive activity, Monica tearfully ordered her son to leave her house.

Restless and troubled, the thirty-year-old Augustine decided to move from Carthage to Rome. Disenchanted with Manichaeism, he became a skeptic in search of a new faith. While in Rome, Augustine's search for a new faith led him to Neoplatonism, a revised version of Plato's philosophy. A year later he moved to northern Italy to take a teaching position in rhetoric. Upon arriving in Milan with his mistress and his young son, Adeodatus, he rented a villa, and when he was not teaching, he studied Neoplatonism.

The Neoplatonists taught that (1) God is pure, perfect being. (2) From God emanates universal mind, then a world-soul, and finally the realm of matter. Each wave has less being than the preceding one because it emanates further away from God. The whole universe is a series of gradations or emanations from God. (3) Men rise to God by living a strict ascetic life and by engaging in mystic meditation as a way of salvation.

For a while Augustine was fascinated by Neoplatonism, which had certain similarities with Manichaeism.[1] But under the influence of Monica, who had come to live with him, Augustine began to attend church where he listened to the sermons of Bishop Ambrose of Milan. These stirred his heart and mind and interested him in Christianity. He left his mistress. Then in July of 386, when Augustine was thirty-two years old, a friend challenged him to answer the question, "What am I doing on this earth?" After his friend left his home, Augustine went out into his garden and heard the voice of a child who was playing nearby. When the child cried "Take up and read," Augustine found the nearest book, a Bible, opened it at random and read Paul's words, "Not in rioting and drunkenness, not in chambering and wantonness, not in strife and envying, but put ye on the Lord Jesus Christ,

1. Christian Science, begun by Mary Baker Eddy in late nineteenth-century America, has major affinities with Neoplatonism.

and make not provision for the flesh to fulfill the lusts thereof" (Rom. 13:13, 14). At once Augustine felt the presence and peace of Christ enter his life. He wrote, "It was as though the light of salvation had been poured into my heart." Augustine had become a Christian. Almost immediately he and his friends went to the country for a retreat. There he thought through his new faith, expressing it in Neoplatonic terms as he wrote his first Christian essays. The next Easter he was baptized by Ambrose in Milan.

Shortly afterwards Augustine returned to Africa, and on the journey his mother died. In response to a request from the bishop of the town of Hippo in northern Africa, Augustine went to Hippo to serve the Christians there. Four years later, cheering crowds jammed into the cathedral and elected the reluctant Augustine as one of the bishops of the town.

As bishop, Augustine faced divisions in the church caused by a group called the Donatists. During the first decade of the fourth century, Christians had been bitterly persecuted by Rome, and some of them had compromised their faith by trying to worship both Christ and the emperor. Desiring a pure church, the Donatists emerged as a group who insisted that those who had so compromised should not be allowed to be members of the church. By the time Augustine became Bishop of Hippo, the Donatists had developed an extensive following in northern Africa. Augustine labored unsuccessfully to bring reconciliation between Donatists and other Catholic Christians in northern Africa. Against the Donatists he argued that God's forgiveness extended even to those who had denied their faith in such acts.

During the thirty-five years Augustine served as Bishop of Hippo, he wrote most of his 230 books which now fill over fifty thick volumes. The three most important are his *Confessions*, *On the Trinity*, and *The City of God*.

Augustine's *Confessions* is a 100,000-word spiritual autobiography that traces his journey to Christ. Written as a diary it opens with the now famous words, "Thou hast created us for thyself and our hearts know no rest until they rest in thee." *On the Trinity* is a brilliant theological treatise reaffirming and explaining the trinitarian nature of God confessed by the Council of Nicaea.

The City of God answers the question being asked all over the Roman Empire in the early fifth century: Why did Rome fall to the barbarians? Some alleged that Emperor Constantine's act making Christianity the official religion caused Rome's downfall. Augustine answered, to the contrary, that Rome became Christian too late. The sins of centuries were so engraved in Roman society that they ate away her strength, and therefore she fell under the barbarians' attack.

In these, and other brilliant works, Augustine described his basic beliefs, as his theological views developed with the passing of years. When he first became a Christian, he sought to synthesize Greek and biblical thought. But as he grew in his understanding of the Bible, he differentiated more and more between its teachings and Greek ideas until his mature theological thought was consistently biblical.

Augustine's Trinitarianism

What were Augustine's theological views? As a lad he had thought of God as the invisible one who could help him escape beatings at school. Throughout his twenties Augustine found God to be mysteriously silent. During those years he wrestled with weighty philosophic questions, the greatest of which was how material substance related to spiritual reality or how becoming related to being. After his conversion he gradually came to a mature understanding of the God of the Bible.

He declared that God, the transcendent one, created all things *ex nihilo*, out of nothing. Thus Augustine rejected both Plato's teaching that the Demiurge merely fashioned the world out of existing forms and matter and the Neoplatonic view that the world is an emanation, or an overflowing, of God. Augustine also rejected Manichaean dualism, asserting that because God created all things, matter is good. In sharp contrast to the Manichaean view, he believed that the universe is neither self-contained nor self-sufficient; it has its source and goal in God, who transcends all things.

At the same time, Augustine emphasized the creative providence of God, which rules over everything from the tiniest atom to the largest star. At creation God implanted seeds of His purpose (seminal principles) in everything. Each seed or principle remains dormant until God wants to change creation. Seminal principles blossom when He decrees. He has an overarching plan for the universe, and He has a plan for every individual life. Events happen according to God's timetable. His providence rules all things and moves history, not cyclically as the Greeks had claimed, but as the Bible taught, in linear fashion toward the time of Christ's return.

Augustine's major theological contribution was clarifying and expounding the trinitarian view articulated by Athanasius. Augustine taught that God had revealed Himself to be eternally Father, Son, and Holy Spirit, with the Holy Spirit proceeding from the Father and the Son (*Filioque*). The Christian church had always believed in one God. The plurality of the Father, Son, and Holy Spirit, however, seemed to some to deny God's unity. A group called the Modalists taught that there is only one God who successively revealed Himself in three temporary forms or modes of activity (Father, Son, and Holy Spirit).[2]

Others sought to explain the plurality of the Godhead while maintaining its unity by saying that the Son was subordinate to the Father, and the Spirit to the Son. Son and Spirit were seen as creations of the Father. Such was the *Arian* heresy described in the previous chapter. Athanasius and Augustine, in contrast to the Arians and Modalists, held that the three persons of the Trinity are co-equal, co-eternal, and of the same substance.

Augustine pointed out that the word *persons* is inadequate to describe the members of the Trinity, but he followed Athanasius in using the term because it helps to describe the eternal distinctions within God. Each person eternally and equally possesses the whole substance and power of the Godhead, and yet each is distinct from the others. The persons of the Trinity differ one

2. Another title for Modalism is Sabellianism. Named after the influential theologian Sabellius, this movement originated in Asia Minor in the third century A.D. Sabellians usually presented the Son and the Holy Spirit as being revelatory and temporary modes of God the Father. Unitarianism is a modern descendant of this view.

from another by the relations in which they stand to each other. Each possesses full personality. The divine Son is the self-reproduction of the Father, of whom He is eternally begotten. The Holy Spirit is the eternal reproduction of both the Father and the Son (i.e., the Spirit proceeds from both). "Father, Son and Holy Ghost mean a divine unity in an inseparable equality of one and the same substance" (*De Trinitate* 1. 7. 4).

Augustine's effort to understand and explain the Trinity rests upon "faith seeking understanding" (*fides quaerens intellectum*). His is a deductive approach, based on the authority of Scripture and the church. His *Confessions*, begun in A.D. 413, clearly state his conviction that Scripture is uniquely and even verbally inspired by God (cf. *Confessions* 13. 4-32). Augustine, along with the early church fathers, declared that the Bible revealed God to be a glorious Trinity.

For Augustine the Trinity resolved the age-old problem of the one (being) and the many (becoming). The Trinity functioned in the changing world of becoming through the person of the divine Spirit who orders all things providentially. Yet the Trinity also was beyond the world, transcending all things in the person of the Father. Jesus Christ was the divine bridge between being and becoming. He was divine love and grace incarnate. In the one, glorious God Triune, singularity and plurality were brought into harmony, and the cosmos was given unity and order.

Augustine's trinitarian principle accomplished what other great thinkers could not do. For example, Plato had attempted to reconcile the Parmenidean concept of unchanging being with the Heraclitian notion of constantly changing becoming. Material things in the realm of becoming "participated" in ideas, which belonged to the transcendent realm of being. Yet Plato never really succeeded in relating or unifying being and becoming.

For Augustine, the Trinity unified all reality in a way that Greek and Roman philosophy had not. God the Father was seen as the divine essence, the ground of all being. God the Holy Spirit undergirds, supports, and gives continuous existence to all creation, to the world of becoming and matter. In the unity of the Trinity God the Son links together invisible and visible reality;

He connects the realms of being (permanence) and becoming (change). Augustine's vision of the unity of reality inspires people to seek the unity of mankind. Charles N. Cochrane, in his monumental *Christianity and Classical Culture*, clearly explains how Augustine's Trinity unifies all reality in a way that Plato's being, participation, and becoming could not. Augustine argued that the Trinity unifies all reality while preserving a dynamic, creative sense of order in the universe. Plato's ultimate (being) was transcendent but lacked immanence and therefore failed to unify the invisible and visible realms. The Trinity, however, is both transcendent and immanent, unifying and structuring all reality by the dynamic threeness-in-oneness that undergirds the "manyness" and oneness of the universe. Thus in the medieval period Augustine's trinitarian principle became the basis of man's quest for social unity.

Augustine also emphasized the biblical theme that the universe is dependent upon the will of its Creator. Like Origen (c. 185–c. 254) before him, he vigorously attacked the Greek view that history endlessly repeats itself in cyclical fashion. To Augustine this cyclical theory clearly contradicted the scriptural view of history as a continuous, linear movement directed by the creative power of the Trinity toward an ultimate divine goal for the cosmos.

God's providential ordering of history, however, posed for Augustine the problem of evil. He reasoned that if evil exists objectively in reality, then God must be its cause and must contain evil within Himself. Because that is contrary to Scripture, Augustine concluded that evil is a privation, an absence of good rather than a positive reality. Wicked acts spring from the will of man, which is devoid of good and totally corrupted. When a person steals another's property, for example, the act of stealing lacks righteousness and goodness. Sins such as stealing occur when people turn away from God as their only true source of goodness, for God is the highest good. In doing evil they are not choosing any essence, for evil has no positive being. Evil in the cosmos results from the absence of good or the absence of God.

Finally, following Paul's and others' teachings in the Bible,

Augustine believed that God planned or predestined for some persons to be saved. He surrounds those elected to salvation with believers and the Holy Spirit so that they come to have faith in Christ. As Augustine looked back over his own life, he could see how God had worked to prod him toward salvation. God knows in advance who will freely accept His grace. Those people receive special influences to bring them to salvation. Above all, Augustine taught that the Triune God is sovereign; He graciously loves and controls all things.

Augustine's View of the Fall and Original Sin

To the non-Christian world of the fifth century, Augustine's anthropological convictions were as radical as his theological ones. Basing his views on the authority of the Bible, Augustine repudiated the Platonic soul-body dualism. Augustine followed Scripture in affirming the unity and wholeness of man. "From the soul and from the body, which are the parts of a man, we arrive at the totality which is man: accordingly, the life of the soul is not one thing, and that of the body another: but both are one and the same, i.e., the life of man as man" (*City of God* 14. 4). Long before the development of depth psychology and existential philosophy, Augustine explored the intimate relationship between the senses and thought.

Serious study of the Scriptures led Augustine to conclude that before the fall Adam had freedom to will and to do right. Adam was created as a rational being who could receive and understand God's commands. He chose, however, to disobey God and seek his own selfish ends, to seek his own good rather than seeking his good in God. Adam's sin, like all sin, which is rooted not in man's body but in man's soul, thus stems from unbelief. Sin is a product of the will, not a result of ignorance, as Plato believed, or the result of evil invading man from the outside. Sin sprang from Adam's giving priority to his own will rather than to God's will. To Augustine the will of man is not coerced by outside forces; it is an autonomous expression of the inner man. Augustine's analysis is that man's actions are preceded by suggestion, inner desire, and assent (or refusal), in that order. The desire or the "love" of a person's soul determines the direction the will chooses to move. Adam desired and therefore willed to put his first love, himself, above God. So he ate the forbidden fruit in a vain attempt to become like God. Thus the fall, resulting from man's free desire and choice to put himself before God, was a sin of pride.

As a result of the fall man lost his freedom and power. The seductions of the senses enshackled him. Sin enslaved his will and distorted his judgment. Before Adam sinned he both knew what was right and had the power to perform it. When he sinned, not only did he lose the ability to do good, but even his moral judgment was affected.

Thus through one act of rebellion human nature was fundamentally altered, and Adam entered into a state of sin. Through Adam the whole human race was plunged into the bondage of sin, which produced people's various sinful acts. The perfect image of God in man became twisted, deformed, and partially useless. After the fall, Adam's moral bondage and intellectual blindness was passed on to all his descendants, an inheritance known as original sin.

Historically, two views of the origin of the soul predominated Western thought before Augustine. Creationism, espoused by Pelagius (see below), maintains that each soul is a new, innocent creation of God. Traducianism, by contrast, teaches that an individual's body and soul are both derived from his ancestors. God created Adam directly, but thereafter human beings have been given life through natural processes. Augustine, Luther, and many other major Christian thinkers have been Traducians. According to Augustine, there is something inherited from the whole human race in each person; all human beings inherit the shattered remnant of the image of God. The vestiges of the imago dei are still evident in the human capacity for self-transcendence and in people's ability to experience God. Human rationality also reflects the image of God (cf. De Trinitate 14. 4. 6). By "rational," Augustine meant more than our reasoning powers. The human memory to him symbolized a unique capacity for self-transcendence: "And where shall I find Thee? If I find Thee without my memory then I do not retain Thee in my memory. And how shall I find Thee if I remember Thee not?" (*Confessions* 10. 7–17). Augustine repudiated the Greek tendency to deify self-consciousness and instead recognized that man's capacities, especially his *imago dei*, point beyond the self to God.

Mankind, however, can be delivered from this slavery to sin and powerlessness because the image of God in man, though terribly crippled, is not totally destroyed. The Triune God accomplishes man's salvation. God begins by freeing people from their intellectual blindness, which is at its roots a moral problem. This necessitates a rebirth of their affections and desires so that love of God replaces love of self at the center of a person's being. Only God's powerful and irresistible grace can cause such a regeneration and reordering of life. This grace, or unmerited favor of God, is an infusion of love into individuals by the Holy Spirit. The grace of God changes the loves and desires of the human heart; it recreates and renews the image of God within a person. God's grace frees the enslaved will and brings immediate justification and forgiveness. Gradually grace begins to transform human nature. This wholly unearned and undeserved grace is given to those chosen (predestined) by God. God predestinates whom He wills "to punishment and to salvation" (*Enchiridion* 107).

The Pelagian Controversy

Augustine's teaching on sin and grace displays the sharp contrast between Greek and Christian thought. To think that humanity could either know or attain goodness by itself, Augustine argued, was utter foolishness. The Greek (and Pelagian) notion that man could perfect himself through knowledge, education, or will power contradicted the Bible and human experience. The biblical teaching that man is fallen and can only be redeemed by the free gift of the sovereign grace of God led Augustine to denounce the Greek hope of human self-perfectibility as absurd. "No one, no not one, has been delivered, or is being delivered, or ever will be delivered, except by the grace of the Redeemer" (*Original Sin* 34).

Building on Paul's teachings in Romans 5 about the "two Adams" (Adam in Genesis 3 and Christ as the Second Adam in the New Testament) Augustine taught that Adam's fall fundamentally altered human nature. Augustine developed a famous play on words that sums up his thinking. Prior to the fall man had the power not to sin and the power to sin (*posse non peccare et posse peccare*, literally "able not to sin and able to sin"). When Adam sinned, he lost the former and kept the power to sin so that after Adam all people inherit his fallen nature and are not able not to sin (*non posse non peccare*). By this Augustine meant that human beings apart from grace have lost moral free will and are "dead" in sin (Eph. 2:1). Only God's sovereign grace can break this bondage to sin and free the will to serve Him. When a person is saved by grace, he receives a new nature, which, through the work of the Holy Spirit, grows in holiness and righteousness, a process called "sanctification." But in this life, perfection is not attainable. In heaven, however, another fundamental change takes place. Believers lose the *posse peccare* and, being perfected in Christ, receive the power not to be able to sin (*non posse peccare*). (Cf. *On Correction and Grace* 33 and *Enchiridion* 28.)

Pelagius, a British monk who came to Rome around A.D. 390, sharply contested Augustine's view of sin and salvation. Pelagius was a well-educated Christian moralist, trained in law, who taught among aristocratic circles in Rome that Christians could attain perfection in this life. Apparently scandalized by the debauchery of the Roman populace, he vigorously encouraged them to reform their lives. Pelagius stressed that man's will is free. Individuals, therefore, have the natural capacity for self-perfectibility: "If I ought, I can." Denying that original sin is inherited from Adam, he declared sin to be isolated actions rather than a state of being. He insisted that all persons are created innocent and have the power not to sin. Adam's sin injured himself only and, beyond that, merely set a bad example for his descendants. Although people can be justified by faith in Christ, Pelagians taught that the unassisted human will takes the initiative in salvation, not God's sovereign grace. Physical death does not result from Adam's disobedience but simply is a part of nature. By such teachings

Pelagius minimized the seriousness of sin. He therefore rejected Augustine's view that grace is necessary to transform a person's nature. Denying that grace is a life-changing, irresistible force, Pelagius taught that God's grace simply remits people's sins, and that individuals can freely choose to accept or reject God's gracious offer of salvation.

The debate between Augustine and Pelagius focused on a basic issue at the heart of all world views. Is man good or sinful, autonomous or dependent, finite or infinite? Pelagius, like the ancient Greeks, came down resoundingly on the side of autonomous, self-sufficient man. The following statements summarize Pelagius's views:[3] (1) Adam was made mortal and would have died whether he had sinned or not. (2) The sin of Adam injured himself alone and not the human race. (3) Newborn children are in the same state Adam was before his fall. (4) The whole human race does not die because of the sin and death of Adam; nor does it rise because of the resurrection of Christ. (5) People can be saved by obeying the law as well as by believing the gospel. (6) Even before the coming of Christ some individuals lived sinless lives.

The debate between Augustine and Pelagius waxed hot for years. In A.D. 431, one year after Augustine's death, the church at the Council of Ephesus officially resolved the dispute by sustaining Augustine's view and condemning Pelagianism.[4] Posthumously the Bishop of Hippo triumphed. His staunchly biblical views would dominate Christian thought for hundreds of years. The Augustinian view that the natural man is fallen and in a state of sin continued to be widely affirmed. Despite the Council of Ephesus, however, the Pelagian view that man's nature is essentially good, unaffected by the fall, had gained a following. Moreover, a semi-Pelagian view developed, which held that though natural man is vitiated by the fall, he remains able to cooperate

---

3. Pelagius's follower Coelestius was charged with teaching these doctrines.
4. The Council of Carthage (A.D. 418) also condemned Pelagius's views and supported Augustine's convictions that all people are sinful both by nature and by deeds and that God's grace is necessary for both salvation and righteous living.

with God in redemption. If Augustinians regarded the natural man spiritually *dead*, and Pelagians considered the natural man *alive and well*, semi-Pelagians maintained that human beings are *sick*. While, for Augustinians, only the grace of God can save individuals and perfect their standing before Him, and, to Pelagians, man is capable of saving or perfecting himself, semi-Pelagians saw salvation as accomplished by man's and God's working together to perfect man. The biblical teaching on this matter, which confirms the Augustinian position, is summarized in Ephesians 2:1: "You he made alive when you were dead through trespasses and sins."

Though Pelagian views nearly disappeared from the medieval church, semi-Pelagian views spread. Semi-Pelagians (John Cassianus, Vincent of Lerins, Faustus, and others) held a position that, though Augustinian in part, sought to preserve some autonomy for man. Many semi-Pelagians held that, while grace is essential for salvation, people cooperate with God in redemption. They generally rejected Augustine's belief in predestination and irresistible grace, arguing that such a heavy emphasis on the divine initiative diminishes human effort, responsibility, and autonomy. Semi-Pelagianism has grown to be a major influence both in Roman Catholicism and in some Protestant sects. Though in theory semi-Pelagians seek to balance the divine initiative with human responsibility, in effect they affirm the alien Greek notion of human autonomy and reject Augustine's emphasis on the sovereignty of God's grace.

Through the centuries, Augustine has been criticized on two major counts. Some have argued that he exaggerated human sinfulness. His followers counter that he faithfully presented the biblical view of man's radical sinfulness (see Rom. 3). Others have complained that his understanding of grace as irresistible violates the free will of man. These critics take offense to his teachings that God chooses (predestines) some to eternal salvation and others to eternal damnation. Augustinians generally have answered that grace restores and guarantees man's freedom of will, which without grace is in bondage (see *The Spirit and the Letter* 30). They also point out that God's predestining some to receive grace is not whimsical or capricious but is based on His foreknowledge (knowledge in advance) of man's rebellion. God, the "Eternal Now," knows all things and plans and acts accordingly. "Since he did foreknow that man would make bad use of his free will—that is, that he would sin—God prearranged his own purpose so that he could do good to man, even in man's doing evil" (*Enchiridion* 38). Predestining grace saves some. Justice condemns others. God is not to be accused of unfairness in choosing some to salvation. Rather He is to be praised for both His justice and His grace.

Augustine was one of the great theologians of the Christian West. More fully than any of his predecessors, he explained how God exists as a Trinity of persons and how God's grace is the source of man's salvation. He strongly affirmed human sinfulness. Sinful human beings live in a universe where the gulf between being (permanence) and becoming (motion) puts salvation beyond their reach. The trinitarian principle bridges this gulf, however, providing redemption and unifying being and becoming. Augustine's mature thought sharply distinguished between Greek and Christian positions. His biblical theology has powerfully influenced Christians in all ages. He used Scripture to construct a thoroughly biblical world view, which emphasizes the grace of the Triune God and presents man as totally dependent on the living God of Scripture.

For Further Reading

Battenhouse, Roy W., ed. *A Companion to the Study of St. Augustine.* Grand Rapids: Baker, 1955.

Bourke, Vernon J. *Augustine's Quest of Wisdom.* Milwaukee, 1945.

———. *The Essential Augustine.* Indianapolis: Hackett, 1973.

Burleigh, J. H. S. *Augustine: Earlier Writings.* Philadelphia: Westminster Press, 1953.

Burnaby, John. *Amor Dei: A Study of the Religion of St. Augustine.* London: Hodder, 1938.

———. *Augustine: Later Works.* Philadelphia: Westminster Press, 1955.

Cochrane, C. N. *Christianity and Classical Culture.* London: Oxford University Press, 1939.

Geisler, Norman. *What Augustine Says.* Grand Rapids: Baker, 1982.

Gilson, Etienne. *The Christian Philosophy of Saint Augustine.* New York: Random, 1960.

Przywara, Erich. *An Augustine Synthesis.* New York: Sheed and Ward, 1936.

Warfield, B. B. *Studies in Tertullian and Augustine.* New York: Oxford University Press, 1930.

6
Medieval Scholasticism: The Thomistic Synthesis
W. Andrew Hoffecker

Medieval Thought Before Aquinas

The Nicene formulation may be seen as the infant stage of a growing synthesis of Greek and Christian ideas. In the later Middle Ages such a synthesis developed into mature adulthood.

Medieval Christianity before Aquinas was largely a mixture of Platonic and biblical thought. Early church fathers in the first three centuries stressed spiritual reality at the expense of the physical. Theologians during this period sought above all to uncover the "spiritual" sense of biblical passages. They emphasized speculation about abstract theories and depreciated the concrete and tangible aspects of the world. Developing the soul, for example, was considered so important that the body was thought to be simply a covering to be discarded at death. Every church father worth his salt published a work praising the virtues of virginity, not because fornication was rampant, but because people believed virginity was the highest calling for both men and women. By the late fourth century celibacy became a prerequisite for nuns and monks who pursued monastic life, as well as for those who entered the priesthood.

As the medieval period progressed, Scholasticism, a systematic method of study used by scholars to understand all reality, began to dominate intellectual life. Scholastics believed that all knowledge could be arranged in an orderly and detailed way. Aquinas, for example, in his major work dealt with God, man, and nature. You cannot get much more comprehensive than that! In their study Scholastics borrowed heavily from Greek ideas. By stressing technical language and concepts, Scholasticism made reason the supreme means to knowledge. Reason, however, was to be supplemented with biblical revelation. Scholastic theologians devoted themselves to studying classical Greek and Roman writers, as well as the Bible and the early Christian fathers. Their goal was to fuse these traditions into a distinctive medieval synthesis or world view.

Aquinas's Life and Writings

When Thomas Aquinas was born in 1225, Scholasticism was in its golden age. By the time of his death in 1274 Thomas was considered preeminent among the Schoolmen. He influenced philosophy more than any other individual between Augustine in the fifth century and the Reformers in the sixteenth century. Although few people in his time were able to receive an education, Thomas was so privileged because his father was a government official. Thomas studied the traditional curriculum of the seven liberal arts at Naples and subsequently graduated from the University of Paris, one of only six universities in all of Europe. He became a professor of theology in the Dominican order, which was founded in the thirteenth century to propagate Christianity by strenuous missionary and educational activity. Except for serving briefly in the papal court in Rome as an adviser, he spent the remainder of his life teaching in the University of Paris.

Like many other medieval scholars, Aquinas was a prolific writer. He wrote over forty volumes, most famous of which are *Summa Contra Gentiles* ("A Summary Against the Gentiles"), an apologetic theological handbook for missionaries to use in converting the heathen; and *Summa Theologica* ("A Summary of Theology"), a systematic theology textbook, which powerfully influenced the Roman Catholic Church. Also significant are his commentaries on the works of "the philosopher" Aristotle.

Thomistic Synthesis

Thomas's scholastic synthesis rests upon his appreciation for Aristotle. Until the thirteenth century Aristotle was unknown in Europe because his writings had not been translated into Latin. For centuries Platonic and Augustinian perspectives had dominated intellectual life. The famous Moslem philosopher Averroes first translated and interpreted Aristotle's works. He so dominated the field that he became known as simply "the commentator" on Aristotle's thought.

Averroes concluded from his study of Aristotle that philosophy, rational truth, is superior to revealed truth. His conclusion caused an uproar in Paris. Freethinkers, as few as there were during the Middle Ages, flocked to the University of Paris to take courses on this newly rediscovered Greek marvel and to read the writings of "the commentator." Church leaders became alarmed at the attention paid to this pagan philosopher and his Moslem disciple. A council in 1210 forbade the reading of Aristotle's *Physics* and *Metaphysics* and Averroes's commentaries. Like banning books in Boston, however, prohibition only instigated an increase in their sales!

But by the 1240s Thomas's teacher at the University of Paris, Albertus Magnus, encouraged his brilliant pupil to study Aristotle's works. Thomas, in turn, was struck by how convincing many of the arguments were. Yet he was disturbed that Averroes had used Aristotle's rational method to reach three non-Christian conclusions: (1) the world is eternal; (2) the soul is not immortal; and (3) human free will and responsibility are impossible. Aquinas was captivated by Aristotelian thinking, even though he recognized that much of it would have to be reworked to fit Christian theology. Indeed he thought this not only could but must be done. While Aristotle had made errors, the major problem was that Averroes had misused Aristotelian method. Aquinas's task, as he saw it, was to refute Averroes's errors and to reclaim reason as an appropriate tool for Christian theology. Thus he attempted to forge a middle way between most Christian philosophers who staunchly opposed Aristotle's works and who argued that they were susceptible to atheistic conclusions, and a minority of scholars who read the Greek philosopher uncritically, that is, without any correction from Christian revelation.

Thomas's efforts gave birth to the most elaborately developed synthesis of Greek and Christian thought to have appeared. He contended that even though Aristotle was a pagan, his ideas were

adaptable to the Christian faith. With slight modification primarily in the form of additions, Aristotle's views of the *unmoved
mover*, man as a rational animal, and the primacy of reason could
be used to support Christian theology. Such was Thomas's goal,
and it was no small task. For his labors he was designated Doctor
of the Church in 1567, canonized as a saint in 1623, and finally
proclaimed official interpreter of orthodox theology during Roman
Catholicism's struggle with modernism in the latter part of the
nineteenth century. To many Catholics he is still known as the
"angelic doctor." In the aftermath of Vatican II, an ecumenical
council held in the early 1960s, however, many Catholics are
reappraising Thomism in light of contemporary thought. But
regardless of how contemporary Catholics come to evaluate
Thomas's theology, his ideas dominated centuries of theological
reflection.

Aquinas's View of God: Baptized Unmoved Mover

Aquinas's God has sometimes been referred to as a "baptized"
unmoved mover. That is because Thomas began his discussion of
God by accepting virtually without criticism Aristotle's philosophical argument for an unmoved mover, the first cause of existence.
Thomas began by ignoring that Aristotle's depiction of God as
basically impersonal, aloof, and uncaring contradicted
Christianity's understanding of God as personal, dynamic, and
actively involved in creation. Thomas accepted Aristotle's explanation and terminology for God and "baptized" it by attributing
biblical characteristics to this otherwise impersonal force in order
to use it as a starting point for Christian theological discussion.
In so doing he took two incompatible and previously unrelated
notions of God and fused them together in an uneasy alliance.
Many subsequent thinkers have questioned this synthesis because
the Aristotelian and biblical world views, from which these views
of God originated, are so disparate.

Thomas stressed that God's uniqueness is rooted in His essence.
Indeed God's very essence is "to be." Whereas all other beings
and objects in creation exist by virtue of their dependence on or
relation to some higher cause (ultimately God), God's very nature

is to exist. Stated another way, *whether* any being exists or not is different from *what* it is, but not so with God. His very essence necessitates His existence. A person, for example, *is* a human being because of his internal form or soul. But he *exists* because God causes him to exist. We can distinguish what he is apart from his existence because he does not exist independently, that is, by his own self-creative power, but only because God gives him life. God's uniqueness is clear from our inability to distinguish between God's essence and existence. In Him alone are essence and existence the same. While all other creatures are dependent on Him, God necessarily exists. Thomas thereby joined the Aristotelian notion of the unmoved mover as a necessary being with the biblical idea of God as the self-sufficient and self-existent "I AM" of Exodus 3:14.

Since God is eternal, first cause, and sovereign good, Aquinas stressed these attributes. He denied that God is like man in any univocal sense, that is, without any qualification. We know God only by analogy. When we attribute something to God that we also affirm of human beings, we understand that the quality is absolute in God and only relative in ourselves. If, for example, we say that God is wise and that John is wise, the term *wise* must be interpreted differently in the two cases because only God is wise in an absolute sense. His wisdom is perfect, complete, or exhaustive. In contrast, human beings have only limited wisdom; even the wisest of philosophers lacks God's perfect wisdom. The same is true of any attribute we affirm of God and men. Human beings, therefore, are analogous to God. God's uniqueness is fully protected when Thomas states,

> It is more appropriate to say that the creature is like God than vice versa. . . . Since what is in God perfectly is present in other things by way of imperfect participation; whatever they are alike in belongs to God absolutely, but not so to the creature (*Summa Theologica* 1. 29).

His method of knowing God by analogy enabled Thomas to affirm God's uniqueness as first cause so that God stands alone as *the* self-subsistent being. The notion of analogy also permitted

Aquinas to say that some relation exists between God and His creatures. While we may be said to be like God, we are also unlike God: "The ideas we conceive of the perfection noted in creatures are imperfect likenesses out of all proportion to the divine essence . . . " (*On the Power of God* 7. 6).

To avoid the mistake of conceiving God to be like His creatures, Thomas advocated a popular medieval principle called the *via negativa*. This "way of negation" denied that we can know God's essence, what He is. Only God knows that. Because God's essence is transcendent it is inscrutable to man. Therefore, if we are to know Him, we must begin by denying of God those qualities we know to be most inappropriate. For example, we know that God is *not* material. He also is *not* finite, *not* mutable (changeable), *not* subject to time.

The rationale behind the *via negativa* is that the more qualities we are able to deny of God, the nearer we come to knowing Him because we remove from consideration elements that make God similar to other things. Since God is unique, not like anything else, we deny the most obvious qualities that would make Him similar to His creatures. The more we are able to deny about God, the closer we are to understanding Him appropriately, as "distinct from everything else" (*Summa Theologica* 1. 14) Paradoxically, by affirming what God is not, we gain some insight into what He is.

When we combine the positive way of knowing God by analogy (*via analogia*) with the *via negativa*, we begin to see the very complex way medieval theologians used the Scholastic method to affirm anything about God. Aquinas was not the first to formulate these two methods, but he carefully developed them as theological tools and integrated them into his great Scholastic synthesis. Although he used both methods, the way of negation was the more fundamental because it best protected God's transcendence. By using it theologians could avoid the sin of idolatry—identifying God with any part of His creation. What was lost, however, by the use of Thomas's subtle Scholastic method was a simple dependence on the Scriptures as the most reliable source for understanding God's nature and being. As we saw in our study of the biblical world view, the writers speak of God in unsophisticated terms, using simple, familiar images from everyday family and rural life (e.g., loving heavenly Father, faithful husband, shepherd, King and Lord).

This appraisal of Aquinas as a synthetic thinker is not meant to imply that his view of God was not Christian or that his ideas were so colored by Aristotle's philosophy that all biblical ideas were lost. Nevertheless, Aquinas did not develop his view of God by using the statements of Scripture alone. Instead, he used Scholastic categories of thought, which were an adaptation of Greek rationalism, in order to explain the Christian faith.

While using Aristotle's philosophy to describe God, Thomas also reiterated fundamental teachings of the Scriptures regarding the God of Christianity. He affirmed the Trinity and explicitly rejected Arius's heresy. God is the Triune Redeemer. The Father sent the Son to be a mediator between God and man. By His sinless life and suffering on the cross, which offered an atonement for the sins of the human race, Christ merited salvation. His passion was a true sacrifice. By His death, resurrection, and ascension Christ is both Lord and Savior of the church.

In extended sections of the *Summa* Thomas discussed the traditional attributes of God—His love, justice, mercy, power, etc. Elaborating on God's power Aquinas affirmed that all power in the created order ultimately comes from God alone. God causes all things to move in accordance with their natures. This led him to argue that God's act of creation was continuous: "If the divine action should cease, all things would drop into nothingness" (*On the Power of God* 5. 1). Since God providentially orders all things, Thomas rejected any notion of fate or chance as determining forces in the world. God's care of creation means all things are ordered to achieve their respective ends.

The implications of providence are carried over into his view of predestination. Since God governs all things, He predestines some people to eternal life and abandons others to the consequences of their sin in eternal damnation. Nevertheless, Thomas repudiated Averroes's use of Aristotle to present a totally deterministic view of the world. He held that despite God's providence it was not contradictory to say that God holds us responsible for our sins. That is because God does not cause us to sin, but He merely permits sin.[1]

Thomas Aquinas's synthesis of Aristotelian and biblical views of God in his *Summa Theologica* stands as a landmark of medieval theology. When we examine medieval epistemology later in our study, we will see how closely related Thomas's view of God is to his understanding of knowledge.

Aquinas's Anthropology: A Triple Synthesis

Closely related to his theology was Thomas's view of man. As was his discussion of God, his explanation of anthropology was synthetic. It was in fact a triple synthesis. He fused Aristotelian, Augustinian, and Pelagian ideas together into a bold new understanding of human nature. Thomas's fundamental assertion was that man is a union of body and soul in the Aristotelian sense. Soul is the form of the body, and human beings endowed with reason possess the highest type of soul. Various lesser kinds of souls exist such as vegetative and animal, but human beings alone have the capacity for rational thought. That we can reason, reflect, and understand indicates that we are high in the created order. Nevertheless, humanity is not the highest, or even the next to highest, order of being. Above men are angels, and above them is God, who is the highest perfection. Thus man is integrated hierarchically into the rest of the created order, a great chain of being. Human beings are distinguished from those under them by their rationality, which is proof of their immortality, and people are distinguished from angels and God by their finitude and sin.

Thomas attempted to synthesize the Aristotelian elements in his anthropology with Augustinian and Pelagian teachings. His views can be labelled either semi-Pelagian or semi-Augustinian,

---

1. God's predestination is a significant part of the biblical and Augustinian understanding of God. Aquinas's view, as we shall see below, slightly altered these perspectives by allowing considerable freedom to man's will. We will find the biblical and Augustinian views revived with new emphasis in the Reformation.

depending on whether Pelagian or Augustinian features are interpreted as dominant. Clearly, both are present.

Aquinas believed that when God created Adam, God gave him reason and a special endowment, *donum superadditum* (superadded gift). Before the fall this gift enabled Adam to seek and attain the highest good of obeying God and doing His will. But when Adam fell, he lost this gift of original righteousness, and human nature became corrupt. As a result of original sin man became a disordered being. With Augustine, Thomas believed that original sin is passed on from generation to generation by heredity as a stain on human nature. This stain exerts a corrupting effect on man's will, resulting in concupiscence, a strong and inordinate desire. The common translation of concupiscence as "lust" is correct as long as we do not limit this word to mere sexual desire. Concupiscence is a strong desire in all people that, when followed, results in *actual* sin.

A crucial question when examining Aquinas's view is How pervasive is original sin? Does it merely affect the will, or does it also affect all other dimensions of human existence including man's rational powers? How serious are original sin's effects upon the will? Is human will totally crippled, morally and spiritually, so that humans are unable to do anything good apart from God's grace (Augustine)? Or, at the other extreme, does sin merely hinder an unfallen human nature from doing the good (Pelagius)?

Thomas sought a compromise between these two views and used all the tools of Scholasticism to forge his synthesis. *Prior* to the fall man could attain what Aquinas called the four natural virtues (prudence, justice, temperance, and courage), described by ancient Greek philosophers such as Plato and Aristotle, and the three supernatural virtues listed by the apostle Paul in I Corinthians 13 (faith, hope, and love). After the fall, however, man can only achieve the natural virtues. Original sin has rendered people incapable of exercising faith or hope and doing acts of love. We are no longer able to achieve the *highest* good we once were (i.e., in Adam) capable of performing.

But the fall did not totally debilitate human nature either. Aquinas believed that human beings retain the ability to discern and perform the four natural virtues. People are able to exercise prudence, execute justice, embody temperance, and manifest courage. While Thomas did not deny original sin, he believed that its effect upon the human race is not as radical as Augustine had taught. Though Adam's corrupted nature is transmitted to his descendants, our rational powers are not impaired. People through their thinking both know and seek the good they ought to perform. Also, human will is not totally corrupted. We are morally free and capable of doing some good, limited though that may be.

This differentiation between various types of virtues and of man's varying ability to perform them is a clear example of Aquinas's distinction between the realms of nature and grace. "Nature" refers to that part of creation which is ordered by natural law—the physical, natural world order, including human life and its institutions. "Grace" refers to transcendent, meta-physical reality ruled by God's supernatural law as indicated in the following diagram:

GRACE	GOD'S SUPERNATURAL LAW
NATURE	GOD'S NATURAL LAW

The virtues are categorized and hierarchically ordered whereby we lose the ability to achieve one group (the theological virtues resulting from grace) while retaining the ability to perform the other (the natural virtues). Because the natural virtues remain unaffected by sin, they are still "natural" to man. Thomas's view of nature and grace as they pertain to the virtues before and after the fall is illustrated in the following diagram:

	SUPERNATURAL	LOST AFTER
GRACE	VIRTUES	THE FALL
NATURE	NATURAL	RETAINED AFTER
	VIRTUES	THE FALL

In his *Treatise on Grace* Thomas said:

> In the state of corrupt nature [man] falls short of what nature makes possible so that he cannot by his own power fulfill the whole good that pertains to his nature. Human nature is not so entirely corrupted by sin, however, as to be deprived of natural good altogether. Consequently even in the state of corrupt nature a man can do some particular good by virtue of his own nature such as build houses, plant vineyards, and things of this kind.

Thomas's position manifests definite Augustinian elements. All people are guilty of original sin and actual sin, and only the grace of God can save them from the result and penalty of sin. But Pelagian elements also have a central role. Reason is unscathed by the fall, and the will is only partially debilitated by sin since it remains morally free in all choices except those requiring supernatural assistance. Augustine, by contrast, emphasized that the will is morally and spiritually bound by sin in *all* moral and spiritual matters (*non posse non peccare*). He also made no distinctions between different classes of moral choice.

How is mankind to be redeemed according to Aquinas? Because everyone inherits original sin and commits actual sin, redemption is made possible through the free and undeserved grace of God. No merely human act can merit saving grace. Christ's sacrifice on the cross was the only act worthy of the saving grace of God. Because of Christ's deity and His sinlessness, His death was more than adequate to pay for the sins of humanity. His "overpayment" is available to mankind in the treasury of superabundant merits in heaven, which God distributes through His grace. God's grace, which is necessary for salvation, is an endowment infused or poured into the soul, thereby restoring the superadded gift to human nature, cleansing sin, and giving man power to perform the theological virtues again.

Aquinas distinguished between two types of grace. Operative grace is the divine help given to man wherein "God is the sole mover." But while God moves the soul (man is a passive recipient), man is also a mover, an active participant in salvation. Because both God and man are active, salvation "is attributed to the soul as well as to God" (*Summa Theologica* 111. 2). Thus grace is both operative (given by God alone) and cooperative (man works with God), and Thomas believes that people can merit rewards from God. Although no one can deserve God's grace in the state of original sin (only operative grace suffices), after we are redeemed, we cooperate with God and become able to merit rewards for our labors. In the Thomistic scheme we can say that man is motivated by both grace and works.

Thomas's view of grace and merit became the object of intense debate in subsequent centuries. In the sixteenth century, Reformers such as Martin Luther and John Calvin denied any distinction between operative and cooperative grace and repudiated any suggestion that people could merit God's grace. Good works do not contribute to salvation but result from God's gift of sovereign grace.

In keeping with his view of grace Thomas reinterpreted the doctrine of justification. We noted in our study of the New Testament that justification is an *objective*, forensic act by which God *declares* man to be righteous on the basis of Christ's work on the cross. The justified receive a new standing with God because of faith in Christ's death on the cross and resurrection from the dead. Thomas, by contrast, viewed justification as a *subjective* process by which God actually *makes* men righteous by infusing grace into them (through the sacraments, as we will note below).

Thomas's reinterpretation of grace and justification had significant implications for the *medieval* view of the Christian life. Thomas believed that it is possible for some Christians, "the saints," to do more than God requires in His law. The treasury of merits contains not only Christ's merits but also those of the saints, who have earned rewards for doing works beyond what the law commands. Works of supererogation add more merits to the treasury. The saints accumulate merits by taking upon themselves "the Three Vows" of poverty, chastity, and obedience, none of which is commanded by the law (Ten Commandments), and therefore exceed what the law requires. In the truest sense of the word, they are "meritorious." Thomas wrote "There are no sins so grave that entering religion [taking the vows and entering a monastery] would not be suitable satisfaction [compensation] for them" (*On the Perfection of the Religious Life*).

How do sinners receive grace in Thomas's view? Thomas endorsed the medieval conviction that God distributes His grace through the seven sacraments of the Roman Catholic Church: baptism, confirmation, the Lord's Supper, penance, ordination, matrimony, and extreme unction. As mentioned above, grace is dispensed not by imputation but by infusion. Since the sacraments operate by infusing grace into believers, they are considered to be miracles. By participating in the sacraments a believer is not merely declared righteous; he or she is actually *made* righteous by God's miraculous act. Participation in the sacramental life of the medieval church was therefore considered absolutely indispensable to the Christian life. The sacraments are synonymous with means of grace.

Upon this concept of salvation and the meritorious life was built a primary institution of medieval life, the monastery and its ideal of a disciplined, ascetic life. Many Christians had for centuries extolled the virtues of the monastic and celibate life as a higher calling. They interpreted Jesus' command for self-denial as best fulfilled by forsaking life in the world, and its attendant pleasures, and separating themselves away from the world in a life of seclusion. Thomas's support of this ideal is another example of his distinction between the natural and the supernatural orders.

GRACE	SUPERNATURAL VIRTUES	SACRAMENTS	ASCETIC LIFE IN MONASTERY
NATURE	NATURAL VIRTUES	DAILY LIFE	ORDINARY LIFE IN THE WORLD

Just as Thomas distinguished between natural and supernatural virtues, so he separated the spiritual from the sacred in the area of vocation or calling in life. Those who separated themselves from the world, refrained from marriage, and joined the monastic life were designated "religious." They were following a higher calling than those engaged in a secular life. In their confession of sin, reception of the sacraments, and knowledge of the Bible, lay Christians were dependent on those who were more spiritual, whose calling enabled them to perform meritorious works. The monastic ideal and the sacraments entrusted to the clergy made a sharp distinction, if not a dualism, between ordinary Christians (the laity), who lived and worked "in the world," and the visible hierarchical church, which was the sole dispenser of grace.[2]

Summary

Two ideas have been prominent in our study of Thomism. First, Thomas's synthetic approach offered a radically new interpretation of Christianity that rejected the older Platonic syntheses of the early Middle Ages. His new synthesis powerfully affected his views on God and man. Although he often used biblical teaching to correct Aristotle, Aristotelian interpretations and methods frequently shaped Thomas's theology because he did not recognize their incompatibility with biblical principles.

Christians can applaud Thomas's attempt to reclaim Aristotelian concepts from their misuse by Islamic thinkers. But Thomas too quickly accepted these ideas without subjecting them to criticism from biblical revelation. He also looked too hastily elsewhere, outside the biblical revelation, for his first principles, which he believed could support the Christian faith. In using Aristotelian categories he bypassed biblical ideas, which are altogether sufficient as a foundation for the Christian world view. While his synthesis was not as radical as Pelagius's use of Greek ideas—for Pelagius clearly stepped outside the realm of Christian belief and made grace virtually irrelevant—Aquinas's ideas illustrate how synthetic thinking alters the distinctive biblical perspectives on God and man.

A second idea that dominated his thought arose from his synthetic approach. Aquinas constantly distinguished between

2. See our discussion below in the epilogue, that the biblical world view entails defining all of life as religion. In this perspective no one area of life is religious; nor are some people more religious than others. Every activity in life stems from an ultimate (i.e., religious) commitment. All of life is lived *coram dei*, before the face of God.

nature and grace. Whether we see it in his differentiation between soul and body, or in his separation between the clergy and laity, or in his portrayal of the sacraments as the means of grace, or in his distinction between saints and ordinary Christians, it is clearly the recurring theme of his theological world view. Some scholars have called this element the "Thomistic dualism," pointing to its similarity with the more exaggerated dualism that dominated Plato's philosophy. Defenders of Thomas have contended that although he makes a distinction between various elements mentioned above, the relation between higher and lower is not as sharp as a dualism. Rather, they say, there is a continuum between the two—a point of contact. Instead of a fundamental break, grace (the higher order) completes nature (the lower order); the secular finds its fulfillment in the sacred.

Those who criticize Thomas point out that his sharp distinction is an inevitable consequence of attempting to unite two radically different and inharmonious traditions. On the one hand is the Aristotelian emphasis, which attributes to man an autonomy made possible by his rational faculty. On the other hand, Christian revelation stresses a limited view of man and his capacities that is due to the fall into sin. Thomas's distinctions imply a fundamental division in reality in which the natural order functions by its own natural laws, and the supernatural order is ruled by God. Thomas and his followers would never have countenanced a radical separation between these two. Others, however, especially in later periods, such as the Enlightenment of the seventeenth and eighteenth centuries, seeking to be freed from Christian thinking altogether, made such a distinction in order to affirm an autonomous natural order unrelated to supernatural law.

Thomas influenced the Middle Ages immeasurably. Although he challenged the Platonic-Christian synthesis, he merely replaced it with another synthesis. In so doing he sought to provide a rational support for the Christian faith. We will examine how Aquinas did this in a later chapter on epistemology.

Thomism eventually came under attack by Renaissance thinkers. In the late Middle Ages Europe experienced a rebirth of interest in the arts and letters. It was a time of economic, social, political, and—underlying all of these—religious change. Serfdom was disappearing, towns were springing up in the place of manors, new political institutions were emerging, and calls for reform in the church were being heard from such diverse sources as John Wycliffe in England, John Hus in Bohemia, and Girolamo Savonarola in Italy. New intellectual changes also made a profound impact on Western Christianity as Renaissance voices became more secular and humanistic. The motto *homo mensura,* "man is the measure," reflected the Enlightenment's almost unrestrained confidence in man's capacity to judge things without any reference to a God who transcends him. As this earth was increasingly considered more important than eternity, the Thomistic synthesis eventually bent to the breaking point under the strain.

For Further Reading

Chenu, M. D. *Toward Understanding St. Thomas.* Chicago: Henry Regnery, 1964.

Chesterton, G. K. *St. Thomas Aquinas.* London, 1947.

Copleston, Frederick C. *A History of Philosophy,* vol. 2. Garden City, N.Y.: Doubleday, 1962.

———. *A History of Medieval Philosophy.* New York: Harper and Row, 1972.

———. *Aquinas.* Baltimore: Penguin, 1955.

Gilson, Etienne. *The Christian Philosophy of St. Thomas Aquinas.* New York: Random, 1956.

———. *The Spirit of Medieval Philosophy.* New York: Charles Scribner's Sons, 1936.

———. *The Spirit of Thomism.* New York: P. J. Kenedy and Sons, 1964.

Grabmann, Martin. *Thomas Aquinas: His Personality and Thought.* New York: Russell and Russell, 1963.

Maritain, Jacques. *St. Thomas Aquinas.* London, 1946.

Pegis, A. *Basic Writings of St. Thomas Aquinas*, 2 vols. New York, 1948.

Pieper, Josef. *Scholasticism: Personalities and Problems*. New York: Pantheon, 1960.

Vignaux, Paul. *Philosophy in the Middle Ages: An Introduction*. Cleveland, Ohio: Meridian, 1959.

III.
POST-SYNTHESIS
WORLD VIEWS

7
Biblical Roots Rediscovered:
The Reformation

W. Andrew Hoffecker

Background to the Reformation
The Protestant Reformation brought profound changes to all of European culture. Its impact resulted in large part from its leaders' recovery and promotion of a biblical world view. The term "Reformation" indicates that men such as Martin Luther in Germany and John Calvin in Switzerland deliberately rejected many of the ideas of the medieval period. They sought to reestablish the doctrine and spiritual life of New Testament Christianity in the sixteenth century church. The Reformation, therefore, was basically a spiritual restoration of biblical ideas. More specifically, its leaders repudiated the synthesis mentality that had dominated Christian thought for centuries.

Many secular historians have argued that economic, political, and social issues inspired the major transformations of the sixteenth century. While these forces influenced the development and course of the Reformation, spiritual and moral issues were of primary importance. Above all else the Reformers sought to correct the doctrine and life of the Christian church. Religious convictions in large measure produced their economic, political, and social concerns and helped change Western European practices in these areas.

Two major world views molded intellectual and religious ideas prior to the Reformation—the Greek and the biblical traditions. In the ancient period Greek and Jewish cultures grew out of very different theological and anthropological perspectives. Before Christ's birth some Jewish philosophers attempted to synthesize Old Testament ideas with those of prominent Greek thinkers.

After the appearance of Christianity, the possibility of continuing such a synthetic approach was a constant threat to the integrity and uniqueness of the newly revealed faith. New Testament writers such as the apostle Paul issued repeated warnings against the danger of syncretism—the borrowing and assimilation of foreign elements into the Christian faith. As centuries passed, such dangers of synthesis increased rather than diminished while scholars debated which *form* of Greek thought would predominate in the synthesis. As we saw in the preceding chapter, Aquinas's *Summa Theologica* made Aristotle's influence primary in the church.

After 1300, theologians became more dependent on Greek philosophy to provide a basis for Christian theology. They often failed to recognize how incompatible Greek and Christian world views were, and how New Testament writers elevated Scripture far above all competing claims of authority. Medieval synthesizers tended to make tradition, philosophy, or history more important than the Bible as a basis for interpreting reality.

Understanding the history of medieval syntheses is important to our perception of what motivated Luther, Calvin, and other Reformers to repudiate medieval thought. In their opinion medieval thinkers had made a conscious and thoroughgoing attempt to fuse these two radically different traditions (Greek and Christian) into a new theological system. The Reformers resolved to reverse this trend. Their attack upon extravagances of the papal court, sale of indulgences and church offices, and excessive church taxation were part of a larger campaign to return the church to its biblical moorings.

Luther and Calvin thought that neither Platonism nor Aristotelianism should serve as a philosophical foundation for Christian theology. Instead they advocated a return to a biblical world view in which Scripture alone is authoritative for what Christians believe and do. Their cry was *ad fontes*, "back to the sources," meaning that they wished to return to the Scriptures of the Old and New Testaments. Luther said simply, "The Bible is our vineyard, and there we should all labor and toil" (*Babylonian Captivity of the Church*).

At the close of the previous chapter we noted various changes that occurred in the period following Aquinas, changes that severely undermined the authority and reputation of the church. Despite the church's position of cultural leadership, the papacy suffered a serious blow in prestige when the papal court moved to Avignon, France. The papacy was further weakened by the Great Schism during which two, and then three, popes claimed to be the one true successor to the apostle Peter. In addition, several popes became embroiled in contests for political power and were more involved in political struggles among Italian princes and support of renaissance arts than in promoting the spiritual vitality of the church. In the two hundred years prior to Luther's revolt, other Christians urged church leaders to correct ecclesiastical and spiritual abuses. But the calls went unheeded.

Martin Luther's Spiritual Pilgrimage

The person who succeeded in bringing reform to the church where others had failed came from a humble background. Martin Luther was born in 1483 and raised to be a devout Catholic by his peasant parents. As a child he learned the creeds, the Lord's Prayer, and the Ten Commandments and revered the church and her saints. He was twenty years old before he read the Bible, and he later reported that he was surprised to find that it contained so much more than he had expected. Luther studied for a career in law, but the unexpected death of a friend and a narrow escape from lightning in a thunderstorm led him to enter an Augustinian monastery in 1505. Deeply troubled about the state of his soul, he became a conscientious, if overscrupulous monk, and he severely punished himself for his sins. He later declared that if ever a man were saved by monkery he would have been that monk!

> I myself was a monk for twenty years and so plagued myself with prayers, fastings, wakings, and freezings that I almost died of cold. . . . What else did I seek through this but God who was to see how I observed the rules and lived such a rigid life? (*Werke* 49, 27).

In 1507 he was ordained to the priesthood, but he continued a life of study and became a professor of theology at the University of Wittenberg in Germany. His duties included lecturing on various portions of the Bible.

Luther completed his doctorate in 1512 and was rewarded for his practical abilities and his brilliance as a scholar and theologian with the administration of eleven monasteries. He also developed into a powerful preacher and used his talent to communicate forcefully the simple message of the Bible acquired from his scholarly research. His study of Augustine led him to become an Augustinian in more than name, and to reject Aristotle and the tradition of Christian theology that rested on Aristotelian foundations. In 1516, while lecturing on Romans, he understood for the first time in an intensely personal way Paul's teaching of justification by faith. Previously his own sense of guilt and sinfulness had led him to fear God's justice. Commenting on his conversion he said:

> Night and day I pondered until I saw the connection between the justice of God and the statement that "the just shall live by faith." Then I grasped that the justice of God is that righteousness by which through grace and sheer mercy God justifies us through faith. Thereupon I felt myself to be reborn and to have gone through open doors to paradise. The whole of Scripture took on a new meaning, and whereas before the "justice of God" had filled me with hate, now it became to be inexpressibly sweet in greater love. This passage of Paul became to me a gate to heaven . . . (*Lectures on Romans*).

A personal faith relationship to God through Jesus Christ transformed his life and his perspective. In 1517 his view that salvation results from simple faith in Christ caused him to challenge the Roman Catholic Church's claim to provide indulgences as pardons for sin. Indulgences were papers, purchased for a sum of money, that released a person from performing a work required by the sacrament of penance. Precedent for such a practice extended back to the crusades, when wealthy individuals purchased an indulgence instead of personally fighting in a crusade.

Anyone participating in such a venture, whether by actually going to the Holy Land or by contributing funds, automatically received the promise that he would not be punished for his sins in purgatory.

In Luther's time the monies secured for indulgences were to be used for building St. Peter's Cathedral in Rome. Luther was persuaded that such practices were contrary to the teaching of the Bible. Only a right relationship to God by faith brought forgiveness of sin and salvation. Therefore he challenged what he considered to be traffic in the grace of God.

On October 31, 1517, Luther nailed his 95 Theses on the door of the castle church in Wittenberg. Posting such notices, which simply called for debate and discussion of the listed items, was common practice in medieval times. An unexpectedly positive response to Luther's theses, however, brought revolutionary change to the church. The key thesis, number 62, stated, "The true treasury of the church is the holy gospel of the glory and the grace of God." By these words Luther boldly rejected the medieval notion of a treasury of merits administered by the hierarchy of the church. Other theses affirmed human depravity, the necessity of lifelong repentance (as opposed to instant remission of punishment by cash payment), and the full and free grace of God in Christ. Luther's theses challenged several dogmas and practices of medieval Catholicism. They contributed to his being excommunicated by the pope and branded an outlaw by imperial edict after a dramatic meeting before Emperor Charles V at the Diet of Worms.

Luther's ideas were beginning to take definite shape in 1520. Three of his principles became the watchwords of Reformation theology.

1. *Sola Scriptura:* As the inspired Word of God, Scripture is the only authoritative basis for all Christian doctrine. Tradition—oral and written teaching from early church fathers and medieval theologians—which was used to validate the sale of indulgences and other ecclesiastical practices, including the addition of several sacraments, was not to be used as an authority on the same level as the Bible.

2. *Sola gratia:* "Grace alone"—coupled with *sola fide,* "faith alone"—describes the biblical view of redemption. Salvation is solely the result of God's sovereign grace in sending Christ. His death on the cross and resurrection from the dead is the only cure for human sin. Righteousness is imputed to man by God on the basis of Christ's atoning work on the cross. The human response to God's grace is faith in God's promises, specifically that God will save all who believe that Christ's death and resurrection were accomplished for them. Salvation is wholly the result of God's grace, and we appropriate salvation not by our own efforts or works, but solely on the basis of faith in God's provision. Following the apostle Paul in the book of Romans, Luther taught that believers are justified in God's sight not through human efforts but through simple faith in God's promises revealed in Christ. How far Luther had come from his monastery days when he believed he had to make himself worthy of God's grace!

3. The priesthood of all believers: The church does not need a priestly class to mediate between believers and God. Rather, every person is his own priest and has immediate access to God through Christ. Christ is our great high priest who replaces all human priests. By virtue of our faith in Christ we stand before God as our own priests and do not need any human institution to intercede for us.

These three ideas were basic to the Reformation and became fundamental doctrines of Protestantism. All changes in doctrine, spirituality, and church organization that resulted in the formation of various Protestant groups were premised on these principles.

Luther's Revival of Biblical Theology and Anthropology

Luther's views of God continued to develop as he deepened his knowledge of the Bible and probed the implications of his three primary principles. During his earlier years in the monastery he experienced guilt and anxiety because he feared God and His justice. After experiencing God's grace, however, Luther came to understand God's justice in light of His love. Rejecting any notion of God that did not originate in the Bible, he openly ridiculed Aristotle's *prime being*. Moreover, he criticized Thomas for drawing his views of God from Aristotle rather than from Scripture. Luther's Augustinian convictions led him to denounce even more strongly Aristotle's influence on medieval interpretations of man. Repudiating Aristotle's statement from *On the Soul* that "the soul dies with the body," Luther retorted:

> It is as if we did not possess the Holy Scriptures where we find a superabundance of teaching on the whole subject, of which Aristotle has not the faintest inkling. Yet this defunct pagan has attained supremacy; impeded, and almost suppressed, the Scriptures of the living God (*An Appeal to the Ruling Class*).

Based upon the Bible, specifically Genesis and the writings of Paul, Luther concluded with Augustine that the problem of sin was rooted in the unbelief of Adam. The image of God after the fall was "so marred and obscured by sin" and is "so utterly leprous and unclean" that we can scarcely understand it. The image of God is "almost wholly lost" (*Commentary on Genesis*). Medieval anthropologies exhibit the dangers of forming Christian views under the influence of synthesis thought. For Luther the greatest sin is pride, our unwillingness to admit our sinful, fallen condition. Sin now exercises such dominion that a man's will lies prostrate and helpless until the grace of God frees him.

So central was the idea of mankind's lack of moral freedom to Luther's whole anthropology that he penned *The Bondage of the Will*, a strident reply to the great Christian humanist scholar Erasmus, who had defended human free will. In it Luther wrote:

> When a man is without the Spirit of God he does not do evil against his will, but he does it of his own accord. . . . And this readiness . . . he cannot by his own powers omit, restrain, or change. . . . It means that the will cannot change itself and turn in a different direction. . . . Free choice without the grace of God is not free at all, but immutably the captive and slave of evil since it cannot of itself turn to the good.

Here is an excellent summary of Augustine's principle of *non posse non peccare*. Like his theological predecessor, Luther was primarily concerned to show that God's grace is absolutely essential for salvation. If people were capable of choosing moral and spiritual good, then salvation would be a cooperative effort between God and man. Luther repudiated this semi-Pelagian position because, if people were able to initiate a relationship with God, grace would merely be an aid to human effort and not the necessity the Bible says it is.

Luther's theology revived major emphases of Augustine. The Reformer denounced Aquinas's distinctions between operative and cooperative grace, and natural and supernatural virtues. Until God's grace frees people from their bondage to sin and evil, they have no "free" will. The only truly "free" will is one that is free to do the good. Because sin cripples the human will, our wills possess no such power. Sin utterly destroys human capacity to do what is morally good. Only by the grace of God are we capable of moral goodness.

Luther's Three Treatises

Luther's initial break with Rome was rendered virtually irreparable when he published three major treatises in 1520. These treatises summarize his thought. His first tract, *An Appeal to the Ruling Class*, was a clarion call to the German nobles to reform the church. In it he attempted to demolish what he called "three walls" that "the Romanists" had erected to strengthen the clergy's control of the church. Luther strongly denied that the Bible distinguishes between Christians in terms of laity and clergy. Peter's statement "You are a kingdom of priests" (I Pet. 2:9) means that all Christians, not just a select few, are priests. Medieval theologians had improperly exalted a priestly class, the clergy, above common believers and called them "religious" by virtue of their supposedly higher office. But Luther pointed out that Peter's teaching on the priesthood of all believers means that, because of God's grace, every Christian stands in Jesus Christ before God and needs no one from a special class to mediate between God and himself.

The second "wall" that Luther levelled was the primacy of the pope as an interpreter of Scripture. Every believer ought to read the Bible for himself and not depend on the pope or the church to interpret it for him. After all, popes have erred in the past, and spiritual authority was given to all the apostles in the New Testament, not just to one of them. Every Christian ought to take up the cause of the faith, understand it, and defend it.

The third "wall" constructed by medieval theologians to keep the church under the clergy's control was the idea that only the pope could call a council to reform the church. Luther believed that the church was in desperate need of reform, and since the clergy were unwilling to carry out this responsibility, he urged secular rulers, the German nobles, to demolish the third "wall" by convening a general council to initiate reform. This is why the treatise was addressed to the German ruling class. Because the first two "walls" improperly invested power in popes and priests, Christians ought not to wait for them to instigate much needed reform. These reinterpretations of the role of Christian believers and their position in the church testify to the radical nature of Luther's breach with Rome.

In his second treatise, *The Babylonian Captivity of the Church*, Luther focused his attention on other problems with medieval Christianity. Whereas the first treatise attacked the hierarchical structure of the church, the second opposed placing the sacraments of the church under total control of the clergy. In so doing, the hierarchy held the church captive, much as the Babylonians did the Jews in the sixth century B.C. Luther argued that Christ had instituted only two sacraments during his earthly ministry, baptism and the Lord's Supper. Church leaders in the Middle Ages, however, without biblical warrant, had increased the number to seven. In addition, medieval theologians placed the clerical hierarchy in control of the sacraments. The clergy, furthermore, abused this authority by insisting that the merit that saves people from their sins is distributed only through the sacraments.

Luther also repudiated the medieval position that the sole value of a sacrament lies in its relation to accumulated merits distributed by clergy who perform the sacrament. Rather, he contended, the value of the sacraments rests upon the promise of God. Thus God alone, not the clergy, administers His grace, not according to works of merit, but according to believers' faith in the promise of God's Word. Therefore, Luther agreed that sacraments are significant because they communicate God's grace to participants. But confession of sin and pious living are more important than ritualistic participation in the sacraments. Luther thus sharply dismissed the medieval view of the Christian life as resting primarily upon participating in the sacramental life of the institutional church. God established other means of grace in addition to the sacraments by which all believers are to maintain a daily relationship with God, such as prayer and Bible reading.

Luther's third treatise, *Freedom of the Christian Man*, probably best summarizes his theology. It is a classic Reformation statement of the nature of the Christian life, specifically of the relation between law and faith in Christian experience. Christians are free in the sense that they are no longer bound to obey the Old Testament law in order to establish a right relationship with God. Rather, they are justified by faith in Christ, which God gives to them as a free gift. A person's works are of absolutely no value in obtaining salvation. People are redeemed not because of their own good works but because of Christ's death for them on the cross. Those who acknowledge that Christ bore their sins and accept Christ as their Lord and Savior have Christ's righteousness imputed to them. At the same time, every Christian is bound to his neighbor by the law of love. Good works do not justify a person in God's sight. They are, however, the results of justification, which Christians perform out of a spontaneous desire to obey God's will. Thus, Luther presented a Reformed view of the relationship between law and gospel, which sharply contrasted with the prevailing view expressed in the sale of indulgences and faith in a treasury of merit.

Luther's major contribution to the Reformation was his revival of Augustine's interpretation of biblical Christianity. Luther stressed the gulf between God and fallen man and emphasized the utter necessity of God's grace and mercy in procuring human salvation. In so doing, he disavowed the semi-Pelagianism and Aristotelianism of his predecessors. Echoing Paul, he declared that without God human beings are lost, and reasoning and knowledge are of little use unless they are based on the Bible. Catholics have maintained that Luther overemphasized human depravity in reaction to Thomist and Renaissance optimism about natural man and his capabilities. Luther's followers answer that in being captive to the Word of God he, like Augustine before him, simply reiterated and explained biblical teaching about God and man.

Architect of Reformation Theology: John Calvin

If Luther was the soldier who fired the opening salvo of the Reformation, Calvin was its chief scholar who consolidated Protestant gains. He attempted to reform not simply doctrine and church organization, as Luther did, but also the social-political order according to the Word of God. Born in Noyon, France, in 1509, just eight years before Luther hammered his 95 Theses to the church door at Wittenberg, Calvin was a second generation Reformer. He studied at several schools in pursuit of a humanist education.

After his father died, he gave up the study of law and turned to theology. Like Luther, he experienced a dramatic conversion, although he was not driven by overwhelming guilt and fear as was his German counterpart. When severe persecution broke out against Protestant Reformers, Calvin traveled for a time in France under assumed names and settled in Basel, Switzerland, where he began to write his *Institutes of the Christian Religion*.

Of the many contributions Calvin made to the Reformation, the *Institutes* was his most enduring. By the time the final edition was published in 1559, it had grown from a short (six-chapter) exposition of Christian doctrine to the most significant theological work of the Reformation. Originally it was a discussion of the Ten Commandments, the Apostles' Creed, and the Lord's Prayer. In its final form of eighty chapters it was organized into four books on the subjects of God, Christ, the Holy Spirit, and the church.

In 1536, Calvin reluctantly agreed to help William Farel, who threatened him with divine wrath if he did not join the Reformation effort at Geneva. Calvin and Farel tried to make the city a model Christian community by enforcing a high code of morality.

But liberal Genevans balked at the reforms. Expelled by the city, Calvin journeyed to Strasbourg where he pastored a church of French Protestant refugees for three years. They were the happiest years of his life. He found a wife, wrote a Protestant liturgy to replace the Catholic order of worship, worked with German Reformers to reunite the church, and began his commentaries, which eventually covered forty-nine books of the Bible.

Again Geneva beckoned him. By public acclamation Calvin returned in 1541 because his successors failed in their leadership. Under Calvin's guidance Geneva became the international center of the Reformation movement. His theological, social, and political views gained admirers in many countries as Protestant refugees from all over Europe flocked to Geneva where they established their own local churches. Calvin became the only international Reformer by carrying on extensive correspondence with these refugees when they returned to their homelands as missionaries for Protestantism.

Calvin's Theology: The Sovereignty of God

Calvin's ideas, like those of Luther, were basically a revival of Augustinianism. The fundamental principle informing every chapter of the *Institutes* is his view of God as majestic and sovereign over all creation. God's sovereignty is not some abstract, speculative idea. Rather it is a dynamic principle, a concrete life-informing reality, that shaped Calvin's discussion of every doctrine. Calvin desired that believers' knowledge of God "consist more in a living experience than in vain and high-flown speculation" (*Institutes* 1. 10. 2).

Of all God's attributes the most important to experience personally is His providence because this attribute most concretely displays His sovereignty. God's providence is inseparably related to His work as Creator. But if God were merely Creator, He would be unrelated to the creation, just as a watchmaker no longer is involved with the operation of a watch after he has assembled it. Therefore, Calvin viewed God's providential care as permeating the created order: "He sustains, nourishes, and cares for everything he has made, even to the least sparrow" (*Institutes* 1. 16. 1). God's secret plan governs all of existence, from inanimate objects to animals and human life as well. God's inscrutable will directs everything.

The implications of this view of God are obviously extensive. Calvin insisted that his view led neither to fatalism nor to rejecting human accountability. Repeatedly, he emphasized that his primary concern was to explain what the Bible taught on this difficult subject. God does not function as an absentee landlord. He is intimately involved with creation. Calvin cited numerous passages from both the Old and the New Testaments to support God's pervasive control over what He has made. While affirming God's providence, he dismissed notions of fate, chance, and fortune as "pagan inventions."

At the outset, therefore, Calvin discussed the doctrine of God as Creator and preserver, not as some abstract, impersonal first cause or unmoved mover. Implicit in the notion of God as Creator is that God is personal and that He wills and orders what He has made. Unlike Aquinas's view, Calvin's idea of God as personal was not added after he had first proved His existence (as Aquinas did in adapting Aristotle's rational proofs of an unmoved mover or first cause). Calvin rejected as unbiblical all ideas of God as merely a prime mover who initiates "a certain universal motion, actuating the whole machine of the world and all its respective parts" (*Institutes* 1. 16. 1). God is personal and actively participates in creation.

Thus Calvin discussed God's providence not merely for its intellectual content, but for its immensely practical religious value to the faithful. Belief in God's providence instills in them great comfort that all of life is in the control of a loving heavenly Father. At the same time, it induces a proper awe and fear of God, for in His plan God has also told Christians their responsibility to discover and fulfill His will. Seeking to reconcile God's sovereignty and human accountability, Calvin emphasized submitting to God's will and recognizing and accepting how God uses circumstances to teach us obedience to His Word.

The Christian heart, since it has been thoroughly persuaded that all things happen by God's plan, and that nothing takes place by chance, will ever look to him as the principle cause of things, yet will give attention to the secondary causes in their proper place. . . . As far as men are concerned, whether they are good or evil, the heart of the Christian will know that their plans, wills, efforts, and abilities are under God's hand; that it is within his choice to bend them whither he pleases and to constrain them whenever he pleases (*Institutes* 1. 17. 6).

Christians not only understand and experience God's providence by faith but also submit their wills to God's sovereignty in order to obey His commandments. Calvinists are relieved from the anxiety that plagues unbelievers who have no sense that God's purpose and plan are being worked out in everyday life. While assuming their own responsibility to order their daily living according to biblical principles, they recognize and accept by simple faith that whatever happens is under God's providential care.

Calvin's Anthropology: Creation, Fall, Redemption

Because God is a majestic sovereign who rules over His creation, all things He created, including man, are to serve and glorify Him. Calvin's motto describes our task: "My heart I offer unto thee, O Lord, promptly and sincerely."

Because human beings have sinned, they have not lived up to their original purpose. Like Luther, Augustine, and Paul, Calvin sharply contrasted man's original nobility and integrity as the divine image with his later deformity and wickedness after the fall.

The Bible portrays fallen mankind as devoid of goodness and power. No human work remains untainted by the corruption resulting from the fall. While the divine image is not utterly destroyed, it is hopelessly distorted. Punished for his sin by being deprived of wisdom, truth, and righteousness, Adam displayed ignorance, vanity, and wickedness. The fallen Adam passed these traits on to his posterity in the guilt and corruption called "original sin." Not only is original sin an inherited corruption, but it is also, Calvin maintained, an imputed guilt, a judicial verdict imposed by God as in a court of law. Reiterating Paul's teaching in Romans 5, Calvin taught that Adam sinned not simply for himself, but as a federal representative for all mankind, much as Christ, the "Second Adam," died as a representative for human sin.

Our inherited depravity means that every individual's will is enslaved to sin, and we are totally incapable of doing good. Fallen human beings have no moral free will. Because our wills in their natural, unredeemed state are slaves to sin, only those who have been set free by the grace of God are free moral agents. Disagreeing with many philosophers, Calvin insisted that human will and reason are so crippled by sin that they cannot function as originally intended; people are unable to do good and worship God. Calvin held that, of all of the church fathers, only Augustine recognized the full extent of human depravity. Sin has so corrupted human nature that man in his total being (reason, will, affections, etc.) is able to do the good that God requires of him only through God's grace.

Calvin's view of salvation is that, in love and obedience and as a substitute, Christ paid the penalty for sin on Calvary in order to rescue those whom God freely chooses to be saved. In redemption, God's grace is *imputed* (placed in the account of) believers rather than *infused* (poured) into believers. Calvin explained the doctrine of salvation under his discussion of the work of the Holy Spirit, who applies the work of Christ to the believer. The Spirit both creates repentance and faith in hearts and renews the image of God in those chosen to be redeemed. Following Paul in Ephesians 2:8-9, Calvin stated that faith is the means by which believers are united to God, but faith itself is a gift from God. Good works follow faith but are not the basis for salvation. In salvation, as in creation and the ordering of the world, Calvin's recurrent theme is human dependence on God's sovereignty.

Calvin used the term *election* to explain how God's sovereignty operates in salvation. Only after understanding man's sinful condition can we appreciate the necessity of election. Those who do not assert God's election, in Calvin's opinion, succumb to various forms of Pelagianism, which teaches that humans either can obtain their own salvation without God's grace or need grace to assist them in their effort to save themselves. Calvin's doctrine of election or predestination opposes both the Renaissance *homo mensura* ("man is the measure") and the medieval notion of cooperative grace, both of which attribute autonomy to man.

In explaining election Calvin sought to affirm only those ideas clearly taught in the Bible. He condemned as speculative thinking any theology that went beyond the explicit teaching of Scripture. His primary argument, therefore, was that the Bible indisputably teaches election by using such terms as *elect, predestine, choose,* and others. For example, in the Old Testament, God chose Israel to receive His special revelation in the covenant with Moses. God selected Israel not because of any innate merit or quality the Jews possessed, but simply because He wanted to show His grace by redeeming them as a people (see Deut. 7:7-8). Even within Israel not all individuals were chosen, but only a "remnant" (Gen. 45:7; Isa. 10:21). Calvin cited God's sovereign choice of Jacob and rejection of Esau as an example of election (Rom. 9:21). Thus, election is both collective and individual in the Bible. From Abraham through the prophets God called a people to be His own.

Calvin noted numerous passages in the New Testament that illustrate God's sovereignty in election and predestination. For example, Jesus' statement "You have not chosen me but I have chosen you" (John 15:16),[1] and Paul's words, "He chose us in him before the foundation of the world. . . . He destined us in him to be his sons through Jesus Christ . . ." (Eph. 1:4ff.),[2] affirm God's sovereignty in election. Calvin concluded that the Bible clearly teaches predestination. God's sovereignty of grace in election is necessary because people are dead in sin; lacking true freedom of will they are unable apart from enabling grace to choose God for themselves. Without God's sovereign predestina-

1. Cf. John 6:39, 44, 45; 13:18; 17:9.
2. Cf. Rom. 8:29; 9:10-13.

tion all of mankind would be eternally lost in sin. In His plan of redemption God chooses to redeem a portion of mankind to glorify His holy name. The reason He has chosen such a method of salvation lies in His sovereign will alone.

Finally, Calvin answered objections proposed against election. His responses took several forms. (1) Previously he had argued that freedom of will was an invention of false philosophies. If human beings are "dead in sin" (Eph. 2:1), then only God's grace can save them. The scriptural teaching about original sin answers many objections to the doctrine of election, for human depravity is an important presupposition of the necessity of God's sovereign predestination. (2) Some objected that election is unjust, that it renders our sense of responsibility meaningless, and that it destroys incentives to moral action. Calvin replied that in the Bible God Himself is the highest principle of justice. As the Old Testament example of Job makes clear, human beings cannot presume to accuse God of being unjust if God chooses some and rejects others. Questioning God's actions assumes that we can call God to account, which would put us or our claims above Him. That is the height of human arrogance. God's justice transcends all human conceptions of justice.

Contrary to common opinion, argued Calvin, God's sovereignty does not negate human responsibility. While the two *appear* to be irreconcilable, Scripture affirms *both* that sovereign grace is the only means by which we can be saved *and* that we are still accountable for our actions. Even though finite human reasoning is incapable of resolving this apparent conflict, we must affirm both to be true. God's sovereignty and human accountability are both taught in the Bible, and their relationship is indeed a great mystery. Divine sovereignty alone validates human responsibility. Views that teach human freedom as the sole basis for moral accountability attribute to human choice an autonomy that the Bible gives to God alone. Calvin's view is more balanced than his detractors often acknowledge. Christians are to affirm both God's sovereignty over the entire created order, so that all things are determined by God's inscrutable will, and our moral and spiritual accountability. In a mysterious way, above human understanding, God holds people responsible for their actions.

A classical New Testament passage that teaches both predestination and human responsibility is Acts 2:23. In his Pentecost sermon Peter contends that God predestined Jesus' death on the cross as part of the divine plan of salvation. Yet Peter also holds those who crucified Jesus accountable for putting to death the Son of God. Neither God's predestination nor human accountability is compromised, as both are unequivocally asserted. Without fully understanding *how* both can be true, Christians are called upon to emphasize them equally because they are both taught in the Bible.

(3) In defending election Calvin also appealed to our own existential experience that we are unable to perform what God requires in His Word. He cited Paul's statement in Romans 7:15-20 that even though we know and want to do good, we still do evil. We find in God's Word that grace is both necessary and promised to us as is confirmed in our own experience. Moreover, the doctrine of divine election is not intended to make believers anxious about whether they are elected or not, but rather to forestall such anxiety by engendering assurance of salvation and comfort. Far from being merely a speculative idea about how God is related to His creation, God's sovereignty in predestination, when rightly understood, is of great practical value in everyday life. It gives us confidence that God exercises personal care over all events. Belief that God is both Lord and Savior of our personal lives prevents despair.

At the end of the sixteenth and the beginning of the seventeenth centuries, Jacob Arminius, a Dutch theologian, proposed an alternative to the view of predestination shared by Augustine, Luther, and Calvin. Arminius believed that God's foreknowledge preceded His predestination, and that therefore God's election is not absolute, but conditioned. God chooses individuals based on His knowing beforehand whether they would freely accept or reject Christ and His work of salvation. Arminius sought a middle ground between Calvin's belief in God's absolute predestination and Pelagius's teaching on human autonomy. Unlike Pelagius,

Arminius believed that original sin not only crippled the human will but rendered it totally unable to do any good thing apart from God's grace. Without God's preparatory grace men are dead in sin. Arminius also believed that Christ did not pay the penalty for everyone's sin, but that Christ's suffering is available only to those who choose to accept it. God forgives the sins of people who repent and believe. Salvation, therefore, is a cooperative effort between man and God, much as Thomas Aquinas taught in his medieval synthesis.

Arminius's theology strongly swayed Protestant thought, particularly evangelicalism, on both sides of the Atlantic. John Wesley popularized Arminian ideas in England's Evangelical Awakening of the eighteenth century and made them central to Methodist theology. Many American denominations, such as Baptists, independents, and holiness groups, are committed to Arminian views.

Summary of the Reformation

The theology and anthropology of the Reformers illustrates how thoroughly they revised the doctrine and the life of the Christian church.[3] The view they formulated successfully challenged the synthesis mentality that had dominated the church for centuries. And they did not invent a new form of Christianity, a perspective never before known in the church. Not motivated by a spirit of novelty, the Reformers developed the biblical ideas on which the church had originally been founded. They sought to eliminate all alien philosophical systems from Christian thought and to return to the teachings of Paul and Augustine to reshape every area of doctrine and practice.

Because the Reformers' assumptions differed so sharply from those of their predecessors, radical changes occurred. Old authorities that mixed the Bible with philosophy, history, and tradition

3. For purposes of simplicity we limit our study of Protestantism as a world view to Luther's and Calvin's ideas. Thus we omit a diverse group called radical Reformers and Anabaptists and other Reformation sects. Because we believe their ideas have greater significance for the social implications of the world view, we reserve our discussion of their ideas for our treatment of society in volume 2.

were rejected in favor of those who consciously accepted the Bible alone as the basis for faith and life. Luther opposed the authority of both pope and emperor. Calvin took the Reformation vision further to rethink the whole of Christian doctrine. Their work divided the Western church into two parts, a division that has lasted to our present day. Catholics initiated a Counter Reformation both to answer the charges of Protestants and to reform abuses that hindered their own ministry. Central to the Counter Reformation was the Council of Trent (1545-63), which reaffirmed most medieval doctrine, including Thomas Aquinas's synthesis of Aristotelian and biblical ideas.

The Reformers were not infallible, and some of Luther's and Calvin's followers have modified their views. But these two pillars of the Reformation strongly asserted God's sovereignty and forced people to recognize that the only alternative to God's sovereignty was an allegiance however strong or weak, to human *autonomy*, which became the byword in the modern era. We will turn our attention to this major change in our next chapter.

For Further Reading

Althaus, P. *The Theology of Martin Luther*. Philadelphia: Fortress, 1966.

Bainton, Roland H. *Here I Stand: A Life of Martin Luther*. New York: Abingdon Cokesbury, 1950.

Bangs, C. D. *Arminius: A Study in the Dutch Reformation*. Nashville: Abingdon, 1971.

———. *The Reformation of the Sixteenth Century*. Boston: Beacon, 1952.

Chadwick, Owen. *The Reformation*. Baltimore: Penguin, 1968.

Dickens, A. G. *The Counter Reformation*. New York: Harcourt Brace Jovanovich, 1963.

Duffield, John, ed. *John Calvin*. Grand Rapids: Eerdmans, 1966.

Leith, John. *An Introduction to the Reformed Tradition*. Atlanta: John Knox Press, 1977.

McNeill, John T. *The History and Character of Calvinism*. New York: Oxford University Press, 1954.

McNeill, John T. and Ford Lewis Battles, eds. *John Calvin: Institutes of the Christian Religion.* Philadelphia: Westminster Press, 1960.

Niesel, W. *The Theology of Calvin.* London, 1956.

Ozment, Steven. *The Age of Reform: An Intellectual and Religious History of Late Medieval and Reformation Europe.* New Haven: Yale University Press, 1980.

Parker, T. H. L. *John Calvin: A Biography.* Philadelphia: Westminster Press, 1975.

Pelikan, J. and H. T. Lehmann, eds. *Luther's Works.* 55 vols. St. Louis: Concordia, 1955-76.

Schwiebert, E. G. *Luther and His Times.* St. Louis: Concordia, 1950.

Wendel, Francois. *Calvin: The Origin and Development of His Religious Thought.* New York: Oxford, 1954.

8
From the Renaissance to the Age of Naturalism
John D. Currid

The Renaissance

While Luther, Calvin, and other Protestants in northern Europe wrestled with the problems of reforming the doctrine and life of the Christian church, another great movement, the Renaissance, was already well under way in southern Europe. Like the Reformation, the Renaissance sought to find a foundation that could provide meaning and unity for all life. Because these two movements provide antithetical answers to the same basic questions, they should be viewed and considered alongside one another.

Historians often classify the Renaissance (c. 1400–1600) as the great period of rebirth in secular learning and the quest for knowledge. Many surmise from this that the Middle Ages (including the so-called Dark Ages), which preceded, were devoid of great art and architecture, literary masterpieces, and speculative philosophy. Nothing could be farther from the truth, however, as a brief look at some of the achievements of the Middle Ages confirms. During those years (500–1400) the magnificent Romanesque and Gothic styles were born; the Abbey of St. Denis was built in Paris; the English cathedrals of Winchester and Durham were constructed; the early universities, such as Oxford and Cambridge, were founded. In reality, the Renaissance, was not so much a rebirth of the forgotten fields of art or philosophy as it was a change in thinking about these and other fields. Whereas medieval thinkers emphasized man's religious nature and his relationship with his Creator, Renaissance philosophers made man himself the central focus of all inquiry and expression.

Influential in shifting attention from the supernatural to man and the natural was the Italian philosopher Petrarch (1304–74). As a young man on his first visit to Rome he was very impressed by the grandeur of the ancient ruins of the city. Comparing the ancient city to the existing one, he concluded that the earlier civilization was much greater and thus needed to be revived. Consequently, Petrarch spent the remainder of his life attempting to restore pagan culture, especially the ideas and ideals of Rome and Greece. Many major thinkers of the Renaissance period sought to achieve this same goal. So in one way the Renaissance was a rebirth; it was an attempt to reclaim the humanistic and naturalistic values of the ancients.

The Ancient Roots of Naturalism

Naturalism is the oldest philosophy in Western civilization. Although it had earlier roots, naturalism was first systematically presented by Thales and the Milesian School, which he founded in the sixth century B.C. Thales and his followers, Anaximander and Anaximenes, tried to discover one physical substance that underlay all things in the universe (*corporeal monism*). For Thales, that one substance was water; for Anaximenes, it was air. Significantly, all members of the Milesian School looked within physical nature for the absolute and ultimate reality. The thought that reality was found only in nature, and not in "supernature," was the cornerstone of naturalism.

Naturalistic expression reached a much more fully developed stage with the appearance of the Greek atomists (beginning in the fifth century B.C.). Democritus and Leucippus were the originators and primary spokesmen for the atomic theory. The theory stated that reality is merely a matter of atoms in motion through space. There is no other reality; even human thought, soul, and emotion could be explained as a result of the physical clash of atoms. Using this theory, atomists explained motion and change solely on the basis of physical principles.

To demonstrate how far the atomists took the idea that reality is only physical let us examine briefly the thought of Epicurus (341–270 B.C.). Although he strongly supported Democritus's thought, Epicurus believed that his mentor had not adequately explained how people obtain knowledge. If all things were merely physical, how does one account for human thought? Epicurus asserted that objects emit physical atoms, which the senses transmit to the mind, which then produces a physical atomic replica of the object. Every human faculty, even the ability to reflect, meditate, and have emotion, is a consequence of physical reactions. Epicurus's explanation exhibits a second cornerstone of naturalistic thought: man could be understood only as the sum of his physical parts, merely as an anatomical being. Man was seen as a part of nature, not separate from and above other parts.

These naturalistic beliefs of Greek philosophy influenced the general thought and thrust of the Renaissance. And yet Renaissance humanism was not simply a revival of Greek naturalism. The major thinkers of the Renaissance differed from the Greek naturalists by not denying outright the existence of God and the supernatural realm. As the movement developed, only gradually did it reject the traditional Christian conceptions of God, the universe, and man's place within it. The shift from the Christian world view to the naturalism of the nineteenth century can be traced in the writings of philosophers of the seventeenth century.

Thomas Hobbes (1588–1679)

Thomas Hobbes became one of the great thinkers of the pre-Enlightenment period despite a stormy youth and upbringing. His father was a cruel, ignorant man who served as the vicar of a church. After reportedly engaging in a slugfest with one of his parishioners at the church door, Hobbes's father abandoned his son. Fortunately, an uncle took care of Thomas, preparing him for adult life and even sending him through scholastic studies at Oxford University. After his formal education was completed, Hobbes became the personal tutor for the very wealthy Cavendish family. While serving in this position he formulated and presented his extensive thought, especially in the fields of political theory and philosophy.

Hobbes was a follower of British scientist and philosopher Francis Bacon (1561–1626), whom he knew personally. Hobbes was especially influenced by Bacon's emphasis on the superiority of the physical sciences over any speculative inquiry of the supernatural. Reality was, to Hobbes, as to the ancient Greek naturalists, merely *matter*, which has "no dependence upon our thought, and is co-extended with some part of space." In other words, reality is nothing more than the movement of physical bodies or matter in space.

Man, according to Hobbes, is nothing but a body made up of matter; each individual is simply a material entity moving through space. Hobbes, therefore, introduced a mechanical anthropology, one in which people are mere parts of nature. In that respect Hobbes displayed the greatest common ground with the ancient Greek naturalists, especially the atomists.

Like many pre-Enlightenment skeptics, however, Hobbes was not a "pure" naturalist, since he believed in the existence of a supernatural being. This being was not the Christian God of the Bible, but rather a "God" whom he adapted to his mechanistic understanding of reality. This "God" had no personal intimacy or relationship with man or nature, but was simply "the first of all causes." In Hobbes's view, God is totally transcendent, apart from nature. He caused all things to exist and move, but He has not intervened in the world since creating it. This theological perspective is known as *deism*.

Deism became the primary religious belief of intellectuals during the Enlightenment, and it was promoted by philosophers such as Rene Descartes (1596–1650). The basic views of deism may be summarized as follows:

1. God set in motion an orderly system called nature and then let it run its own course. At first glance it seems as if the deist has a proper Christian understanding of God, as Creator, the first cause, and the one who brought order out of chaos. But, in reality, deism is *reductionistic*: unlike theists, proponents of deism assert that God does not personally intervene in the day-to-day affairs of the universe. He merely set in motion an orderly system and then refused to act upon it. God is the cosmic bystander. As

James Sire explains, "To the deist, then, God is distant, foreign, alien" (*The Universe Next Door*, p. 49).

2. Nature is a closed system and humans cannot know anything beyond the natural realm. Whereas theism is grounded in the belief that man can know truth because God has revealed it to him through written revelation (the Bible) and natural revelation (the physical world), the deist denies that God intercedes with the written Word or by any other means. Nature is a closed system, which God does not directly break into for any purpose. People can learn about God only through studying nature, which God set in motion at the beginning of time. This important shift in thought from theism to deism underscores the impersonal, mechanistic theology of Renaissance thinking.

3. Human beings are merely a part of nature. Unlike Christian thought, which teaches that man is specially made in the image of his Creator and is thereby capable of a unique, personal relationship with God, deists conclude that man is simply locked into the closed system of nature. People cannot have a direct relationship with God. They cannot transcend nature any more than God can break into nature. Man and God are thus eternally disengaged.

The philosophical currents unleashed by Renaissance humanism and furthered by Hobbes, Descartes, and others supplied a total world-and-life view that transformed all aspects of the southern European culture. The fundamental presupposition that nature—in particular, man—should be the central focus of all inquiry and expression, while "squeezing out" God, was present in every aspect of society, including such diverse fields as art, literature, and the sciences. A good example of this anthropocentric perspective is Michelangelo's Great Room in the Academy in Florence, as described by Francis Schaeffer:

> . . . we come finally, at the focal point of the room, to the magnificent statue of David (1504). As a work of art it has few equals in the world. Michelangelo took a piece of marble so flawed that no one thought it could be used, and out of it he carved this overwhelming statue. But let us notice that

the David was not the Jewish David of the Bible. David was simply a title. Michelangelo knew his Judaism, and in the statue the figure is not circumcised. We are not to think of this as the biblical David but as the humanistic ideal. Man is great! (*How Should We Then Live?*, pp. 71–72).

Like art, drama was secularized during the Renaissance. The first instance occurred in the fifteenth century in Florence, when public festivals and plays severed any ties with the church. Playwrights soon centered on the themes and stories of secular society, man, and nature. In 1471 Pliziano wrote the *Orfeo*, the first purely secular play written since the Middle Ages began. Theater and secular drama had been important in antiquity, but they had disappeared with the decline of Greece and Rome. Renaissance leaders attempted to recapture a secular interpretation of drama and theater.

The Enlightenment

If Renaissance humanism began to reject theistic presuppositions, the Enlightenment, which followed (1660–1798), even further accentuated the importance of man and nature and de-emphasized the supernatural. The Enlightenment was primarily a period of rational thinking in which people believed that truth could only be discovered by reason, logical analysis, and argumentation. Prominent thinkers of the time, such as Descartes, Spinoza, and Leibniz, insisted that man could achieve certainty in his knowledge, and that it was attainable mainly through the process of mathematical reasoning. Such an approach, of course, denied that truth could be revealed supernaturally or from outside of human rational processes.

Confidence in human reason led Enlightenment thinkers to teach that individuals and society could be perfected by developing and implementing reason. Voltaire called such conviction "the idea of the limitless perfectibility of the human species." Man's reason was seen to be all-powerful, the source of truth, even the basis for human and socio-economic perfection.

Like the Renaissance, the Enlightenment promoted a world-and-life view in which all aspects of society, culture, and life reflected the beliefs of the prevailing philosophical system. Since truth was understood during the Enlightenment period as logical, systematic, and ordered, it followed that everything in life ought to be logical, systematic, and ordered. So, for example, the artistic style of the Enlightenment, called Baroque, demonstrated an admiration for the love of harmony and symmetry in classical Roman art. The Baroque masters Monteverdi, Milton, and Bernini expressed emotion and imagination, but only within the confines of an order that reason established. In both art and literature, Enlightenment masters opposed whimsical and fanciful expression. An artist or writer was expected to represent faithfully the manners, customs, and poses of his subjects (*realism*). There was no room for emotional interpretation. The Enlightenment master, furthermore, centered his work upon man and reason. As Dr. Samuel Johnson stated: "A blade of grass is always a blade of grass whether in one country or another. Men and women are my subjects of inquiry." Such themes revived ancient Greek naturalism. As Socrates had said, "I am a lover of knowledge, and the men who dwell in the city are my teachers, and not the trees of the country."

Most contemporary scholars argue that Enlightenment thought was antithetical to traditional Christianity and theism. Not all the philosophical rationalism of this period, however, was antireligious or atheistic. The rationalist systems of Descartes, Voltaire, and Rousseau continued to promote the deistic claims of the Enlightenment, for deism was quite consistent with rationalistic presuppositions. It was logical, orderly, and systematic: a God set in motion an orderly universe and then He let it run according to the natural laws He logically built into it.

Enlightenment thought, as that of the Renaissance, was not a total reversion to ancient Greek naturalism since most rationalists believed in some form of supernatural being. The core of rationalism, however, originated with the Greeks and, in particular, with the theory of the Pythagoreans and Plato that reason is self-sufficient as the basis for truth. Indeed, Plato taught that only through intellectual or rational cognition could man understand the world of forms, the world of reality. Like the intellectuals of the Renaissance, the humanists of the Enlightenment rejected traditional theistic or Christian ideas and reverted to pre-Christian thinking.

Two catastrophic events in the eighteenth century shattered the rationalist view of an orderly, perfectible universe. In 1756 a great earthquake destroyed much of Lisbon, Portugal, killing many of its residents. The disaster prompted people to ask, If nature and reality are rational and ordered, why were many people killed in a seemingly irrational act of nature? The second event that hastened the downfall of rationalism was the French Revolution of 1789–96. From the beginning of the Enlightenment, France and her aristocratic order had epitomized structure and order of rationalism. With the overthrow of the French Empire from within, a symbol of world power and harmony came to an end. These two developments eroded confidence in a rational universe, human reason, and social perfectibility.

The Romantic Revolution (1798–1837)

The demise of rationalism in the second half of the eighteenth century led to dramatic changes in man's view of the world. Instead of viewing reality as rational and ordered, people turned to mystery, imagination, and feeling as the basis of truth. This Age of Romanticism originated with the German secular philosophies of von Goethe (1749–1832), von Schiller (1759–1805), and Lessing (1729–81). Rebelling against the rationalistic thought of the Enlightenment these authors emphasized emotion. Von Schiller summarized their position when he said, "All creatures drink in joy from nature's breast."

This romantic world view, initiated by the German philosophers, was integrated into all aspects of European society and culture. The great romantic poets of England, Wordsworth, Coleridge, Byron, Keats, and Shelley, however, did the most to popularize this new understanding of the universe. Byron's stanza from *Childe Harold* exemplifies the romantics' emphasis upon man's inner feelings and emotions as the source of knowledge and truth:

> Could I embody and unbosom now
> That which is most within me, could I wreak
> My thoughts upon expression, and thus throw
> Soul, heart, mind, passions, feelings, strong or weak
> All that I would have sought, and all I seek
> Bear, know, feel, and yet breathe—into one word,
> And that one word were Lightning, I would speak;
> But as it is, I live and die unheard,
> With a most voiceless thought, sheathing it as a sword.

Wordsworth in *The Tables Upturned* expressed a similar conviction:

> One impulse from a vernal wood
> May teach you more of man,
> Of moral evil and of good,
> Than all the sages can.

The music of the romantic period also displays romantic themes, as it expresses the composer's imagination and emotions. During these years Ludwig von Beethoven (1770–1827) and Felix Mendelssohn (1809–47) composed their grandiose music of self-expression, which evokes from listeners such powerful sentiment and passion.

Romanticism, then, like rationalism, was a form of humanism; it elevated man to a position of prominence in knowing and valuing. While rationalists emphasized man's mind, romanticists accentuated his feelings as the basis for discovering truth. Both philosophies, however, shared a belief in the reality of a supreme deity, which distinguishes them from the "pure" naturalism of the ancient Greeks. A brief examination of a key romantic theologian will clarify the romantics' view of God.

Friedrich Schleiermacher (1768–1834)

Schleiermacher was raised in a very religious atmosphere. His parents entrusted his education to the devoutly religious Moravian Brotherhood. Despite rebelling against some of their basic Christian doctrines in his youth, he eventually continued his studies in the field of theology at the University of Halle. Throughout the remainder of his life he served as pastor, tutor, and university instructor. In addition, Schleiermacher published many influential works, including *Speeches on Religion* (1799), *Monologues* (1800), *The Christian Faith* (1821), and a variety of collections of his sermons.

A particularly formative period in the life of Schleiermacher was between the years 1796 and 1802, when he served in an ecclesiastical position in Berlin. During that time he fell in with a circle of romantics, some of whom were to have a great impact upon his later thought. Schleiermacher came to agree with much of romantic belief; yet he also wanted to retain much of his Christian convictions. Throughout his life, therefore, he sought to harmonize romanticism and theism. In his famous *Speeches on Religion to Its Cultured Despisers*, he pleaded for his romantic friends not to discard religion because rationalists had distorted it by subordinating it to reason and conscience. Of all people, romantics are closest to the unique characteristic of religion because of their emphasis upon feeling. Schleiermacher concluded that religion is the *"feeling* of absolute dependence on the infinite."* That a God exists can only be known and posited on the basis of an individual's self-consciousness, that is, in his own religious feeling that he has a relationship with a deity. A true knowledge of God, therefore, does not arise from contemplation. It is an affair of the heart rather than understanding, of faith rather than reason.

Rooted in his definition of religion was Schleiermacher's view of true Christianity not as a set of dogmas but as an inner individual experience. Dogmas are necessary in the church as concrete symbolic expressions of religious experience, but they are secondary to man's religious consciousness of his relationship with Christ. Accordingly, Schleiermacher understood the Bible as simply the textbook of Christian dogma and doctrine. The Scriptures are only a reflection of "the original translation of the Christian feeling." As such, the Scriptures are subordinate in authority to man's own feeling or intuition about God, religion, and truth. Schleiermacher denied that the Bible provides concrete, rational truth revealed to man by God. The only absolute truth in Christianity comes from the inner experience of man; objective theological knowledge does not exist.

Schleiermacher's theology illustrates how humanistic and man-centered romantic religion was. Compared to biblical presuppositions, which teach that God and His revealed Word are the final, absolute authority regarding truth, romanticism concluded that man's own inner consciousness, feeling, or intuition serves as the ultimate arbiter of truth. With the arrival of the Enlightenment, reason was considered the basis of authority, thereby replacing the Word of God. Now with the advent of the romantic period, reason was supplanted by subjective intuition. Although their emphases were different, romantic poets and Enlightenment philosophers both rejected truth based upon supernatural revelation.

Along with redefining religion as man's feeling of absolute dependence and the Bible as the first century Christians' experience of God, Schleiermacher also altered the traditional view of human nature and redemption. For centuries Augustine's view of fallen man's original sin and the absolute necessity of God's grace dominated Christian theology. But as we have seen, Renaissance and Enlightenment thinkers rejected human depravity. And although Schleiermacher did not repudiate the doctrine of human sinfulness, he radically reinterpreted it along romantic, subjectivist lines. Sin is not human rebellion against God; nor do we inherit Adam's sinful nature. We are a mixture of God-consciousness (our original righteousness) and God-forgetfulness (our original sinfulness, which is a tendency to subordinate God-consciousness to our other desires and needs). Doubting the story of the fall as an historical event, Schleiermacher regarded Adam as a representation of what all men have always been, are now, and will be in the future: imperfect but perfectible creatures. Adam's fall was not a one-time event in history, but a story of sin emerging in every person's life. Thus Schleiermacher rejected Augustine's threefold state of humanity (original righteousness, original sin, future perfection) and substituted in its place a view of all people as created imperfect yet capable of self-perfection in history. Man was no longer a sinner under God's judgment but a potentially self-perfecting creature.

Schleiermacher's romantic ideas in theology and anthropology also radically transformed the traditional view of Christ as the incarnate Son of God, who redeems sinful men by His death on the cross. Schleiermacher frankly dismissed the early church formulations such as the Nicene Creed as mere intellectual speculation about the deity and humanity of Christ. Christ's divinity was His highly developed God-consciousness. Though Schleiermacher did not deny Christ's death on the cross, he relegated it to the periphery of his views by saying that His death was not substitutionary, but rather an example of God's love. He described redemption as "mystical": "The Redeemer assumes the believer into the power of His God-consciousness, and this is His redemptive activity" (*The Christian Faith*, par. 100).

Later in the nineteenth century other German scholars followed Schleiermacher's lead of reinterpreting the Christian world view. Not all were romantics. But thinkers such as F. C. Baur (1792–1860), David Friedrich Strauss (1808–74), and Adolf von Harnack (1851–1930) developed the main ideas of Protestant liberalism. They stressed the immanence of God at work in history, at the expense of God's transcendence, and Christ's prominence as a moral teacher or prophet, instead of His deity. They viewed redemption as Christ's communicating the love of God through example rather than by His once-for-all death on the cross and resurrection from the dead. They viewed human beings as imperfect yet perfectible, and human sin more as a vestigial appendage, a part of man's animal nature that he would eventually discard, than as a state of spiritual depravity. Liberal theology gained many adherents, and its effects are still evident in much of the popular theology of the twentieth century. Most theologians correctly evaluate liberalism as a denial of the Protestant heritage. In its extreme form, as expressed by H. Richard Niebuhr, liberalism taught that "a God without wrath brought men without sin into a kingdom without judgment through the ministrations of a Christ without a cross."

The basic assumptions shared by the romantics and their liberal successors may be summarized as follows:

1. They believed that rationalism as a system had failed. Individuals could find truth not through reasoning and mathematical formulas, but only through the human emotions, feelings, and imagination.

2. They concluded that a rediscovery of nature would feed the imagination of man in his quest for truth. Nature evokes feelings of awe and wonder in human beings as they experience its beauty. Rationalism never allowed such emotion.

3. Romantics placed man at the center of all reality. As a type of naturalism, romanticism made man's subjective feelings and the natural world central to obtaining truth. While agreeing with the ancient Greek naturalists on this point, most romantics were not consistent naturalists since they allowed for the existence of the supernatural.

Rationalistic deists, romantic Christians, and Protestant liberals bear striking resemblance to medieval synthesists, who sought something external to Christian teaching on which to base their world views. They postulated as ultimate something in creation other than God and His revelation to explain their revised world views. Deists posited a natural order discerned by human reason. Schleiermacher and his followers based Christian teaching on romantic, subjective intuition. Protestant liberals chose various critical methods (primarily historical study and scientific research) to support their redefinition of Christian truth in wholly modern terms. Such efforts totally transformed the Christian world view from its God-centered emphasis until it bore little difference from naturalism.

Modern Naturalism (1830)

By emphasizing man and nature, the Renaissance, the Enlightenment, and the Romantic Revolution paved the way for a complete return to the ancient naturalism of the Greeks. Thinkers throughout the three periods selectively used the Word of God in their systems, but they gradually pushed God further and further from the center of their understanding of reality. The ancient naturalists taught that there is no supernatural. Modern naturalists revived the ancient world-and-life view, which maintained that the universe is a closed, autonomous system. Examining the life and views of its earliest exponent will help us understand the perspective of modern naturalism.

Ludwig Feuerbach (1804–72)

By the 1830s, faith in romantic idealism had begun to wane throughout Europe. In Germany, in particular, many were abandoning the philosophical idealism of Kant and Hegel. People seemed disenchanted with every influential philosophy on the continent. About that time, Ludwig Feuerbach offered a distinct philosophical approach that broke from romanticism. He quickly gathered a vast intellectual following.

Feuerbach began his career studying theology, but soon changed to philosophy at the urging of G. W. F. Hegel. Feuerbach's views became so radical, especially his opposition to Hegelian thought, that he was denied an academic post throughout his home country. His main influence was through the writing of philosophy, including such works as *History of Philosophy from Bacon to Spinoza* (1833), *The Essence of Christianity* (1841), and *Principles of the Philosophy of the Future* (1843).

Above all, Feuerbach repudiated all romantic views of philosophy based upon feeling or emotion. Believing that truth and existence are concrete, he concluded, "There is nothing beyond nature and man." He stated further that "any solution that seeks to go beyond the boundaries of nature and man is worthless." Arguing for a closed system, he denied the existence of the supernatural, a view, of course, that was held by the ancient Greek naturalists. Thus *Premise 1: Reality is a closed system in which there is no God; there is only man and nature.*

Feuerbach further postulated that nature, which encompasses all existence, consists entirely of physical entities. As a materialist, he defined the universe and reality as simple matter. Even his understanding of human thought reflected this conviction, as the following quotation illustrates: "Thought from existence, and not existence from thought." Many of the Greek naturalists would have agreed with Feuerbach on this point, since quite a few of them were *corporeal monists*, who sought ultimate reality in the physical elements of the universe. Thus *Premise 2: Reality is composed of physical objects alone.*

Feuerbach agreed with the ancient Greek naturalists that man is merely part of nature. He is the most perfect creation of nature, but like a tree, a rock, or a river, man exists solely because of material processes. He is what nature made him to be. From Feuerbach came the famous saying that expresses the oneness of man and nature: "Man is what he eats." And so, *Premise 3: Man is no different from anything in nature.*

Disavowing any view of eternity, immortality, or afterlife, Feuerbach believed that nothing transcends nature, and the ideas of eternity are merely false desires and hopes created by man. "Thought about the historical past has an infinitely greater ability to arouse man to great deeds than daydreams about theological eternity." Therefore *Premise 4: Death is the end of man.*

Feuerbach determined, as well, that nature contains no inherent values. There is nothing greater than nature; it is absolute and ultimate reality. So, for example, while man may consider it unethical to kill, no such principle is innate to natural law. How then is man to distinguish right from wrong? Feuerbach answered that man must define his own value system: "Man is a god to man." To determine how to act, Feuerbach urged, "Follow your inclinations and desires, but follow all of them: then you will not be the victim of any of them." With no objective standard of truth, each man is his own criterion for deciding moral questions. Feuerbach reiterated the ancient Greek naturalists' ideal of *homo mensura*: "Man is the measure." Thus *Premise 5: The universe has no ethical character.*

The naturalism of Feuerbach, which reflected ancient Greek naturalism, captivated philosophical thought in Germany and in the rest of Europe. Most subsequent philosophies that opposed romanticism and promoted materialism were directly or indirectly derived from his work. Like the rationalism and romanticism of earlier periods, modern naturalism is a world-and-life view in which all aspects of society and culture reflect the underlying philosophical system. The impact of naturalistic belief can be seen most dramatically, however, in the fields of natural science, literature, and society.

The Natural Sciences

Feuerbach's materialism rapidly found wide support in the natural sciences, a field marked by a flurry of discoveries after the recession of romanticism in 1830. Scientific naturalists claimed, as had Feuerbach, that nature is the only reality: there is no God, and man is merely a part of the closed system. Even man's thought processes are entirely physical: "There is no thought without phosphorus and . . . bluntly speaking, thoughts are in the same relationship to the brain as bile to the liver and urine to the kidneys." La Mettrie summed up the position in poignant words: "Let us conclude boldly then that man is a machine, and that in the whole universe there is but a single substance with various modifications." This scientific world view rested upon the conviction that the whole universe—including all living things—is not only composed of natural objects but also shaped and directed by natural processes alone.

Naturalistic thought reached its height in the nineteenth century with the appearance of Charles Darwin (1809–82) in the field of natural science. Darwin's career as a natural scientist began when he served as botanist, or "naturalist," on a five-year global expedition of the *H. M. S. Beagle* (1831). Some years earlier he had studied theology at Cambridge University, although he had no heart to become a minister. On the voyage Darwin became intrigued with the problem of the origin of diversity, in other words, why there is such a wide diversity among animals within the same species. So, for example, on his visit to the Galapagos Islands, Darwin observed that different islands sustained different types of turtles, closely related to one another, but each distinct in some physical respects. After his return to England he described his observations in the book *Voyage of H. M. S. Beagle* (1839). He concluded in that work that evolution occurs within a species (*micro*-evolution). In other words, in animals or plants of the same species different traits emerge as a result of an adaptation to differing natural environments. Furthermore, Darwin hypothesized that in order to survive, plants and animals have to develop new capacities to adapt themselves to their surroundings. Consequently, in the struggle for existence, only species that adapt successfully to nature survive. This process is known as natural selection.

After more years of observation and experimentation Darwin, in *On the Origin of Species* (1859), postulated an even more dramatic and divisive theory based upon natural selection. In this monograph he stated three principal axioms, each built upon his investigation while serving with the *H. M. S. Beagle*. First, Darwin argued that the world is not static but always evolving. Species change constantly, although usually at an unrecognizable rate. So, for instance, over many centuries sheep have developed from a small, short-haired animal into a much larger creature with a greater amount of wool. Second, this evolutionary process has occurred at a steady rate, never accelerating or slowing. And, lastly, Darwin posited that all mammals have descended from one common ancestor. From the advent of animal life, the principle of natural selection has directed the development of various species, which have arisen from this common ancestor. These species then in turn have evolved into other species: "It's quite conceivable that a naturalist might come to the conclusion that each species had not been independently created but had descended from other species" (*macro*-evolution).

What caused the greatest uproar, however, was Darwin's contention that man too descended from an original ancestor. He stated specifically in the *Descent of Man* (1871):

> The main conclusion here arrived at, and now held by many naturalists who are well competent to form a sound judgement, is that man is descended from some less highly organised form. The grounds upon which this conclusion rests will never be shaken, for the close similarity between man and the lower animals in embryonic development, as well as in innumerable points of structure and constitution,

both of high and of the most trifling importance . . . are facts which cannot be disputed.

According to Darwin, then, all of nature, including man, is in the grip of an evolutionary process and the struggle for survival. In addition, Darwin deduced that "such survival occurred not according to some ordered plan but as the result of chance operating among the countless creatures produced by nature's unlimited tendency towards variation." Although Darwin made a cursory reference to God as the "Creator" at the end of *On the Origin of Species*, it is nevertheless clear that his system contained no room for God. Darwinian thought was "pure" naturalism at its best.

Literary Naturalism

As Darwin's theories shaped the natural sciences, naturalistic philosophy also influenced the literature of the nineteenth century. Emile Zola, one of the earliest literary naturalists, in his essay "The Experimental Novel" described the purpose of the novelist: "A novelist must be only a scientist, and analyst, and anatomist, and his work must have the certainty, the solidity, and the practical application of a work of science." What a radical change this was from the romantic understanding of the intention of literature!

As the naturalist writer saw it, his task was to reveal man and nature for what they are as physical entities. Consequently, the literary naturalist depicted man as merely part of nature, without purpose or meaning, and subject to the forces of nature beyond his control. So, for example, Stephen Crane, in his work, "The Open Boat," portrayed man as being at the mercy of the whims of nature. The story concerns four men who survived the sinking of the steamer Commodore and were attempting to reach land safely in a small boat. Forces beyond their control, however, prevented them from reaching shore, even after they had come close enough to see people on the beach. As one of the sailors exclaimed:

If I am going to be drowned—if I am going to be drowned—
if I am going to be drowned, why, in the name of the seven

mad gods who rule the sea, was I allowed to come thus far and contemplate sand and trees? Was I brought here merely to have my nose dragged away as I was about to nibble the sacred cheese of life?

Clearly in the story, nature decided whether they would make it to shore; nature chose man's destiny, whether he would live or die. There was no supernatural hand to save man from the clutches of terror and death, only man and nature struggling endlessly together.

Naturalistic thought was revealed most forcefully in Crane's poetry. In one brief poem, for example, Crane wrote:

A man said to the universe:
"Sir, I exist!"
"However," replied the universe,
"The fact has not created in me
A sense of obligation."

For Crane, human life is merely a part of the natural scheme of things, subject to natural processes and the impulses of nature. Man is not special. Other authors who may be categorized with Crane and literary naturalism include John Steinbeck, Sinclair Lewis, Frank Norris, and Jack London.

In the field of biblical literature, naturalistic thought had a great impact as well. During the latter part of the eighteenth century and throughout the whole of the nineteenth century, numerous volumes appeared that denied the supernatural and miraculous elements in the Bible. This critical trend originated with the deists of the Renaissance and Enlightenment, who, as we saw earlier, repudiated the notion that the supernatural and the natural have any interrelationship after the initial creation event. The example of Thomas Jefferson, a well-known deist and Founding Father of our country, comes to mind. He penned a gospel of Jesus in which he excised every miracle and supernatural passage from the biblical writings. It was in the Age of Naturalism, however, that criticism of biblical literature hit its peak. Writings of men such as D. F. Strauss (1808–74) and J. E. Renan (1823–92) questioned and, in fact, denied the historical character of the Gospels and the authenticity of any supernatural events described within those writings. This new thrust in biblical studies provided the impetus for the so-called "Quest of the Historical Jesus," in which scholars tried to discover what the man Jesus actually believed and did.[1]

During the Age of Naturalism the traditional understanding of the Old Testament, the mighty acts of God within a historical context, also came under scathing attack. Accordingly, an event such as the Exodus from Egypt, though considered remarkable, was explained from a naturalist perspective. The Israelites were able to cross the Red Sea as described in Exodus 14 because they walked on a sand-bar, which just happened to be in their path. In addition, the plagues that afflicted Egypt (Exodus 7–12) were merely natural phenomena that coincidentally occurred one right after another. In short, many biblical historians of the nineteenth century were greatly influenced by the prevailing naturalistic world view, and they thus attempted to de-supernaturalize biblical literature.

Society

Karl Marx (1818–83) and Friedrich Engels (1820–95), the formulators of the communistic system of society, owed much of their foundational thought to Feuerbach. At the beginning of their work Engels even admitted their dependence upon Feuerbach: "We were all enchanted by him and for a time became Feuerbachians." Many of the naturalistic principles espoused by Feuerbach became essential doctrines of communism: (1) There is no God. According to Marx, there is no reality or truth in man's religious desires. He stated, "Religion is the enemy of all progress," and "man makes religion, religion does not make man." Religion and belief in God are only expressions of an oppressed man who yearns for a better life. (2) Man is part of nature. Marx derived this idea mainly from Darwin and his theories of evolution, which we saw directly stemmed from the philosophy of Feuerbach. (In

---

1. This was the title of Albert Schweitzer's 1906 survey of nineteenth-century biblical studies.

fact, Marx sought to dedicate *Das Kapital* to Darwin, who flatly refused to have his name associated with Marx's work.) Concerning Darwin's influence upon Marx's view of man and history, Marx commented, "The Origin of Species serves me well as a basis in natural science for the struggle in history." (3) Human beings must abolish religion and replace it with a naturalistic, corporeal world view. That is to say, since only the physical universe is real, man's efforts, inquiry, and expression should be focused on the natural order alone.

Although Marx and Engels clearly depended on Feuerbach for their understanding of nature and man, they later departed from his views of society and history. Most importantly, they criticized Feuerbach for not having derived any social consequences from his materialism. Engels wrote of Feuerbach's limited application of his naturalistic philosophy that it "had to be replaced by a science of real people and their historical development." Marx and Engels claimed that their work on communist theory correctly expounded the implications of naturalism for history and society.

As we have repeatedly shown, modern naturalism is a world-and-life view in which all areas of life and culture reflect the basic presuppositions of the philosophy. The naturalistic perspective of Feuerbach—that ultimate reality is impersonal, material, finite, and atheistic—strongly influenced nineteenth-century life. As the presuppositions of modern naturalism took hold of Western culture, they reflected and to a large extent restored the ideas of ancient Greek naturalism. The distinctive contribution of modern naturalism was its scientific explanation of the origin and development of life and its extensive documentation of this evolutionary process.

Conclusion

Beginning with the Renaissance in the fifteenth century and continuing through modern naturalism in the twentieth, there was a gradual yet sustained movement away from theism. In theism God is the sovereign Creator of all things, who supports and maintains the universe. He is the central focus of reality.

Deists began to "squeeze out" God by reducing His role to that of an impersonal watchmaker who no longer acts in and through history or communicates with man. Modern naturalists went one step further by rejecting God altogether. And so the downward trend in theological thought from the outset of the Renaissance through naturalism was clearly a movement from theism to deism to atheism.

As God became less and less important in secular thought, nature (including man) became increasingly prominent. In theism, nature and man were seen as dependent on God for their existence and continued subsistence. With the advent of deistic thought, however, nature was viewed merely as having been set in motion by God and allowed thereafter to run on its own. No longer dependent upon the providential hand of God, nature had become a closed system and the primary focus of concern. With the advent of modern naturalism, nature became the *only* concern, as the physical universe was assumed to be all that there is. Thus, as God became less significant to secular man, nature was promoted to His place.

For Further Reading

Allis, Oswald T. *The Five Books of Moses*. 2nd ed. Phillipsburg, N.J.: Presbyterian and Reformed, 1949.

Collins, James. *God in Modern Philosophy*. Chicago: Henry Regnery, 1959.

Copleston, Frederick C. *A History of Philosphy*, vol. 7, *Modern Philosophy*, Part I, "Fichte to Hegel." Garden City, N.Y.: Doubleday, 1963.

Dillenberger, John, and Claude Welch. *Protestant Christianity*. New York: Charles Scribner's Sons, 1954.

Gay, Peter. *Deism: An Anthology*. Princeton: Van Nostrand, 1968.

———. *The Enlightenment: An Interpretation, The Rise of Modern Paganism*. New York: Alfred A. Knopf, 1967.

Henry, Carl F. H. *God, Revelation and Authority*, vol. 1. Waco, Tex.: Word, 1976.

Herbert of Cherbury. *De Veritate*. Bristol, 1957.

Jones, W. T. *Hobbes to Hume*. New York: Harcourt Brace Jovanovich, 1969.

Mackintosh, Hugh R. *Types of Modern Theology*. New York: Charles Scribner's Sons, 1937.

Niebuhr, Richard. *Schleiermacher on Christ and Religion*. New York: Charles Scribner's Sons, 1964.

Schaeffer, Francis A. *How Should We Then Live?* Old Tappen, N.J.: Fleming H. Revell, 1976.

Sire, James W. *The Universe Next Door*. Downers Grove, Ill.: Inter-Varsity, 1976.

Stone, Edward, ed. *What Was Naturalism?* New York: Appleton-Century-Crofts, 1959.

Tillich, Paul. *Perspectives on 19th and 20th Century Protestant Theology*. Edited by Carl Braaten. New York: Harper and Row, 1967.

Wladyslaw. *Nineteenth Century Philosophy*. Belmont, Calif.: Wadsworth, 1973.

9
Naturalistic Humanism

Gary Scott Smith

Introduction

A major ideological fruit of naturalism is secular humanism. This chapter seeks to clarify the nature, roots, and goals of humanism, to evaluate that philosophy from a Christian perspective, and to assess its impact upon American society.

Because the word *humanism* has many definitions, much confusion surrounds its use today. Individuals as different as Roman Catholic philosopher Jacques Maritain and the militantly atheist foe of Christianity Madalyn Murray O'Hair have claimed to be humanists. Marxist revolutionaries and humanitarians in the mold of Albert Schweitzer insist they represent this philosophy as well. Supporters and critics offer contrasting evaluations of humanism, sometimes because they disagree sharply about what this word means. Any label that can attract groups as divergent in belief as Marxists, existentialists, naturalists, socio-political liberals, and even some Christians must be an ambiguous or multifaceted one. We must, therefore, state the meanings of the term very precisely. In this chapter we are not using the word *humanism* to mean "devotion to human interests," or humanitarianism, or the study of Greek and Latin classics, or the pursuit of the humanities as opposed to the social sciences. These broader definitions allow all the groups mentioned above to consider themselves "humanists." Rather, we discuss humanism as a philosophy or a world view that is concerned with *merely* human interests. This system of thought rejects all belief in the supernatural or metaphysical and exclusively emphasizes the mundane

161

or temporal. And it considers man the "center and sanction"—the only standard for evaluating life. Such humanism differs sharply from the long and rich tradition of Christian humanism. Proclaimed first by such Protestant Reformers as John Calvin and Philip Melancthon, Christian humanism has more recently been advocated by C. S. Lewis and Jacques Maritain. Inspired by their devotion to God, Christian humanists have labored arduously for both humanitarian and educational causes.

Varieties of Humanism

By delineating the various forms of modern nontheistic or naturalistic humanisms and by tracing the historical development of this philosophy, we can better understand its influence in contemporary American life. All varieties of naturalistic humanism repudiate theism and consider man the supreme being in the universe.

One type is Marxist humanism. Proponents of this view consider religion to be an impediment to social progress because it often strengthens the bourgeoisie's control over society. Marxist humanists seek primarily to improve social and economic conditions through restructuring the political order and implementing the techniques and findings of modern science. Other humanists (as well as many Christians) criticize these Marxists for condoning violence, accepting determinism, refusing to allow political democracy, and denying civil liberties to dissenters.

Equally condemnatory of traditional religion is atheistic humanism. This form of naturalistic humanism is chiefly promoted in the United States by the Atheist Association (formerly "The American Association for the Advancement of Atheism") and American Atheist Women under the leadership of Madalyn Murray O'Hair. The Atheist Association exists to educate people about "the falsity and superstition of all religion [and] to enforce complete separation of church and state." Both groups aggressively attack organized religion, especially through the courts.

More important and influential is religious humanism. A diverse group, it includes clergy and laity affiliated with a range of congregations, synagogues, and fellowships such as the humanistic wing of the Unitarian Universalist Association, the Ethical Culture Societies, the Fellowship of Religious Humanists, and the Society for Humanistic Judaism. Through their main voice, *Religious Humanism*, these humanists seek to promote upright conduct and support many aspects of traditional biblical morality. Their goal, however, is to spread a "religious world view . . . within a naturalistic framework."

A final variety of humanism, which has the most adherents and is the most significant form in America, consists of those who explicitly accept and promote secular (sometimes also called variously liberal, scientific, or naturalistic) humanism. Some in this camp simply ignore traditional religions; many of them are agnostics. Outstanding proponents of this view include philosophers John Dewey, Bertrand Russell, Corliss Lamont, and A. J. Ayer; psychologists Erich Fromm, Abraham Maslow, and B. F. Skinner; and scientists Julian Huxley and Francis Crick. Advocates of this position offer an alternative to religious orthodoxies based upon man-centered ideals. This group founded the American Humanist Association in 1941 and has expressed its views principally through two periodicals, *The Humanist* and *Free Inquiry*. Members of the association promote humanism through discussion groups, educational programs, television and radio, books, and humanist "counselors."

Secular humanists and religious humanists joined to publish Humanist Manifesto I in 1933 and Humanist Manifesto II in 1973 to explain their views in a systematic creed. These creedal statements succinctly express major humanist convictions about ultimate reality, humanity, knowledge, society, and ethics. In 1982, conferees of seven different groups largely representing these two varieties of humanism created the North American Committee for Humanism. Support for key humanistic ideas in America, however, is much greater than the membership of these organizations. For numerous reasons, many Americans, wittingly and unwittingly, accept humanist conceptions of man, morality, and social relations.

While these four types of humanism—Marxist, atheistic, religious, and secular—have different emphases and approaches, they do share certain common traits.[1]

The diverse forms of naturalistic humanism have always been based on respect for individual dignity, on confidence in human reason, and on belief in man's possibilities for improvement. Humanists affirm the supreme value and self-perfectibility of human personality. They regard the scientific method as the primary means of discovering truth and claim to support free, independent critical thought. According to Paul Kurtz, former editor of *The Humanist*, "The only authority is the authority of intelligence, the only master is reason."

Historical Development of Humanism

These four varieties of modern naturalistic humanism[2] share the same complex roots. The earliest ones stretch back to classical Greece, especially to the philosophy of the Sophists, who lived during the fifth and fourth centuries B.C. Sophists insisted that anything beyond the temporal realm and humans' common understanding is a matter of indifference and agnosticism. Their leading philosopher, Protagoras, repeatedly appears in humanist literature as a type of patron saint. He is best known for penning the central doctrine of humanism, "Man is the measure of all things." By this he meant that man, individually and collectively, is the sole criterion for verifying knowledge.

Other Greek philosophers also contributed to the development of humanism. Socrates helped to introduce the critical method of thinking upon which humanism rests. Naturalists Democritus and Aristotle laid the earliest foundations of the scientific tradition, which in the nineteenth century provided a mechanistic explanation for human origins. And like the ancient Greeks,

---

1. Humanist Manifesto II declares that "the varieties and emphases of naturalistic humanism include 'scientific,' 'ethical,' 'democratic,' 'religious,' and 'Marxist' humanism. Free thought, atheism, agnosticism, skepticism, deism, rationalism, ethical culture and liberal religion all claim to be heirs to the humanist tradition."

2. In the remainder of this chapter the single word *humanism* is used to denote secular or naturalistic humanism.

humanists often emphasize that they impose no theological creeds, revere no authoritative Holy Book, and accept no dogmas, rituals, sacraments, and clergy.

Humanists disagree about whether Judeo-Christian tradition is a major source of their philosophy. Some humanists see the teachings of Old Testament prophets and especially of Jesus as instrumental in, or at least supportive of, their views of human dignity, solidarity, equality, and social justice. Generally, humanists argue, however, that their philosophy is little expressed in the biblical record, which makes humans "infinitely inferior to deity" and teaches people to expect God to rescue them from their plight.

The modern humanist world view has clear antecedents in the European Renaissance, which began in the fourteenth century. In their efforts to revive learning, Renaissance leaders revolted against the otherworldliness of medieval Christianity. They turned from preoccupation with personal immortality to trying to achieve the best life possible in this world. As they did, they relied increasingly on reason and less and less on the authority of the Roman Catholic Church and the Bible. Leading Renaissance artists, philosophers, and authors insisted that people could attain the good life through their own efforts.

An even more important source of modern humanism is the Enlightenment of the seventeenth and eighteenth centuries, whose philosophers and poets sang praises to man's natural goodness. Their faith in the perfectibility of man and human society was based on three doctrines: the effectiveness of human reason, natural rights, and a universal law of progress. Enlightenment thinkers asserted that human reason enables people to understand the world and to live successfully in it. Such philosophers were confident not only in human reason but also that the universe itself is ruled by reason. English scientist Sir Isaac Newton confirmed this idea in the seventeenth century when he demonstrated that the laws of nature are the laws of a rational universe.

During the Enlightenment the belief developed that the laws of nature, which guide man's physical behavior, imply natural rights and duties that should guide moral conduct of individuals and institutions. Most Enlightenment thinkers retained Thomas Aquinas's doctrine that natural law is part of God's eternal law. Eventually, however, in the writings of British political scientist Thomas Hobbes and French social philosopher Jean Jacques Rousseau, natural rights became totally independent of God. They were seen as inalienable, as rooted in the natural order of things, requiring no higher justification.

Meanwhile, British scientist Francis Bacon, French philosopher Rene Descartes, and the French Encyclopedists developed a doctrine of human progress. Based upon their belief in the goodness and grandeur of man and their confidence in the scientific method, these writers explained that human history is moving irreversibly upward from primitive beginnings to an age of enlightened reason. Such ideas were also expounded in deism, the predominant religious expression of the Enlightenment, and later by German philosopher Immanuel Kant, by Auguste Comte (the founder of positivism), and by Karl Marx.

In the nineteenth century Darwin's extensive documentation of evolutionary change in nature seemed to offer powerful confirmation of this belief in human progress. Darwin taught that every species tended to "progress toward perfection" as the result of natural selection. Progress seemed to be the order of nature. English social scientist Herbert Spencer applied the concept of development to society. Like mankind, human societies followed a law of evolution from simple to complex, through a process of successive differentiations. At the same time, Darwin's explanation of the survival of the fittest as the mechanism of evolution provided a scientific rationale for naturalism (and therefore for humanism), which previously had been lacking. Darwin's discoveries offered an alternative to the Judeo-Christian explanation of origins that seemed plausible to many educated people. Interpretations of the world and life taught by many in both the physical and the social sciences made humanistic principles even more attractive to increasing numbers of Americans in the twentieth century.

Modern humanism, itself, then, has emerged through a long

historical process of evolution. Philosophers and scientists in ancient Greece, the Renaissance, the Enlightenment, and the nineteenth century all contributed to its development. Central to the humanist tradition is a belief in man's innate goodness, rationality, and self-perfectibility, and in the empirical method as the principal means of obtaining truth. Prior to the late nineteenth century, belief in humanism was limited to an influential educated elite. During the past one hundred years more and more people from all walks of life have accepted humanist interpretations of the cosmos and life.

God: A Human Projection

Having examined the historical development of humanism, we turn now to an analysis of contemporary humanist convictions about ultimate reality and humanity.

Humanists are skeptical about the supernatural. They do not believe, as one of them quipped, "that poltergeists, vampires, or little green men with pointy heads exist independently of the *National Enquirer*." More substantively they repudiate belief in "a perfect, omnipotent and benevolent creator who performs miracles, responds to prayers and proclaims a fundamental set of eternal moral principles." The preface to Humanist Manifesto II declares, "Humanists still believe that . . . faith in the prayer-hearing God, assumed to love and care for persons, to hear and understand their prayers, and to be able to do something about them, is an unproved and outmoded faith." For humanists there is nothing beyond the natural realm. As Humanist Manifesto I states, the universe is "self-existing and not created." Because the metaphysical dimension cannot be measured or tested by empirical methods, humanists contend, it cannot be known and belief in it must be rejected. Humanist Manifesto II states, "We find insufficient evidence for belief in the existence of a supernatural; it is either meaningless or irrelevant to the question of the survival and fulfillment of the human race."

Humanists use anthropology, sociology, and psychology to explain the origins of beliefs in God and religion. People devised religions to account for their experiences of sacredness and transcendence and to provide hope in immortality. "Man created the gods," insisted the leading British humanist Julian Huxley, "to protect himself from loneliness, uncertainty, and fear." The need for religion, Sigmund Freud declared, arose from the "child's feeling of helplessness and the longing it evokes for a father."

Humanists contend that religion developed because some things seem beyond human control. People created religions in an attempt to put themselves in proper relationship with powers that seem unpredictable and mysterious. Religion grows out of men's feelings of impotence and dependence and their need for consolation and assurance about this life and the next. Through worship, prayers, and sacrifices people believe they can win favors from these unknown powers.

To humanists, then, "man has created God in his own image, rather than the reverse," as British playwright George Bernard Shaw once remarked. According to Ludwig Feuerbach, a German philosopher who strongly influenced Karl Marx, men projected their own noblest traits onto the universe and called this ideal image "God." Freud theorized that man's belief in a primordial myth about killing his father led him to regard "Providence" as a greatly exalted Father, softened by human prayers and placated by signs of man's remorse. For Marx, man's invention of God had even less laudable motives. Marx argued that the bourgeoisie used the God-concept to keep workers subjugated. Capitalists warned laborers that a flaming hell awaited the disobedient, but that eternal rewards in heaven would be given to those who were morally upright, obeyed civil laws on earth, and respected authority. Such promises, Marx maintained, scared workers into submission and diverted their attention from changing the oppressive conditions under which they lived in this world. Thus God is a tool of oppression, and religion is "the opiate of the people," a tranquilizer that dulls their sensitivity to the exploitation and pain they experience.

Since God does not exist, humanists continue, Jesus Christ obviously was not God. Jesus was at best an outstanding moral teacher and at worst a Jew who accepted the world view of His day. Corliss Lamont describes Him as "one of the supremest personalities of all history and a radiant martyr for the cause of humanity, a great good man instead of God." More skeptical humanists such as Paul Kurtz, editor of *Free Inquiry*, state that Jesus was not even a great moral teacher. Only an unbalanced person would make some of Jesus' claims for deity and threaten hell for unbelievers.

Over and over again, humanists proclaim that religion is declining and will eventually die. "The god-hypothesis, invented by man to provide an explanation of the meaning of existence," one of them wrote, "has served its purpose and is destined to disappear." Christianity cannot survive because its world view seems implausible to modern man. The growth of scientific knowledge has undercut the traditional Christian outlook and rendered it unbelievable.

While desiring to preserve the best ethical teaching in religious traditions, many humanists applaud the decline of these "obstacles to human progress." They insist that Christianity in particular has been thoroughly tried and found wanting. "When you survey the bloody story of Christendom, the cruelty of the churches and their obstruction of truth," wrote British positivist A. J. Ayer, "you are inclined to . . . regard the acceptance of Christianity by Constantine as a disaster." "Religions, even the highest of them," declared Aldous Huxley, author of *Brave New World,* "consist at most times and in most places of one part spirituality to nine of superstition, magic, priestcraft and bad science."

Man the Measure

Believing that God does not exist or at least has no relevance for human life because He cannot be known, humanists assert that man is the supreme being in the universe. "As non-theists," declares Humanist Manifesto II, "we begin with humans not God, nature not deity." "We are ourselves the ultimate and irrefutable arbiters of value," British philosopher Bertrand Russell argued. "It is for us to determine the good life, not for Nature—not even for Nature personified as God." Humanists maintain that if God did exist, human beings would be "underlings" to a

supernatural dictator. Humanists repudiate the Christian contention that human dignity rests upon their creation in the image
and likeness of God and their relationship with Him. They reason
instead that the idea of God's existence necessarily impairs rather
than improves man's responsibility and worth. If God is omnipotent, argues Paul Kurtz, then we are "helpless creatures." If
humans are dependent upon God for their existence and suste-
nance, then the relationship between Creator and created "is
analogous to that of master to slave." Put simply, if God exists,
humans cannot be autonomous, and so humanists reject belief in
God. They aver that human beings are their own authority, not
subject to any superior powers or higher forces, whether God,
fate, economic conditions, or historical necessity.

Thus humanists agree with naturalists that we are not created
in the image of an all-powerful God. Rather, humanity is an
integral part of nature and cannot be differentiated sharply from
the natural order within which it evolved. But humanists disagree
with naturalists' contention that people are insignificant because
they are part and parcel of nature. For humanists, as for the
ancient Greeks and seventeenth-century rationalists, man has
value because he is the pinnacle of the evolutionary process, a
fact most evidenced by his rational abilities. "What distinguishes
man from animals," writes one humanist, "is that he evolved by
a mechanism that belongs to him alone, and which he alone can
modify and improve."

For humanists we are neither sick, nor sinful (as Christians
contend), nor alienated (as Marx maintained), nor inauthentic
(as existentialists hold). Humanists agree with Pelagius that we
are fundamentally good as we are. Individuals do not need to
become their true selves by obeying a divine will, by conforming
to a cosmic design, by participating in the historical process, or
by assuming their autonomy in the continuous exercise of choice.
Man is his own rule and his own end. He is free to create the
kind of world he wants, governed only by his own desires. Since
there is no God, people must rely upon themselves to improve
their lives and the world.

Humanist Manifesto II expresses the humanist conviction that "no deity will save us; we must save ourselves." By this is meant generally that people must strive to achieve their own highest potential, or "self-actualization," and labor to build a world order where barriers to individual growth are removed and peace and liberty prevail. According to Humanist Manifesto I, "Humanism considers the complete realization of human personality to be the end of man's life." Traditional religions often inhibit humans from realizing their full potentialities by encouraging "dependence rather than independence, obedience rather than affirmation, fear rather than courage." Those who obtain self-actualization or "fullness of being" experience excitement, joy, community, love, creative fulfillment, and freedom and live courageously and rationally.

Repudiating all belief in heaven and personal immortality, humanists optimistically believe that we are capable of creating the best possible life here on this earth. Christianity's preoccupation with life after death, they declare, has prevented people from enjoying this life and from working fully to improve conditions here and now. "Promises of immortal salvation or fear of eternal damnation," declare the signers of Humanist Manifesto II, "are both illusory and harmful. They distract humans from present concerns, from self-actualization, and from rectifying social injustices." To achieve the good life mankind must employ the scientific method systematically. "Science has emancipated man from the bondage of dogmatic religious mythology," one humanist insists, "and it has provided him with the instruments for remaking and reordering his life, improving and enhancing it immeasurably." Some humanists, such as B. F. Skinner, even believe that people can use scientific methods to create a utopia, a perfect world, a Walden II.

Humanists also place considerable faith in evolution. Only those who "uncompromisingly" accept the full meaning of evolution have a perspective that enables them to "face up to the world as it actually is, assess man's place in it, gauge the possibilities of the future and plan realistically for their species." While stressing that evolution is a mechanism or a process devoid of purpose and intelligence, humanists sometimes ascribe an almost transcendent or rational quality to it. Repeatedly, humanists declare their confidence in the evolutionary process to be great "because of its degree of coherence, predictability and creativity." Evolution in the humanist tradition assumes the character of a universal principle capable of explaining the development not simply of life but of everything in the universe. Christian apologist C. S. Lewis calls evolutionism "the Great Myth" of the nineteenth and twentieth centuries. No longer a hypothesis, it has attained dogmatic status as "the formula [to explain] *all* existence."

In summary, humanists believe that although traditional religion has successfully promoted many sound moral principles, its many detriments outweigh this one good point. Generally speaking, traditional religion has neglected reason, fostered dogmatism and intolerance, persecuted dissenters, and played on people's superstitious fears. Belief in supernatural beings capable of affecting human destiny leads men and women to waste time and energy in petitionary prayer and all kinds of propitiatory practices. Hope in personal immortality encourages people to concentrate on attaining salvation in another world and thus to depreciate and even denigrate life in this world. This belief in divine redemption leads individuals to ignore their own self-actualization. Finally, Christianity, in particular, has often allied itself with the status quo and vested interests, opposed beneficial social changes, and resisted efforts to promote social justice.

A Christian Critique of Humanism

Does humanism offer a more plausible and attractive world view than traditional Christianity? Is its perspective on life and reality more consistent with our world and our experience? If secular humanism were widely accepted, would people enjoy a better life on earth? Students will not be surprised to read that we are convinced the answer to these questions is no. Naturalistic humanism suffers from several major weaknesses.

First and most important, this philosophy ignores an immense amount of evidence for the existence of God. Many humanists declare belief in God's existence to be implausible and incredible, but they cannot possibly examine and refute all evidence for

God's existence to prove their contention. Although physicists cannot see an electron, they know it exists because of its effects. Likewise, people cannot see God, but they do observe His activities in the world. Ignoring considerable evidence of intelligent design, humanists assume the world is the outcome of chance combinations of atoms. Their theory of the origins of the natural world rests upon random, fortuitous events that are highly improbable. Is it plausible that a cold and indifferent process could produce a being like man? Humanists also neglect the observable and permanent changes produced in the attitudes and lifestyles of millions of individuals who attribute those changes to their relationships with God. Moreover, they reject substantial scientific, historical, linguistic, and archaeological evidence for the accuracy and reliability of the biblical record and the physical, bodily resurrection of Christ.

Humanists also fail to appreciate the many contributions of the Judeo-Christian tradition. Rather than impeding human advance, Christians and Jews have consistently supported the freedom, dignity, and individuality of persons, as well as democracy, social justice, and modern education. They have brought medicine, literacy, and material improvements to the ends of the earth and have taught people to value human life and to love others.

Moreover, the humanist view of man is defective. Humanism offers no power to curb human selfishness. The materialism, hedonism, and brutality of the twentieth century testify that people are self-centered and primarily seek their own pleasure and their own good. Humanism is powerless to purge individuals of their greed, covetousness, and self-aggrandizement, evident in constant pursuit of fame and fortune. Humanism provides no compelling reason to follow ideals that might be socially disapproved or that do not bring personal earthly gain. Rarely can this philosophy inspire people to act sacrificially. As Robert L. Johnson writes, "If man is only a part of nature and nature is neutral or indifferent to the human venture, why should man have any special concern or compassion toward fellow human beings?" For that matter, why is man significant? If human beings are simply a product of nature and have no distinct qualities or characteristics that can transcend or survive all other things of nature, then what gives them their worth? If there is no purpose in human history or in the cosmos, if as Bertrand Russell says, "the world is simply there and is inexplicable," then why should we not simply throw up our hands in despair, crying with the atheistic existentialist, "life is absurd"? How can we strive to obtain truth, create beauty and achieve goodness, writes one philosopher, "if we are convinced that we are unimportant accidents in a universe which is indifferent, if not hostile" to such ideals?

At its very core, humanism is inconsistent with man's nature and the cosmic order. Deep within us lies a belief that our lives are meaningful and worthwhile, that our quest for values is significant. We experience an urge to pursue noble things. Such inward convictions indicate that both history and humanity do have a purpose. Does humanism offer "hope to those who are bereaved, strength to the weak, forgiveness to the sinful, rest to those who are weary and heavy laden?" asked Sir Arthur Balfour. "If not," he concluded, "then whatever be its merits, it is no rival to Christianity."

Worse still, humanism logically leads to moral relativism. Since there is no God, there are no absolute values. Because no overruling moral purpose exists, humans must create their own moral and value structures. Thus every human code necessarily is arbitrary and relative—no universal principles exist by which to judge these codes. As exiled Soviet dissident Alexander Solzhenitsyn argues, only belief in a Supreme Being guarantees human freedom and moral responsibility, and erosion of religious faith, therefore, spells the end of moral decency.

In actuality what is good and beautiful and true in the humanist ethical code originated in an earlier religious context. Whether humanists admit it or not, declares Jacques Maritain, "Western humanism has religious and transcendent sources without which it is incomprehensible to itself." Arthur Dakin adds, "The quest for a good life in a good world—nine-tenths of humanism—" is not the "peculiar property of that movement, but is a quest as old and as varied as the race." Humanism's distinctive feature—

its "new naturalism"—is an "impoverishment rather than an enrichment of life."

The Impact of Secular Humanism in America

Having described the varieties, sources, principles, and weaknesses of humanism, we turn now to assess the influence of this philosophy. How great an impact has humanism made on American society? How widely accepted are its distinctive principles? To what extent has this ideology shaped our public and private life? To answer these questions we must first distinguish between humanism and secularization. Humanism, as we have seen, is a philosophy. Secularization, by contrast, is a process "whereby religious thinking, practices and institutions lose social significance." In other words, as secularization occurs, economic, political, and social life are divorced from religious considerations, and religion is relegated to the sphere of private concern.

In America, secularizing forces and hedonistic lifestyles have combined to weaken the influence of religion in public life during the twentieth century, as is evidenced in challenges to religious orthodoxy, traditional sexual morality, and civil and parental authority. The various groups considered above, which forthrightly promote humanism, have done little, however, to accomplish this. They repudiate hedonism and strongly support many basic moral values. True, they do denounce historic Judeo-Christian theology and insist that public life should rest upon a neutral (by which they mean secular) rather than a religious foundation. But even in promoting these views they are limited by their small numbers. All the groups of humanists mentioned above have a combined membership of less than 40,000. Few Americans fully and enthusiastically agree with the Humanist Manifestos. After all, every Gallup poll since the 1940s has revealed that 97 percent of Americans say they believe in God (although "God" is not usually defined in these polls). In addition, over 60 percent of Americans belong to Christian or Jewish congregations, and 45 percent of Americans attend services during a typical weekend.

The secularization of our society is vast. This secularization, however, has resulted primarily from complex, interrelated forces that have encouraged people who hold traditional religious values in their private lives to see public life as beyond God's jurisdiction. Secularization has made deep inroads into American society because of what sociologists call "privatization." By the Civil War secularization had advanced significantly in this country because many Americans did not take their religion seriously, others used their faith to justify what actually were "worldly" values, and the impact of religion had been substantially reduced in the federal government. Beginning in the late nineteenth century, however, more and more devoutly committed Christians and Jews began to confine their religious beliefs to the private dimensions of life— church, home, and leisure—and to ignore the relationship between religious teachings and social, political, economic, and educational practices. While continuing strongly to support the institutional church and to cultivate personal piety, many of these believers came to agree with secularists and nominal adherents of Christianity and Judaism that public life should be neutral or outside the concern of religion. Even though most Americans do not subscribe totally to the humanist credo, many do believe that human beings are innately good and inherently rational and that they can create a better world largely through their own efforts.

Public secularism is evident today in the marketplace, government, schools, the arts, and the media. The biblical conception of marriage as a divinely ordained, permanent institution is increasingly repudiated. Belief that business enterprises should strive to glorify God by serving human needs is not widely held. Neither are the beliefs that political policies and practices should promote righteousness and justice, and that human laws should be based upon God-given moral principles. And many Americans do not consider it necessary for schools to teach children to love and obey God or for the news media to report on God's activity in the world. By law, religion is largely excluded from public elementary and secondary schools, and many colleges founded by Christians are today predominantly secular.

In assessing the impact of humanism upon American society

we must avoid two errors. We should not assign to a small band of zealous secular humanists undue responsibility for the widespread secularization of American society. That would obscure the more subtle, pervasive, and significant social, economic, and ideological forces that promote this trend. At the same time, we must not caricature humanists as bent on the destruction of society and morality. If we do, we will misrepresent their ethical and social convictions and fail to appreciate their commonalities with Christians.

Because Christians and humanists share some common concerns and values, they can work together on many good causes. Both groups affirm the supreme worth of human personality; they support equality of opportunity and individual freedom; they promote human and social welfare; they believe that moral and social improvement is possible. Both Christians and humanists emphasize that humans are ethical beings who should love their neighbors, respect property, tell the truth, and promote peace and justice.

While humanists and Christians base their ethical and sociopolitical views upon different presuppositions, they do support many of the same policies and programs and therefore can work as allies on some issues in a common attempt to build a better tomorrow. As Saint Augustine wrote in his classic work, *The City of God:*

> So long, then, as the heavenly City is wayfaring on earth, she invites citizens of all nations and all tongues, and unites them into a single pilgrim band. She takes no issue with that diversity of customs, laws and traditions whereby human peace is sought and maintained. Instead of nullifying or tearing down, she preserves and appropriates whatever in the diversity of divers race is aimed at one and the same objective of human peace, provided only that they do not stand in the way of the faith and worship of the one supreme and true God. Thus, the heavenly City, so long as it is wayfaring on earth, not only makes use of earthly peace but fosters and actively pursues along with other human beings a common

platform in regard to all that concerns our purely human life and does not interfere with faith and worship.

Humanists agree with so many biblical values because of common grace. Since the fall, God has used His common grace to restrain sin and to promote civilization. In God's providence many unbelievers realize the benefits of following His laws even though they do not acknowledge Him as the lawgiver.

Christians and humanists share one final thing: they both hold religious world views. Although some humanists vehemently argue that their philosophy is not a religion, strong parallels exist between humanism and other religions.[3] For a small group of devout followers, humanism functions as a religion. These adherents eat, sleep, play, and work according to its central doctrines. Like other religions, humanism offers a comprehensive system of beliefs about God, humanity, knowledge, cosmology, society, and ethics. Its advocates insist that there is no metaphysical reality, that man is innately good, and that human reason—employing the scientific method—can solve the many problems people face. Moreover, humanist organizations have developed programs similar to those of organized religions such as weekly fellowship meetings. The American Humanist Association sponsors a group of "counselors" who conduct weddings and funerals and advise people with problems.

Some humanists do admit that their philosophy functions as a religion. If we consider religion, one of them writes, as that "aspect of life which centers around self-chosen ideas to which a person is committed and by which he is influenced," then humanists are indeed very religious. Humanist Manifesto I is religious in tone and rhetoric. It states, for example, that "in the place of the old attitudes involved in worship and prayer the humanist finds his religious emotions expressed in a heightened sense of personal life." Humanists must labor to build one new religious system, Julian Huxley declared, to "replace the multiplicity of conflicting and incompatible religious systems that are now competing for the spirit of man." Such humanists recognize, as do many Chris-

3. See our discussion that all life is religion, in the epilogue.

tians, that humans are fundamentally religious creatures. They will always revere, worship, and serve some person, principle, or program. As Aristotle argued, everyone lives by a philosophy whether he is aware of it or not. Given the "religious nature" of humanism, is it fair to teach this world view or perspective in public schools, which are supposedly "neutral" regarding religious teachings?

Summary

The rise of scientific naturalism during the second half of the nineteenth century provided an alternative to the Christian explanation of the beginning of the cosmos. This development enabled humanist principles to gain much wider acceptance. While only some intellectual elites espoused these views before Darwin's discoveries, in the twentieth century many common people endorsed them as well. Humanists repudiate the Judeo-Christian view that God is Creator and sustainer of the universe, the ultimate basis of reality, and the absolute standard for evaluating both individual and corporate life. They also reject the Judeo-Christian belief that human beings are created in the image and likeness of God and that their worth and meaning derive from their relationship with Him. As a result of common grace, however, humanists do accept some of the moral principles and social values taught by Christianity, although they do not recognize the divine foundation upon which they rest.

Humanism should not be equated with secularization. Humanism is a philosophy of life, a religious world view that espouses many convictions contrary to biblical faith. Secularization is a process. Several different modern philosophies, including humanism, have prompted it. So have hedonism, apathy, and the belief that religious convictions should be confined to private life because the public order should somehow be "neutral" in regard to religion. Christians should oppose any aspects of the humanist world view that are antithetical to the gospel. And we should resist the process of secularization because it diminishes commitment to biblical beliefs and values in both individual and corporate life. In order to accomplish these tasks we must encourage individuals to apply scriptural teachings to all dimensions of their lives, and we must work to base social institutions and practices upon biblical principles.

For Further Reading

Critical Evaluations of Humanism

Braunthal, Alfred. *Salvation and the Perfect Society: The Eternal Quest.* Amherst Mass.: University of Massachusetts Press, 1979.

Dakin, Arthur. *Man the Measure: An Essay on Humanism as Religion.* Princeton, N.J.: Princeton University Press, 1939.

Ehrenfeld, David. *The Arrogance of Humanism.* New York: Oxford University Press, 1978.

Geisler, Norman. *Is Man the Measure?: An Evaluation of Contemporary Humanism.* Grand Rapids: Baker, 1983.

Gordon, Ernest. *Me, Myself and Who. Humanism: Society's False Premise.* Plainfield, N.J.: Logos International, 1980.

Hitchcock, James. *What Is Secular Humanism?* Ann Arbor, Mich.: Servant, 1982.

Johnson, Robert L. *Humanism and Beyond.* Philadelphia: United Church of Christ Press, 1973.

Maritain, Jacques. *Integral Humanism.* New York: Charles Scribner's Sons, 1968.

Packer, J. I., and Thomas Howard. *Christianity: The True Humanism.* Waco, Tex.: Word, 1985.

Smith, Gary Scott. *The Seeds of Secularization: Calvinism, Culture and Pluralism in America, 1870–1915.* Grand Rapids: Eerdmans, 1985.

Webber, Robert. *Secular Humanism: Threat and Challenge.* Grand Rapids: Zondervan, 1982.

Works Supporting Humanism

Ayer, A. J., ed. *The Humanist Outlook.* London: Pemberton, 1968.

Huxley, Julian, ed. *The Humanist Frame.* London: Allen and Unwin, 1961.

Kurtz, Paul, ed. *The Humanist Alternative: Some Definitions of Humanism.* Buffalo: Prometheus Books, 1974.

Lamont, Corliss. *The Philosophy of Humanism.* New York: Philosophical Library, 1957.

Various issues of *Free Inquiry* and *The Humanist*

PART TWO:
EPISTEMOLOGY

Introduction

W. Andrew Hoffecker

Epistemology is the study of knowledge—its nature and scope, the means of attaining and verifying it, and its underlying presuppositions. The idea of scrutinizing our own thought processes is no less intimidating than our previous challenge of examining the theological and anthropological elements in our world views. Nevertheless, we all use various methods of knowing throughout each day, and it is important that we become aware of just how and why we can know something to be true.

Just as important is our becoming aware of why others believe what they do. In the following chapters we shall examine the views of knowledge that underlie the positions surveyed in part one of this book. Having already considered views of God and man should make our study of the epistemologies connected to those views that much easier. Thus our investigation of world views from the Hebrews and the Greeks to twentieth-century humanists has laid a foundation for our present study.

We have already seen that aspects of a world view are always interrelated. A person's view of God affects and reflects his or her belief about human nature and its capacity to understand reality. Similarly, one's beliefs about human goodness and autonomy imply one's views of God and of human ability to know and function in the world. Regardless of whether we begin with theology, anthropology, or epistemology, we find that our ideas evidence a strong correlation. While interdependence of ideas is not the sole criterion for judging the truth or adequacy of a world view, rarely, if ever, do philosophers intentionally try *not* to be consistent in their thinking.[1]

The chapters that follow, therefore, roughly coincide with ones in our first unit. Their correlation is more than chronological; the basic ideas of the corresponding chapters are compatible. Consequently, we frequently encourage readers to note the relationships between the two parts.

For purposes of simplicity and length we have united the biblical material into a single chapter (10). Clearly differences exist between the Old Testament emphasis on the law and prophets and the New Testament stress on Jesus Christ as the unique incarnation of God. Both testaments, however, distinguish between God's general revelation, available to all people, and His special revelation, which was given in unique historical events. If God is sovereign over all matters, then His revelation is the basic source of knowledge. God's majestic rule is not limited to His power manifested in creation, or His providential control of history, or His redeeming activity in the Exodus or at the cross. The Bible presents God as the author and source of truth. Without God, the very notion of knowledge would not exist, for knowledge as a sum of ideas and individual acts of knowing depends on God as the revealer of truth. The biblical writers are as theocentric in their epistemology as they are in their theological and anthropological views.

Accordingly, we find in the Bible an anthropological perspective consistent with this view. Human beings are as dependent on God for knowing as they are for redemption or for life itself. The biblical world view emphasizes not only the limitations of human knowledge due to its finiteness but the damaging effect of sin, which blinds us to the theocentric implications of what we know. God's grace and our repentance are as necessary to a full understanding of reality as they are to our very salvation.

Chapter 11 examines the Greek alternative to the biblical view.

---

1. Possible exceptions to this generalization are variations of skepticism, nihilism, and existentialism. Adherents of these philosophies frequently reject not only the idea that reality is meaningful but also the argument that consistency is desirable.

Though Plato and Aristotle agreed on human autonomy in knowing, consistent with their respective world views they strongly disagreed over how that autonomy is expressed. Their debate over whether reason or sense experience is the basis for knowledge drew battle lines between rationalism and empiricism that have existed in various forms for centuries. Plato, in favoring reason, rejected sense experience as a source of knowledge. According to his theory, individuals start from ignorance and become progressively enlightened only as they leave sense experience behind and study what lies beyond the senses: first mathematics, and eventually perception of the unchanging, absolute, and eternal forms. Plato's epistemology conforms with his high estimation of man's immortal soul and his depreciation of everything physical. Aristotle rejected Plato's concept of an "ideal world" and argued that reality could be known not through reflection but through systematic sensory observation of the physical world.

Chapter 12 explains medieval and Reformational theories of knowledge. The differences between Augustine's emphasis on biblical themes and Aquinas's synthetic, Scholastic orientation are evident in their respective mottos. In affirming "I believe in order that I might understand," Augustine made faith in God the foundation for knowledge of everything else. In contrast, Aquinas adopted an Aristotelian approach exemplified by his motto, "I understand in order that I might believe." By using rational arguments in an attempt to prove God's existence, he made reason the preamble to faith. As we saw in the first unit, Luther and Calvin rejected any synthetic borrowing from the Greeks and joined Augustine in affirming God's revelation in the Bible, rather than reason or the senses, as the starting point in knowing. The practical implications of the synthetic and Reformational epistemologies are that Thomas limited revelation and faith to theology alone while the Reformers argued that faith commitments underlie all fields of knowledge. Thus, Luther and Calvin declared that all of life is religious, not simply our private and public worship of God.

Chapters 13 and 14 correspond to chapters 8 and 9 in part one. In our treatment of rationalism and empiricism we show how the debate that began with Plato and Aristotle extends to the modern era. Continental rationalists and British empiricists continued the Enlightenment thinkers' adamant rejection of old authorities and the modern preoccupation with epistemological issues. Only when we appreciate how complete they considered their break from the past to be can we understand the intensity of efforts by modern philosophers to put all of human knowledge back together on a totally new foundation.

We treat Immanuel Kant (chap. 14) as one of the great watershed thinkers of Western history. In retrospect, widespread acceptance of his "Copernican Revolution" in epistemology effectively eliminated any possibility, at least from a human point of view, that modern thinkers would again embrace the Christian world view. Kant's two critiques of reason pushed the supernatural to the periphery of speculation and established human autonomy at the center of modern thought. Science and religion have not been the same since.

Our concluding chapter examines twentieth-century expressions of human autonomy: positivism, pragmatism, and existentialism. Among proponents of these philosophies, only a few existentialists seriously consider theological questions. Contemporary epistemologies, therefore, reflect different nuances of secular humanism. Some humanists base their hope for human knowledge on scientific and technological advance (derived from positivism's emphasis on empirical verification). Others believe that human choice will enhance human knowledge, (rooted in existentialism's contention that meaning and purpose are not intrinsic to life but can only be affirmed by human choice). Still others argue that knowledge is dependent upon successful implementation of human ideas, (based upon pragmatism's claim that truth or falsity is exclusively a matter of the usefulness of an idea).

Our survey of epistemology reveals a clear and consistent correlation with our study of Western theological and anthropological perspectives. Large numbers of people in Western culture have apparently rejected distinctively biblical ideas, as affirmation of human autonomy has replaced God's supremacy as the basis for knowledge. Contemporary Christians, therefore, face several challenges. We need to deepen our understanding of Christianity's unique claims by studying the Bible and books that defend its infallible authority. We need also to examine the implications of contemporary secularism so that we can counteract humanistic claims for autonomy. Finally, we need to live by our convictions and work to implement Christian ideas in our everyday lives.

I.
BIBLICAL AND CLASSICAL
EPISTEMOLOGIES

10
Biblical Epistemology: Revelation

W. Andrew Hoffecker and G. K. Beale

Introduction

The biblical view of knowledge is both at odds with and the solution to the more widely accepted humanistic view expressed throughout Western history. By revealing Himself God clears our vision, heals the damage done by sin to His image within, and makes us capable of true knowledge and wisdom. The apostle Paul emphasized God's sovereign revelation in II Corinthians 10: 4–6, when he called upon Christians to "cast down vain imaginations and every kind of knowledge that exalts itself against the knowledge of God," and to bring thoughts into "captivity to Christ." By this striking phrase, Paul challenged Christians to think differently from non-Christians, using a theistic view of reality taught by the Bible.

The Importance of Presuppositions

Most important to any system of knowledge is its starting point. By definition, presuppositions are ideas that a person "*pre*-supposes" in all his or her thinking. They not only provide a point of departure for thought, but also determine the method by which knowledge is attained and the goal toward which knowledge is directed. All views of reality, therefore, begin with certain ideas or truth-claims that exercise an enormous, though often unrecognized, influence over what and how we know. Since they are the starting point of knowledge, presuppositions are simultaneously part of what we know and yet not susceptible to proof. They are like the axioms in mathematics, which cannot be proved but are indispensable for the rest of geometry. The idea that parallel lines in the same plane never meet, for example, is an axiom of Euclidean geometry that cannot be proved empirically. We cannot extend a plane far enough to ascertain by means of our senses whether or not parallel lines ever meet. Even though the axiom is unproved and unprovable, it serves as an essential first principle; no problems can be solved in Euclidean geometry without it.

What axioms are to the study of geometry, presuppositions are to all other areas of knowledge. They are the foundations upon which the rest of knowledge stands. For example, we have seen that secularists assume the universe is a closed finite system that operates on the basis of pure chance. Secularists interpret everything they experience in the world in light of that basic idea. Even though some may claim that evidence for their naturalistic view is conclusive and incontrovertible, they cannot prove it. Rather, they assume that this idea is correct, and they use it as a fundamental premise to interpret every event and to attribute meaning and purpose (or lack thereof) to all aspects of reality.

Christians begin with a totally different starting point: the transcendent and personal God of the Bible. Following Scripture, they assume that God exists and reveals Himself. They regard this assumption as not requiring proof because God's existence is the ultimate predication of all being; that is, God is the prerequisite not only for the existence of all other things but also for their meaning. The self-sufficient God of the Bible stands behind reality not only as Maker and sustainer of creation, but also as the author and interpreter of truth, giving meaning to all ideas, events, beings, and laws. Christians affirm God as the basis of all predication just as non-Christians make a world of pure chance their basis for interpreting reality.

These two examples show how presuppositions function in our thinking. All people use them because no one can think without them. They are like the glasses through which a person views the world. If the lenses are tinted green, all colors appear very different than they would through rose-colored glasses. The lens determines what the eye sees. In the same way, our presuppositions, the ideas we use to view the world, men, events, and objects in the world, "color" how we understand them.

Thus there can be no such thing as a "brute" or a "neutral" or uninterpreted fact. All facts are interpreted by a person's presuppositional perspective. The same apparent "fact" can have two completely disparate meanings, depending on whether it is viewed through the presuppositional lens of theism or of atheism. The one lens colors all facts with a theistic tint, the other with a naturalistic one.

Facts are always interpreted in light of a greater field of reference. For example, if a father takes his young son to a baseball game,[1] and the boy has never seen a game before, his lack of understanding of baseball will limit his appreciation of the game. If a player hits a home run in the bottom of the ninth with the bases loaded to win the game, the father will be excited; but the son might only be puzzled by all the commotion. Do both the father and child observe the same fact?

They both view the action on the field: a ball is thrown to a batter who hits it into the center field seats. But since only the father knows the rules of baseball, only he realizes the full significance of what has happened. The son, not knowing the rules, lacks the presuppositional framework for understanding what takes place on the field. In order for him to recognize the meaning of a "home run," the rules of baseball must be correctly organized in his mind as he watches the game. The rules are the "lens" or "framework" through which he can properly perceive the action going on before his eyes. Lacking such a perspective, our little spectator will leave the stadium without fully appreciating what he has seen, unless someone explains how the game is played. Imagine missing out on the thrill of a game-winning home run!

In a similar way, we are not neutral witnesses of the world we live in; we understand the meaning of everything either through a lens of regenerate belief provided by God or through a lens of unbelief affected by sin. One of these two lenses is already over

---

1. This illustration is borrowed from Thom Notaro, *Van Til and the Use of Evidence* (Phillipsburg, N.J.: Presbyterian and Reformed, 1980), p. 48.

our mind's eye *before* we perceive the world. Anything observed in reality can be understood in two fundamentally different ways. An atheistic biologist interprets a human body as an excellent illustration of naturalistic evolution, while a Christian biologist marvels that the same body is a result of God's creative genius. Everything in the universe is subject to this conflict of interpretations—from butterflies and precious gems to apples and granite rock formations.

Non-Christians may even believe that certain "miraculous" events in Scripture actually happened. But they would *interpret* them in radically different ways than would Christians. Nonbelievers would interpret the miracles of Christ, for example, not as demonstrations of His deity and kingship but as unusual phenomena requiring some explanation unavailable to the biblical writers. So it is with other facts in our world. The Bible, therefore, speaks of two kinds of knowledge: (1) a "renewed," "true knowledge" (Col. 3:10), which is a genuine "knowledge of the truth" resulting from repentant faith in Christ (II Tim. 2:25; cf. Col. 2:3–10; I Cor. 10:37); and (2) a knowledge that is "falsely called knowledge," which has "gone astray from the faith" (I Tim. 6:20–21, NASB) and is based on a philosophy of "empty deception" and an ultimate faith in man (Col. 2:8). Such a deceptive philosophy causes the non-Christian to consider Christian truth as "foolishness" (cf. I Cor. 1:18–31). Both of these outlooks are described in this and following chapters.

The Christian presuppositional system focuses our attention on the absolute indispensability of God for all our thinking. Without God as a starting point, we can know nothing about the world of particulars. We can only ascribe a relative meaning to what we know based on our limited, finite perspective. Without God we cannot trust reason, sense experience, intuition, or any other methods purported to give knowledge. While we know some things truly by *reason* (e.g., the law of noncontradiction), others by *sense experience* (e.g., our shoe size), others by *intuition* (e.g., our love for family and friends), and still others by *authority* (e.g., the date Washington crossed the Delaware in the Revolutionary War), none of these methods by itself can provide an adequate basis for *all* knowledge. Nor can any of these ways even establish with certainty the validity of knowledge within its own sphere. Reason cannot validate itself; nor can sense experience, intuition, or other authorities. All means of knowing rest on premises outside themselves. Reason, experience, and intuition can be used in radically different ways depending on one's premises. Only by granting that God exists and has authoritatively revealed Himself are we able to rise above mere opinion and achieve a measure of certainty. If the transcendent, personal God of the Bible exists and has spoken in an authoritative Word, we have a warrant to trust our different ways of knowing.

That does not mean that we will always reason correctly, that we will interpret our senses without error, that our feelings are unerringly correct, and that all our authorities will report truthfully. But God's existence and self-revelation give us the absolutely necessary precondition—authoritative truth—for accepting these ways of knowing as valid within their own spheres. We can use reason to figure out a problem in logic without saying that logic is the only way to truth. Likewise, scientific study of the brain is appropriate even though thinking is more than a biochemical reaction. Thus, God's truth enables us to use each method without reducing all knowledge to any one such method.

Christian epistemology finds in God the ultimate source of both being and meaning, value and interpretation. Those who do not affirm His existence are forced to posit some other source of meaning, or else confess the absence of meaning.

In presupposing God, Christians assert that objective truth exists. God is Himself the basis of truth not just because His words are true (II Sam. 7:28), but because He is the very God of truth (Isa. 65:16). Jesus reaffirmed this when He said, "I am the way—the truth and the life" (John 14:6). Christians are not left in a quagmire of doubt over whether relativity and chance are in control of reality. On the basis of God's existence Christians aggressively challenge truth claims of all epistemologies that exclude God. If God is ultimate, all thinking without reference to Him is vanity and idolatrous and must be brought captive into obedience to His will (II Cor. 10:5). Challenging all systems of thought at their very starting point, the Bible calls us to examine our presuppositions to see whether they regard God or something else—such as our rational powers, individual experience, or empirical data—as the basis for truth. Only by presupposing God can we adequately account for the rest of reality and our experience in the world. True wisdom, in biblical terms, begins with the "fear" (reverential awe) of God (Prov. 1:7).

God's Revelation

Having started with the existence of God, whose attributes we considered briefly in chapter 1, Christians believe secondly that God has revealed Himself to human beings. The word *revelation* in the Bible refers to God's self-disclosure. To *reveal* means to uncover or unveil, to show what was previously hidden or unknown. Apart from God's self-revelation, He would be unknown to man. Because we are made in the image of God, we are so constituted that we can be the recipients of God's revelation; it is adapted to our finite capacity to comprehend it. Even though our knowledge is not exhaustive (only God can know anything exhaustively), nevertheless our knowledge of God is true.

The Bible teaches that God revealed Himself to man because of His grace (Deut. 7:7–8; Titus 3:5) so that man may say with the apostle Paul, "I know whom I have believed" (II Tim. 1:12). God desires us to know Him not just intellectually as an abstract fact, but experientially and personally. Ultimately, of course, God became incarnate in His Son, Jesus Christ. But God's self-disclosure also took place in time and space either as miraculous interventions in history or as verbal communication. In all of these conditions God's revelation was adapted to finite human beings as receivers of divine revelation.

Because God is personal and reveals Himself as a sovereign Creator and Redeemer, revelation never consists merely of data that we believe intellectually. His revelation is both indicative and imperative. It describes and prescribes. First, it explains that God is loving, just, and good. For example, "The heavens are telling the *glory* of God" (Ps. 19:1). All who look at the majestic expanse of the heavens feel compelled to say with the apostle Paul, "Since the creation of the world His eternal power and divine nature have been clearly seen." But God's revelation is also imperative; it demands an appropriate human response in keeping with the character of that revelation. Thus the psalmist prays in 19:14, "Let the words of my mouth and the meditation of my heart be acceptable in thy sight, O Lord, my rock and my redeemer." Similarly, Paul condemns unbelievers for their failure to worship the majestic God of creation: "For even though they knew God [by the creation He had made] they did not honor Him as God, or give thanks; but they became futile in their speculations and their foolish heart was darkened" (Rom. 1:21, NASB).

Because God's self-revelation is indicative and imperative, our response is always to be more than merely recognizing intellectually that God exists and has certain attributes. We are to respond in faith by worshipping God and obeying His commandments.

General and Special Revelation

In the biblical tradition God reveals Himself to man by two means—general and special revelation. As its name implies, general revelation is truth God reveals to all people regardless of time, place, culture, or other historical factors. General revelation is not verbal communication. It is God's revelation of Himself in nature, the human mind or conscience, and the facts of experience and of history so that all people can know Him.

First, God reveals Himself clearly through the majesty and beauty of creation (Ps. 19). Biblical writers use the metaphor of creation's "speaking" or "showing" man what God is like. As we observe the grandeur of a starlit night or the vast expanse of the ocean or a mountain range, we can know Him in the same way that we can know an architect by living in a house he has designed. Thus Paul affirms in Romans 1:21 that all people know God through the creation.

Second, God reveals Himself to all men through their minds, specifically their consciences. In Romans 2:14 and 15 Paul notes that Gentiles, who do not have the law of the Jews, nevertheless know the difference between right and wrong. Even though they do not possess the revealed Old Testament law, they have the ability to distinguish right from wrong. Paul concludes that "what the law requires is written on their hearts, while their conscience also bears witness. . . . " Our consciences are not always reliable guides to right and wrong conduct because they are distorted by sin. That we praise what is right and forbid what is wrong, however, reflects that God's general revelation is present in our conscience.

Finally, the events and experiences of history also reveal God. Those who chronicle the rise and fall of civilizations inevitably connect the moral and spiritual characteristics manifested in a given culture to that civilization's success or failure. Western historians, for example, attribute the fall of ancient Rome to its moral corruption. In the same way, historians praise principles of justice that enable a culture to be strong and unified, and they rightly criticize cultures that foster brutality and injustice. Cultural successes and failures recorded in the Bible likewise are tied to the moral and spiritual qualities of their people. Therefore, observers of a nation like Old Testament Israel know that love and justice are not *arbitrary* categories invented by people to evaluate historical events. They rest upon a genuine system of values that enables us to make valid judgments. As the controller of the destinies of peoples, God manifests His character by His judgments upon nations for all to observe. Though the prosperity of a nation is not in exact proportion to its righteousness, a sufficient correlation exists for people to discern God's involvement in history.

The purpose and meaning of general revelation should now be apparent. Through general revelation God has revealed Himself to all people without exception. They live in God's created order as witnesses of His power and deity, knowing the difference between right and wrong, and evaluating the events of history. Through all such experiences people also know God and gain some insight into the qualities that give meaning and purpose to reality. Every person not only knows *that* God exists, but also knows God's *character*. People are related to God even when sinfully rejecting this knowledge of God. To suppress knowledge of Him is not merely to deny a fact, but personally to reject God

Himself. Willful denial of the God we know to exist indicates that our knowing process is not ethically neutral. If it were, we would not be held accountable for rejecting the God we know. He is not a mere datum to be known abstractly like a mathematical equation. He is a personal and dynamic God who can be known personally. Therefore, man stands guilty for rejecting the God he knows through general revelation. As the psalmist put it, "The fool has said in his heart there is no God" (Ps. 14:1).

If mankind were not sinful, general revelation would be sufficient to enable people to know God and His truth. But as Paul states in Romans 1:18, men "by their wickedness *suppress* the truth"; even though people knew God, they deliberately did not honor Him as God or even thank Him. As a result "they became futile in their thinking and their senseless minds were darkened" (1:21, 22). Paul's striking language vividly describes what is called the *noetic effect* of sin on our knowledge and indicates the pervasiveness of human sin. Since our knowledge is never morally neutral, sin not only cripples our wills but also clouds our knowledge, leading us to deny what we know to be true—that God exists and expects us to worship and obey Him. Because sin has affected man's mind, general revelation needs to be supplemented. People need more than additional information about God. They need to be restored to fellowship with Him; they need to be saved from their sins. General revelation, therefore, provides the basis for God's special revelation, His act of saving grace.

Through special revelation God discloses what sinful human beings need to know about Him, themselves, and the world. God has given special revelation in the form of the incarnation, miracles, and the Scriptures. The supreme example of revelation in history is, of course, the incarnation, by which God manifested Himself in human form in Jesus Christ. So fully is Jesus the revelation of God that He can say to His disciples, "He who has seen me has seen the Father" (John 14:9). Of Jesus the apostle John wrote, "No one has ever seen God; the only Son who is in the bosom of the Father, he has made him known" (1:18). If God were to appear in human flesh, what would He claim in order to make Himself known as God that Jesus Christ did not claim?

Jesus taught with authority, performed miracles, asserted His authority to forgive sins, and died and rose again from the dead to defeat the power of sin and death. He even went so far as to claim that His works and words were not His own but the very works and words of God. On one occasion He even used the greatest name of God, "I AM" (Exod. 3:14; cf. John 8:58), of Himself. Nothing else could so clearly and completely reveal God to man as God's taking on human form in the person of His Son, Jesus Christ. Through Jesus, people were able not only to hear the Word of life but to see and touch it as well (I John 1:1–5).

Before examining special revelation in more detail, we can now appreciate how general and special revelation are interrelated in Christian epistemology. They are both necessary and complementary. Through general revelation God has revealed Himself to all people without exception so that all people know God in their hearts. They not only know about Him; they know Him, His character, and His demands. Creation, conscience, and history reveal God. People have denied this knowledge of God, however, by willfully rejecting what they know of God and by worshipping other things.

Through special revelation God enlightens our minds to a saving knowledge. To accomplish His plan of redemption, God inspired chosen people to write the Scripture so that we can understand correctly God's work in Christ. While general revelation discloses God to mankind, special revelation provides for man's salvation and growth in obedient knowledge of God. Both types of revelation are necessary, and they complement each other.

When combined with our previous study of anthropology, Christian epistemology supplements our understanding of man as the image bearer of God. As sinners our redemption from sin includes renewal in knowledge. Most popular views of knowledge do not make this moral and spiritual dimension essential to knowing. Presupposing knowledge to be ethically neutral (i.e., as consisting of "brute facts" or detached ideas) many believe that the pursuit and accumulation of knowledge requires little more than cultivating our native intelligence and developing our inherent rational capacities. Such thinking has led to the widely accepted idea that people are able to arrive at the facts by means of an unbiased, objective, scientific method. Truth is assumed to be merely an impersonal or abstract idea without any relation to transcendent ideals or beings. Christians, however, by affirming knowledge of God to be paramount, regard knowledge first and foremost as a moral and spiritual matter requiring renewal of the mind and repentance from sin. Christian epistemology, therefore, assumes and is intimately related to the biblical views of God and man.

Scripture as Revelation

Besides the incarnation of Christ, the living Word of God, God also reveals Himself *specially* by means of Scripture, the written Word of God. The incarnation and miracles are indeed events in history, but such events without interpretation would be meaningless, much like a movie without a soundtrack or subtitles. The viewer would be left to project subjectively a meaning onto the events or to deny that they have any meaning whatsoever.

The Scriptures fulfill our need for a meaningful and true interpretation of reality and, therefore, occupy a primary place in Christian epistemology. In the Bible, revelatory events include a narrative of actual historical occurrences plus their meaning. Christ's resurrection from the dead, the most important revelatory event in history, illustrates the necessity of a written Word of God. Without an authoritative interpretation of the fact of the resurrection people might propose any number of meanings to explain it. For example, one school of secular historical interpretation accepts Jesus' resurrection as historical fact, but goes on to explain that Christ's resurrection means only that anything can happen in history. Some secular historians, therefore, have accepted the testimony of biblical writers that Christ rose from the dead, but have denied that Jesus was God or that He overcame the power of sin and death in the world. Seen merely as a most improbable event, Christ's resurrection, however historical, means something totally different from what Christians have asserted for almost two thousand years.

In claiming that the Bible is God's Word Christians mean not only that God reveals certain truths both about Himself and His creation, but also that He interprets His revelation so that it may be truly understood and furnish a knowledge of salvation. Orthodox Christianity affirms that God inspired the authors of the Bible in such a way that what they wrote is what God intends for us to know. The Old Testament writers declared again and again, "Thus says the Lord." On numerous occasions they were specifically instructed to write what God had commanded. In the New Testament, Jesus promised the gift of the Holy Spirit, who "will teach you all things and bring all things to your remembrance whatsoever I have said to you" (John 14:26).

The Bible contains numerous references to the significance of language as a medium of revelation. In fact, verbal communication is the primary means by which God reveals Himself to man. Jesus said in John 6:63, "The words that I have spoken to you are spirit and life," and in His high priestly prayer He said, "I have given them [the disciples] the words which thou gavest me, and they have received them and know in truth that I came from thee; and they have believed that thou didst send me" (John 17:8). In receiving Jesus' words His disciples encountered God and knew Him. No higher sanction could be given for the validity of language as a vehicle for knowing God. As God's image bearers, human beings are constituted rational creatures able to communicate verbally not only with each other but also with God. Thus we are capable of both talking with God and receiving His written Word in the Scriptures.

Some contemporary theologians divide this unified view of biblical truth. They distinguish sharply between propositional revelation (God's revelation by means of propositions or statements, that is, *language*) and revelation through encounter (God's revelation via a spiritual, existential *encounter* incapable of being fully captured in words). These theologians depreciate propositional revelation by contending that true revelation is an event that takes place only as an existential encounter on a personal level.

The well-known twentieth-century theologian Karl Barth popularized this idea, which many contemporary theologians now accept. Barth held that divine inspiration applies only to the *activity* of receiving revelation from God and not to the *content* of the words penned by the biblical authors. The inscripturated words themselves are not to be called the Word of God. Therefore, we cannot directly equate God's Word and the Bible; they are not synonymous. In fact, according to Barth, the Bible contains "error," "fallibility . . . historical and scientific inaccuracies . . . and theological contradictions," so that we should not "take everything in the Bible as true *in globo* [in its completeness]." Nevertheless, this fallible Bible at times and in parts can *become* the "Word of God" when God chooses to reveal Himself to people through particular passages. Consequently, the "Word of God" does not reside permanently in the Bible but only with God Himself.

Thus God reveals Himself through existential, nonverbal, and personal encounters with individuals, which may or may not come through the written words of Scripture. For Barth, revelation is always an event not to be identified with the Bible; revelation occurs only in Jesus Christ, and Scripture merely *witnesses* or *attests* to this revelation. To identify the contents of the Bible with the Word of God would mean that revelation became "frozen into a system of truths" and that God was "imprisoned" and controlled by man. When God chooses to use Scripture as a channel of His Word, *and* man responds in faith to it, then a revelatory "event" has taken place, and the Bible and God's Word *become* identical. This revelation is a nonpropositional, wordless "encounter," which resembles a mystic, existential experience.

While Barth's intention was to prevent what he considered rationalist tendencies in theology, his view poses three difficulties. First, it is contradictory for Barth to say that parts of the Bible can contain both the Word of the God of truth and errors. Second, the supposed errors in the biblical text can be challenged (see our comments in the next section). Third, Barth's contention that the Bible is not the objective, permanent "Word of God," but only a channel through which God sometimes reveals Himself in an experiential, wordless manner contradicts biblical teaching. The words already quoted from Jesus (John 6:63; 17:8) demonstrate that God does reveal Himself through statements (propositions) in human language.

Further, contrary to Barth's distinctions, the Bible refers to itself as God's Word! Psalm 119 describes the written Scripture (in this case, the *Torah*) as the "Word of God" thirty-four times. Paul refers to his own writing as "the Word of the Lord" (I Thess. 4:15), and John is commanded to "write" his Revelation because the statements in it "are true words of God" (Rev. 19:9). The New Testament authors introduce Old Testament quotations by "Scripture says" (e.g., Rom. 9:17; Gal. 3:8), "God says" (e.g., Matt. 19:4–5; Acts 4:24–25; 13:34–35; Heb. 1:5–13; 4:3–4, 7; 5:5), and the "Holy Spirit says" (Heb. 3:7), so that what Scripture says, God says, and vice versa. In fact, the Old Testament writers in various ways declare almost four thousand times that they are conveying the very words of God.

We conclude that those who say God is known only through particular *statements* of Scripture *or* only through a personal *existential encounter* have made a false dichotomy between these two ways of knowing. A unified perspective holds that we encounter or know God as we receive His Word in Scripture, which interprets our encounter for us. Human language is not only adequate but also absolutely necessary to communicate divine truth. To believe in God is not merely to give mental assent to statements about God; believing involves having complete confidence in and knowing God Himself. Such knowledge can be mediated through language. Without Scripture—the Word of God—we cannot encounter God, because we learn about God primarily through His Word. Paul affirms this view in Romans 10:14 and 17:

> But how are men to call upon him in whom they have not believed? And how are they to believe in him of whom they have never heard? And how are they to hear without a preacher? . . . So faith comes from hearing, and hearing by the *word of Christ* (NASB).[2]

The written and spoken Word, therefore, brings man to a

2. The majority of the Greek New Testament manuscripts read "the word of God" at the end of v. 17.

position of encounter with God. As we respond to God's Word, we know God Himself.

The Inspiration of Scripture

A proper view of inspiration rests upon a careful interpretation of several biblical texts on this subject. In John 10:35 Christ states that "the Scripture cannot be broken." The *whole body* of Old Testament Scripture is authoritative on whatever topic it speaks. That is because Scripture is inspired by God and can never be viewed as offering false statements; otherwise its truthfulness would be "broken." In this sense one can speak of Scripture as "inerrant" or "infallible." John 10:34–35 has in view specifically the Old Testament Law but may well include the entire Old Testament Scripture as the "Word of God," which cannot be broken.

The apostles concur with Christ's view of the Old Testament. The classic Pauline text is II Timothy 3:16: "All Scripture is inspired by God and is profitable for teaching, for reproof, for correction, and for training in righteousness." The Greek word for "inspired" literally means "God-breathed." Actually Paul's words speak of a divine "breathing out" or "expiration" rather than "inspiration." The point is that the Scriptures (the original autographs) originated in God and are the written effect of God's speech as communicated through the human authors. Elsewhere Paul also referred to the Old Testament as "the oracles of God" (Rom. 3:2; cf. Acts 7:38).

Another important apostolic text is II Peter 1:20–21: " . . . no prophecy of Scripture is a matter of one's own interpretation, for no prophecy was ever made by an act of human will, but men moved by the Holy Spirit spoke from God" (NASB). The Greek word translated "interpretation" literally means "loosing" or "untying," which stresses that Scripture did not originate in man's efforts, but came "from God." The *manner* in which Scripture was written is expressed by the phrase "men moved by the Holy Spirit." The verb translated "moved" (lit. "born along") is a maritime metaphor also found in Acts 27:15–17, where it describes a ship carried along by wind. Similarly the Old Testament prophets are portrayed by Peter as "raising their sails" (they were obedient and receptive), and the Spirit filled them and carried them along in their writing according to the direction He wished them to go. Thus, at no time did the writers of Scripture determine the content or truth of the message even though their various personalities and backgrounds influenced the style in which they wrote.

The New Testament authors not only affirmed the divine authority of the Old Testament but also ascribed the same authority to their own writings. In I Corinthians 2:13 Paul wrote, "Which things also we speak, not in words taught by man's wisdom, but in those taught by the Spirit" (NASB). In I Thessalonians Paul said he was writing the "word of the Lord" (4:15; 2:13), which "does not come from error or impurity or by way of deceit" (1:3; see also I Cor. 7:10, 12, 17, 40; 14:37; II Cor. 2:17; 13:3; I Thess. 1:5; I Tim. 4:1). Paul also considered the Gospels to be divine "Scripture" on an authoritative level with the Old Testament (I Tim. 5:18). In like manner Peter understood Paul's letters to have the same authority as Old Testament Scripture (II Pet. 3:2). Finally, John was given a divine mandate to write down (1:19) the "revelation of Jesus Christ" as it was communicated to him (1:1). John wrote with the understanding that he was inscribing the very words of Christ (2:1, 8, 12, 18; 3:1, 7, 14; 22:12-16) and of the Holy Spirit (2:7, 11, 17, 29; 3:6, 13, 22; 14:13; 22:17). Thus John was told that the words he was writing are "true words of God" (19:9; also 21:5; 22:6), and that anyone who "adds to them" or "takes away from the words of the book of this prophecy" will be accursed (22:18-19).

And so, according to the witness of Christ and the apostles, what Scripture says, God says. If we assume that God can only speak truth (which we must), then we must also assume that Scripture, as God's regulative Word for our lives, can express only truth (cf. Ps. 119:43, 140, 142, 160).

While all Christians agree that the Bible is inspired, they differ over exactly what inspiration means. A minority of Christians espouse mechanical inspiration, a view that presents God as having dictated His words to men who served merely as passive secretaries. The writers themselves are regarded as having contributed nothing to either the form or the content of Scripture. The obvious differences in style among the various books of the Bible make this view implausible.

At the opposite extreme, others view God's inspiration as limited merely to intensifying normal human mental and spiritual perception. The biblical writers were enabled, therefore, to see spiritual realities more clearly than under normal circumstances. Although their insights were heightened by God's assistance, in this view, nothing new was introduced to their minds as they wrote. Nor were they preserved from error by any special guidance. Inspiration merely involved God's assisting the writers' normal thinking processes. The Bible is really the word of men written with divine help. Such inspiration differs not in kind but only in degree from the spiritual insights evident in theological and devotional writings throughout the history of Christianity. This view contradicts the claims of the biblical writers that their writings are unique because God broke into space and time and "spoke" His Word through them so that what they wrote was not their own. Their writings were not simply more inspired than others'. The words of Scripture stand in a class by themselves because of the unique guidance and control of the Holy Spirit under which they were produced.

A third view best accords with the statements of the biblical writers themselves. Its proponents maintain that the Holy Spirit worked in the hearts and minds of the authors, using their natural talents, styles, vocabularies, cultural milieu, and thought patterns to guide them even to the choice of words that express inerrantly His revelations of truth, history, holiness, and love. Therefore, biblical inspiration should be understood in two ways. First, because the Bible is *verbally* inspired, what God wanted to say is found in its pages exactly in the words He chose to say it. Second, because *all its parts* without exception are inspired, the Bible in its entirety is God's Word.

Some theologians argue, however, that God's inspiration influenced only the "important parts" of Scripture, texts dealing with the theme of salvation or redemption (the teaching of Jesus, the doctrinal Epistles, etc.). Inspiration is not considered to extend to the Scripture's apparently nondoctrinal or historical sections. Since the divine purpose of each biblical book is to communicate truths about salvation, only the materials having that purpose were inerrantly or infallibly inspired. Other materials, which are not inspired and may contain errors, are merely the "husk" within which is found the "kernel" of saving truth. Thus, for example, the Gospels report the truth that salvation comes through Christ, but they may contain historical inaccuracies regarding "inconsequential details" such as time, place, or other matters of historical setting.

Among the problems associated with such a "limited inspiration" viewpoint, one especially stands out in the light of the New Testament evidence about inspiration discussed above. The many texts that speak of Scripture as the "Word of God," or as divinely inspired, never limit inspiration only to certain parts of the Bible. While the primary intention of Scripture is unquestionably to communicate truths about salvation, Scripture itself never states that only portions of the biblical text contain these truths. Is it not precarious to assume that apparently insignificant historical details have no relation to these truths of salvation? For example, in John 10:34–36 Christ refers to a *seemingly* insignificant historical detail in Psalm 82 as part of the whole body of Old Testament "Scripture [that] cannot be broken." Indeed, God's message about man's salvation encompasses every part of Scripture and every part is divinely inspired *to contribute in some way* to this purpose. Paul affirms this most clearly in II Timothy 3:16: "All Scripture is God-breathed and profitable for teaching, for reproof, for correction, for training in righteousness," that is, for purposes essentially concerned with man's salvation.

In conclusion, if we assume that God speaks only truth and that Scripture declares itself to be the written Word of God, then what the whole of Scripture says must be true because it is equivalent to God's speaking. Thus, the writing of the Bible was an act of both inspiration and revelation so that mankind throughout history would have a reliable, authoritative, infallible record of God's self-revelation.

Characteristics of Scripture

How do Christians know that the Bible is in fact God's Word? After all, have not other religions made similar claims for their sacred writings? Our answer to this important question is related to the fundamental presuppositions of Christianity: that God exists and has revealed Himself. Just as Christians confess the absolute self-sufficiency of God, by analogy they confess Scripture to be self-sufficient in its testimony to itself. By this they mean that the Bible is self-interpretative. We have already noted Christ's testimony to the Scriptures. Believers accept the testimony of Christ and the Bible's witness to itself because they find that Jesus' words and the words of Scripture are equally self-authenticating. To seek a higher authority would be to question the Bible's inherent veracity as the self-sufficient Word of God. Christians do not establish criteria for Scripture's truth; the Scripture itself establishes and satisfies its own criteria. To create a standard for explaining the Bible's truth would be to exalt a rational or empirical test above the Bible. Some abstract test would usurp the authoritative position now accorded to God's Word alone. This would mean that Scripture would not be ultimate and would cease to be the foundational presupposition of faith.

Christians therefore confess Scripture to be God's Word because of its very content. The message revealed within the Bible is consistent with the character of the God revealed therein. Moreover, God's Holy Spirit attests to the authority of the Bible. Apart from the witness of the Holy Spirit no one can recognize the Scripture as God's Word. In I Corinthians 2:14 Paul states that the unbeliever "does not receive the gifts of the Spirit of God, for they are folly to him, and he is not able to understand them because they are spiritually discerned." Therefore the same Spirit who inspired Scripture also assures the Christian that it is God's Word. In I John 5:7, 13 we note that the Spirit's task is to witness to the truth. He does so both objectively (in the written Word) and subjectively (in the heart of the believer).

If the above answer appears to involve circular reasoning, it is not alone. All world views involve reasoning in a circle. Since all of life is religious in its orientation, everyone holds a religious commitment to first principles that are ultimate, all-encompassing, and unprovable. Attempts to prove any world view depend on the very presuppositions out of which that world view has grown, inasmuch as there are no neutral or a-religious standards for validating world views. Thus, like all other religious systems, Christianity cannot be demonstrated by rational arguments coming from without. Christian doctrine finds an internally consistent defense in terms of its ultimate presupposition—the God of the Scriptures.

At the same time, the biblical interpretation of the external world does justice to human experience and offers a clear message of salvation to a world lost in the power of sin. The believer sees *confirming evidences* of the Scripture's witness in every aspect of life. Unbelievers, of course, deny its witness. But even their disbelief confirms the Christian's view inasmuch as the Bible often cites skeptical rejection of God's truth as evidence of the noetic effect of sin. Those who deny God also reject what His Word says about our experience.

In seeking to explain the Bible, Christians have noted its four main attributes: *necessity, authority, perspicuity,* and *sufficiency.*[3]

Man *needs* a true interpretation both of creation and of redemption. The necessity of Scripture is the biblical answer to all views that say human reason is independent of God. The assumption of human autonomy implies our ability to know truth apart from God's revelation. Autonomous reason, however, produces mere human opinion and not the certainty that people seek. Only revelation from a transcendent God can give us the absolutes, the universals, upon which certainty rests. Other attempts to assert first principles, such as in Aristotle's major premises (see our next chapter), represent human efforts to postulate universals based on experience of the world without any reference to God and His revelation. Such efforts are doomed to failure because of the noetic effect of sin. The Scriptures, however, provide a basis for

3. See Cornelius Van Til, *A Christian Theory of Knowledge* (Phillipsburg, N.J.: Presbyterian and Reformed, 1969), pp. 52–71.

human rationality in a transcendent God who made and upholds a rational universe that functions according to His Word. Our task is not to *establish* truth but rather to *recognize* God's truth and to *live obediently* under it.

The *authority* of Scripture is implicit in its necessity. Traditionally believers have held that the Bible is the only infallible authority in matters of faith and practice. Indeed, the authority of Scripture rests upon its divine authorship. A fallible Word of God would be a contradiction in terms. As authoritative, Scripture is the standard or rule against which we may measure all human opinions and judgments. Interpretations of God, humanity, and the world are to be judged according to this divinely given norm. We are not left without an absolute point of reference for understanding the world in which we live. God has spoken authoritatively so that we can know truly even if not exhaustively.

That the Bible is *perspicuous* means that its message is clear. The Bible interprets itself insofar as difficult passages receive light from passages that are easier to understand. Because the Bible is basically clear and the Holy Spirit is given to all believers, no priestly class is necessary to mediate the Bible's meaning authoritatively to the laity. The perspicuity of the Bible does not mean that all parts of the Bible are equally clear. But using the principle of allowing the Bible to interpret itself, we are able to understand what we need to know about God and to live obediently in His world.

The *sufficiency* of Scripture means that the Bible is a completed work of God's revelation. The sixty-six books of Scripture are a closed canon. In other words, no additional revelation, prophecy, or teaching needs to be added to God's Word. Various contemporary sects and cults violate this principle by claiming that new doctrines, written or unwritten traditions, visions, or prophecies are equally authoritative with the Bible. Throughout church history various groups have wrongly set up additional authorities supposedly to complete or supplement the revelation of God.

The four attributes taken together indicate why Christians have esteemed the Bible as God's Word throughout history. This understanding of Scripture has enabled Christians to withstand heresies, train their children, change the course of history many times over, and improve society. These principles have challenged believers not only to affirm their faith in the Scriptures but to live on the basis of the certainty provided by the Bible. As ages have progressed and civilizations have risen and fallen, the Bible has maintained its place in the minds and hearts of believers.

Conclusion

Biblical epistemology is integral to the Christian world-and-life view. Knowledge from a Christian perspective is never a mere speculative system of thought abstracted from life like a coldly detached arrangement of facts. Epistemology closely parallels our theological and anthropological views. The biblical view underscores God's sovereignty and mankind's dependence by its emphasis on God's existence and His revelation as the indispensable starting point for knowledge. God is not only Creator and Redeemer of all things including man; He is also their source of meaning and thus the ultimate presupposition of knowledge. As created in God's image, yet fallen because of sin, mankind needs both to be redeemed from sin and to be renewed in His knowledge.

In subsequent chapters we will note alternatives to biblical theism proposed throughout history. Some philosophers have tried to synthesize biblical and other starting points. Such efforts compromise the uniqueness of Christian theism. Others have rejected Christianity altogether. Contemporary thinkers especially have framed world views that deny the necessity of the biblical perspective. Their world views presuppose unaided human reason, sense perception, or simply human existence. Contemporary philosophers either deny the existence of God or make His existence irrelevant to the search for truth. Some even deny that truth exists and cease all efforts to construct a world-and-life view. In our century this abandonment has led many to conclude that there are no absolutes to give meaning and purpose to life, except those arbitrarily adopted for individual situations.

Biblical epistemology, however, opposes all forms of knowledge that exalt man instead of God as the ultimate arbiter of truth. It also calls on people everywhere to repent in their thinking as well as in their manner of living. Without intellectual repentance, human pride will continue to establish itself as the only standard of judgment. From a biblical standpoint undaunted pride eventually leads to spiritual decay and ultimately to God's judgment.

Understanding and articulating radical contrast between biblical and opposing perspectives of knowledge should be one of our highest priorities. Only by doing so can Christians construct a viable intellectual alternative and make a cultural impact in the last years of the twentieth century. By adopting a holistic biblical view of knowledge we can participate in building the kingdom of God by submitting how and what we know to His lordship and living our lives in obedience to His will.

For Further Reading

Boice, James Montgomery, ed. *The Foundation of Biblical Authority*. Grand Rapids: Zondervan, 1978.

Davis, John Jefferson. *Foundations of Evangelical Theology*. Grand Rapids: Baker, 1984.

Guthrie, Donald. *New Testament Introduction*. London: Tyndale, 1970.

Henry, Carl F. H. *God, Revelation and Authority*, 6 vols. Waco, Tex.: Word, 1976.

———. *Revelation and the Bible*. Grand Rapids: Baker, 1958.

Kantzer, Kenneth S. and Stanley Gundry, eds. *Perspectives on Evangelical Theology*. Grand Rapids: Baker, 1979.

Montgomery, John W. *God's Inerrant Word*. Minneapolis: Bethany, 1974.

Nash, Ronald H. *The Word of God and the Mind of Man*. Grand Rapids: Eerdmans, 1962.

Packer, James I. *"Fundamentalism" and the Word of God*. Grand Rapids: Eerdmans, 1958.

Pinnock, Clark. *Biblical Revelation: The Foundation of Christian Theology*. Phillipsburg, N.J.: Presbyterian and Reformed, 1971, 1985.

Rogers, Jack, ed. *The Authority of the Bible.* Waco, Tex.: Word, 1977.

Runia, K. *Karl Barth's Doctrine of Holy Scripture.* Grand Rapids: Eerdmans, 1962.

Schaeffer, Francis A. *He Is There and He Is Not Silent.* Wheaton, Ill.: Tyndale, 1972.

Van Til, Cornelius. *A Christian Theory of Knowledge.* Phillipsburg, N.J.: Presbyterian and Reformed, 1969.

Warfield, B. B. *The Inspiration and Authority of the Bible.* Phillipsburg, N.J.: Presbyterian and Reformed, 1948.

11
Greek Epistemology: Plato and Aristotle

Charles S. MacKenzie and W. Andrew Hoffecker

Early Greek Thought

Greek views of epistemology differ sharply from those of the biblical authors. The Bible emphasizes that God is the source of all knowledge and that human understanding depends upon His communicating truth to us. By contrast, the Greeks held that human beings themselves discover knowledge by using reason or empirical methods alone. None of the Greek philosophers saw God as the basis of knowledge. Instead, they argued either that true knowledge is unobtainable, or that sense experience or rational methods could enable people to find truth. The key figures in the development of Greek epistemology are the Sophists, Socrates, Plato, and Aristotle. Their efforts to probe the nature of the physical universe and to produce cosmologies testify to their concern about how people know.

The first major Greek school of epistemology was the Sophists, a professional school of teachers that taught rhetoric (the art of speaking), grammar, the nature of virtue, history, the sciences, and the arts. Led by Protagoras, Gorgias, and Thrasymachus, Sophists travelled among the Greeks and questioned everything. At their best, they stimulated people to think; at their worst, they wrangled over insignificant trivia.

Indeed Plato painted an unflattering picture of Sophists as having no genuine interest in discovering truth, but as desiring only to make money through skilled debate and training their followers to do likewise. Plato's harsh judgment reflects his disdain for Protagoras's most famous dictum, "Man is the measure of all things." Protagoras appears to have limited knowledge to sense experience, which is relative and subjective because everyone's perceptions are different. For example, to one person a breeze may feel warm and to another it may feel cold. Knowledge is measured and limited by one's perception. Rather than developing a system of knowledge that could obtain objective truth, Protagoras restricted his epistemology to questions about human powers of observation in the physical world and our use of words. In common with other Sophists his philosophy was antimetaphysical, that is, he claimed that knowledge is limited strictly to what the senses experience—concrete, physical objects. He also attacked traditional Greek morality and challenged popular belief in Olympian gods.

Gorgias rejected Protagoras's view that truth is relative and declared that truth does not exist. Believing that no reliable knowledge is possible, Gorgias abandoned philosophy and instead taught young Athenians the art of persuading others to do what they wished them to do. This practice led Socrates to become one of the Sophists' keenest critics. Our word *sophistry*, which describes the skill of using plausible but deceptive arguments, stems from Socrates' criticism of Sophists like Gorgias. They accepted money to train people not to arrive at the truth, but only to win an argument in debate.

Thrasymachus took the radical skepticism of the Sophists to its conclusion. He taught that each person should seek his own self-interest by continually asserting his own wishes. In his system there was no truth or knowledge to hold power in check.

Sophistic epistemology was as inconclusive as other pre-Socratic discussions about the nature of the ultimate and man's place in the world. Though undoubtedly the Sophists stimulated much debate, they provided few lasting answers beyond the commonplace recognition that human perceptions differ and that people gifted in argumentation can defeat their opponents through the skilled and sometimes dishonest use of words. It remained for Socrates, Plato, and Aristotle to probe the deeper questions of knowledge.

Socrates

While the Sophists split hairs and engaged in endless debates "just for fun," Socrates was intensely serious about finding truth. The quest for truth could provide the foundation for living the good life.

Born in Athens in 470 B.C., Socrates grew up in the golden age of Greek culture and power only to see its eventual decline. His own life ended in prison in 399 B.C. At the age of seventy-one he drank hemlock to fulfill the death sentence handed down to him by the court. Ironically, the greatest philosopher Greece had produced in several centuries was executed for supposedly misleading the youth of Athens and for disbelief in the gods of the state. Socrates possessed one of the keenest minds of all time. He claimed to be influenced by mystical impulses, messages or warnings he received from what he called an inner voice or "daimon."

In his effort to overcome the skepticism and relativism of the Sophists, Socrates attempted to find a solid foundation for knowledge. He discovered this foundation within the human soul or psyche. The soul is the part of the human being that seeks knowledge, knowledge to govern one's conduct and to provide a basis for living the moral life. Whereas Sophists taught virtue but denied that anyone could define its essence, Socrates stressed that the philosopher's task is to arrive at a rational understanding of virtue and other qualities such as courage, piety, beauty, and justice. Unless we know with the mind what justice is, how could we ever recognize what is fair? More importantly how could we ever intend to do the right thing in a given situation? Only if I know what beauty is, for example, can I paint a beautiful picture or if I know what justice is can I serve on a jury.

In his quest for reliable rational knowledge Socrates used a method he called "dialectic." The dialectic was a process of dialogue and discussion that involved asking careful questions and proposing reasoned answers in order to clarify ideas and to discover truth. Conversations between Socrates and his friends and opponents in Plato's *Republic, Phaedo, Timaeus,* etc. represent the new Socratic method, the dialogue, in operation. In these long and frequently digressing conversations we witness reason's dialectical quest for rational truth: definitions are proposed, arguments are adduced and rebutted, analogies are drawn, mistakes are corrected, and in the end conclusions are reached. Socrates played the central role in all such dialogues as he asked questions and urged the participants to clarify their ideas. But Socrates claimed no special wisdom on his part. He desired only to be the intellectual "mid-wife," who helped give birth to ideas. The dialogues are concrete illustrations of Socrates' demand that we follow an argument wherever it might lead. They epitomize Socrates' contention that no unexamined idea is worth holding, just as no unexamined life is worth living.

Socrates sought to use this dialectic method to formulate clear, precise definitions. Such definitions enable the mind to distinguish between the particular (one special tree) and the universal (the idea of treeness), which is associated with every tree, whether maple, oak, or lilac. For Socrates, knowledge is what the mind discovers beyond mere facts. Knowledge of a water lily, for example, consists of what a person knows about the lily after it has died, that is, understanding its beauty and delicacy, not simply naming its parts. True knowledge comes from recognizing that beyond the physical world of phenomena there is an order of reality, the forms or ideas, which the mind can discover. Man's effort to see beyond the physical facts of nature, in order to interpret the meaning of particulars, leads him to knowledge of universals.

Even though Socrates was one of the most original and influential Greek thinkers, we know little of his exact ideas because he never wrote on philosophy and never founded a school to publish his ideas. Most of what we know concerning him comes from his famous student Plato. Scholars disagree on how successfully we can disentangle Socrates' original ideas from their discussion in the Platonic dialogues. Nevertheless, what we know of his thought indicates how Socrates sought to counteract the Sophists' skepticism. He denied Protagoras's subjectivism and relativism and issued a clear challenge to philosophers to use reason with integrity.

Plato

Building on what he had learned from his teacher, Socrates, Plato developed an elaborate theory of knowledge that surpassed in detail and complexity Socrates' epistemology. Whereas the Sophists taught that all knowledge is relative because man's experiences of the physical world are so diverse, Plato taught that knowledge is absolute because the true object of knowledge is transcendent, residing in an invisible realm of forms or ideas, which are changeless, eternal, and nonmaterial essences.

For Plato, the forms or ideas are eternal patterns. They are separate from physical things, which are vague copies of these ideas. A beautiful tree is a copy of both the idea (or ideal) of beauty and the idea of treeness. Plato called the realm of unchanging ideas the realm of being. The world of particular, changing objects he designated the realm of becoming.

While these forms are central to Plato's epistemology, they are difficult to define precisely. This is partly because the forms are abstract absolutes, which Plato himself argued are best described by mathematical propositions. Nevertheless, we can make certain claims for the forms to help us understand their nature. First, they are standards (or "norms"). Beyond beautiful objects and just individuals is a concept of beauty and justice. In addition to sheets of white paper is whiteness itself. Pounds of beans, beef, and barley are measured against the standard or idea of a pound itself. These standards—beauty, justice, whiteness, "the pound"— are what Plato considered to be forms. Notice that in the material world there is no perfect pound, no complete justice, no absolute beauty, no total whiteness. Things in the material world merely approximate an ideal. Because Plato's philosophy is based upon these forms, it is called "idealism." Individuals should seek to implement as nearly as possible the ideals of truth, justice, and beauty in their everyday lives.

Most scholars agree that all forms share traits such as the following:

1. The forms have no spatial traits or properties. They are immaterial; they have no size, shape, or location.

2. They are eternal and changeless. Forms are outside of time in the sense that they do not develop or perish. By contrast, change is a trait of all things in the physical universe. Only forms are immutable, absolute *being*.

3. Their existence does not depend upon any other thing. For example, they exist whether we think of them or not. Without just men there would still be justice itself. Beauty and courage would exist even if Rembrandt had never painted and Lincoln had never led our country in the Civil War.

4. The senses cannot perceive the forms. Only the intellect can discern their existence. Our senses only inform us of shadows or copies of the forms, of varying opinions, of shades of white rather than whiteness itself. Physical "things" in the world of becoming are caused by eternal ideas. They imitate or copy forms.

5. The forms alone are real. This is the most difficult consideration for most people to understand because we are accustomed to saying that the real world is the world of sensory cognition. The things I see, taste, or touch are real. But for Plato certain truth (what he meant by "real") abides only in the absolute, unchanging norms (standards) of the forms.

6. All forms are by nature good. As we saw in our initial study of Greek theology, Goodness is the highest form. The human task is to adopt the forms as norms or guides for action. We cannot content ourselves with merely executing what we consider to be "just acts," because our opinions always differ. Therefore, for Plato, the forms are worthy of religious adulation.

The ideas or forms exist as the highest part of a hierarchy of being, which includes the physical world. The lower a person searches in this hierarchy, the closer he is to material things and the more limited is his knowledge, as when one speaks of a specific tree. The higher one ascends in the hierarchy of ideas, the more abstract and universal is his knowledge, as when one speaks of treeness in general.

Plato indicated that there are three ways in which human reason discovers the forms. *First* and foremost, there is recollection or memory. In the *Meno* Plato narrates Socrates' leading a slave boy, who had never been taught geometry, through a geometrical problem. Although the boy makes some mistakes he eventually proposes the correct answer. Since Socrates only asks questions, Plato argues that in some way the truth was already in the boy, acquired in some previous existence, and is now recollected or remembered under Socrates' interrogation. Plato uses Socrates' conversation with the boy to prove the immortality of the soul as a basis for this theory of recollection. Virtually all scholars discount the slave boy story as proof for both immortality and recollection as a way of knowing. Most people would hold that at most the story proves that the lad possessed mathematical talent or ability to think through a geometrical proof rather than that truth is innate and remembered from a previous life.

A *second* way in which people know the forms is through dialectic, which defines, abstracts, and separates essences from the things we experience. Dialectic, as we saw above, is the process of examination through debate that enables people to distinguish essences from common experiences. By separating opinions, feelings, and prejudices from the issue being examined, dialectic helps one find essential truth.

Plato used *eros*—a desire or love—as his final way to describe our search for knowledge. While we usually associate "erotic" with sexual desire and love of physical beauty, these are merely the lowest manifestations of *eros*. Generically, *eros* is a reaching out of the soul to a desired good. Even though its crudest expression may be physical attraction to a beautiful person, eternal beauty, one of the highest forms, is its highest object. *Eros* impels the knower insistently to seek universal beauty, which transcends all particular beauties and causes them to be. The philosopher's task is nothing less than a supreme beatific vision of the highest form, Goodness itself. Plato's description of the eristic search for knowledge accounted, at least in part, centuries later, for the religious quest of Christian mystics who rapturously described union with God. All three of these methods of discovering ideals—recollection, dialectic, and eristic—are basically rational. The soul or mind or rational capacity of man rises to a knowledge of ideas or forms.

In its discovery of real knowledge, the mind, according to Plato, passes through four stages. At each stage or rung of the ladder of reality the mind acts differently or uses a different mode of thought.

At the earliest and lowest stage of knowledge, the mind *imagines* that the shadowy appearances of the physical things it encounters are real. These imaginings are like an individual who cannot distinguish between a reflection in a mirror and the object causing the image. Believing that mere appearances are real, such an individual is at the lowest stage of cognition. At the next stage of knowledge, the mind climbs upward to recognize that the shadowy appearances are not real, but are caused by the physical objects themselves. Someone at this state has progressed to a "common sense" belief in tangible, physical reality. But being preoccupied with material things, he has not yet begun to understand the rational order of reality. In the moral sphere, for example, he may have correct beliefs, but they are not grounded in rational knowledge. Thus we must move higher up the order of being.

In the third stage of knowledge a person penetrates beyond the physical into the intelligible world of meaning, interpretation, and abstraction. This stage of knowledge is demonstrated by the mathematician who solves a geometrical problem. He recognizes that his diagram of a triangle is only a crude approximation because it is only a representation of the ideal triangle. Mathematics functioned in Plato's system as a bridge from the visible and sensible world of appearances (chalk diagrams on the blackboard) to the invisible, intelligible world of forms (thinking activity of the mind). Geometers use figures in their teaching, but their aim is to enable students to "see" the ideal, which can only be apprehended with the "eye" of thought.

The fourth stage of knowledge is that *perfect intelligence* whereby the mind is free of physical objects and deals exclusively with ideas. In this highest stage of knowledge a person totally leaves behind the world of appearances, and, depending only on ideas, sees the unity and interrelatedness of all knowledge. Using abstract reasoning alone the mind ascends to the sublime reality of the higher ideas and finally to Goodness itself.

The stages of knowledge for Plato can be diagrammed as follows:

	OBJECTS OF KNOWLEDGE	MODES OF REASON	
INTELLIGIBLE WORLD (BEING)	The Good Ideas/Forms	True Knowledge or Perfect Intelligence	KNOWLEDGE
	Mathematical Objects	Thought	
VISIBLE WORLD (BECOMING)	Physical Things	Belief	OPINION
	Images/ Appearances	Imagining	

By these stages Plato teaches that the path from ignorance to knowledge is a process, but not a natural or continuous progression. The mind makes its way to knowledge by a series of conversions from lower cognitive states (opinion) to higher states (perfect knowledge).

Plato also illustrated man's epistemological ascent from ignorance to knowledge in his famous allegory of the cave. The allegory depicts mankind as prisoners who have been chained since childhood in a dark cave. Behind them, and between them and the mouth of the cave, is a wall on which other people walk back and forth. Behind these people walking on the wall and carrying figures and other objects is a fire, and behind the fire is the mouth of the cave. The prisoners only see shadows, the shadows cast by those behind them on the wall. Assuming that the shadows on the wall are reality, the prisoners represent people who imagine that the shadowy physical objects before them are reality. Led by their passions and opinions of other people, they are truly prisoners of ignorance and have a distorted view of reality.

If one of the prisoners were to be released and brought to the fire, his eyes would ache and he would long to return to seeing shadows. If the prisoner were dragged into the sunlight outside the cave, his eyes would hurt even more severely, and he would have great difficulty adjusting to reality in the sunlight. But gradually, and only with great effort, he would take the final step and realize by gazing directly at the sun that the sun (being) makes all things visible, and that the sun supports life. It would be difficult for him to reenter the cave. If he did, the prisoners would ridicule his description of reality as viewed in the sunlight.[1]

By his allegory Plato taught that all people live in darkness, under the illusion that shadows are reality. Moreover, he argued that education and reason ought to lead men out of the cave. This can only occur when individuals are "converted" from focusing on the physical world to concentrating on the spiritual world of ideas. "The conversion of the soul is not to put the power of sight in the soul's eye, which already has it, but to insure that, instead of looking in the wrong direction, it is turned the way it ought to be."

For Plato, then, those who understand the reality of the transcendent world of ideas obtain absolute and infallible knowledge. Here was Plato's radical answer to the skepticism of the Sophists.

Aristotle

For twenty years Plato's premiere student, Aristotle, listened to these lofty thoughts as they came from the lips of his master. But as he matured in his thinking, Aristotle altered primary ideas of his teacher and developed his own distinctive philosophical system. Aristotle's interests spanned many disciplines (metaphysics, logic, psychology, biology, ethics, politics, and art), and while he contributed to each of these, perhaps his single most important achievement was his probing of knowledge itself. By dividing human knowledge into several broad fields, Aristotle laid the

---

1. Plato's allegory depicts what will happen when a true philosopher tries to explain the world of forms to an unenlightened public. Athens condemned Socrates for trying to "reenter the cave" with his forms in order to replace the Homeric deities.

foundation for much of Western philosophical speculation and empirical or scientific study. In the latter area his investigation of life forms in the lagoon of Pyrrha established him as the founder of systematic and comparative zoology. Because of his scientific interest at the Academy in Athens, Aristotle shifted his emphasis from the transcendent realm of being, which had been all-important to Plato, to the empirical realm of matter. Thus, Aristotle's epistemology emphasized becoming, whereas Plato's had emphasized being.

Aristotle declared that knowledge consists of facts and the meaning of facts. It includes observation and theory, fact and interpretation, the physical object and the form or idea. Unlike Plato, however, Aristotle saw the form or idea not residing in an ideal realm but in the physical object itself. Treeness is *in the tree* rather than in a timeless transcendent world. Every tree has a universal essence or idea (treeness) contained within it. We never find matter without form or, except for the unmoved mover, form without matter. Aristotle called the idea that form lies within the object "formal cause." The self-contained purpose embedded in any object, which determines what a thing is, is also called its "entelechy."

All things, according to Aristotle, are in the process of moving between pure potentiality (matter) and pure actuality (the unmoved mover). The unmoved mover is the impersonal soul or the intelligible form of the world. Everything in the universe is a mixture of matter and form, potentiality and actuality. The closer things are to pure actuality, the more form they contain. However, in the process of change, the closer things are to pure potentiality, the more matter predominates.

For Aristotle, the rational soul is the formal cause of the body. At birth the mind or soul begins as an empty tablet. The human soul has three aspects, which Aristotle called the *vegetative* (by which it simply lives), the *sensitive* (primarily involving sensing), and the *rational* (focussing on thinking). Human reason has the capacity to analyze, to categorize, to distinguish differences among the forms or essences of things. Reason, therefore, has the potential to obtain knowledge of reality, but it must thoroughly analyze its conclusions. By probing and classifying objects reason can penetrate beyond appearances to the form or essence of things. Thus, by using reason autonomous individuals, unaided by any higher power, can attain knowledge.

Aristotle distinguished three kinds of reasoning. *Dialectical* reasoning proceeds from "opinions that are generally accepted." It clarifies and defines ideas. *Eristic* or contentious reasoning starts with opinions that seem generally accepted but really are not. It questions and separates the true from the false. *Demonstrative* reasoning proves that the premises from which it begins are true.

Aristotle was most concerned to clarify the nature of demonstrative or deductive reasoning. Demonstrative reasoning starts from *archai* or first things (forms), principles or propositions that cannot be proved but that have absolute certainty. These axioms or presuppositions are discovered by observation and induction and become premises from which reason discovers further knowledge by deduction. Knowledge, for Aristotle, rests upon basic premises (*archai*) discovered as man "recognizes" or grasps them intuitively, by the immediate and direct insight of reason.

Once these basic premises are known, a person is able to engage in syllogistic reasoning, on which all knowledge depends. Aristotle defined a syllogism as "discourse in which certain things being stated, something other than what is stated follows of necessity from their being so." A syllogism has three parts: a major premise, a minor premise, and a conclusion.

> Major premise: All men are mortal.
> Minor premise: Socrates is a man.
> Conclusion: Socrates is mortal.

In deductive reasoning, once the major and minor premises are stated, the conclusion follows. Valid demonstration is always reducible to a syllogism. The question remains, How do we acquire first principles, the starting point of deduction?

In the reasoning process, Aristotle argued, people discover the major premises by induction and observation. He argued, for example, that the axiom "the whole is greater than any of its parts" is inherent in reason, but is only made explicit by our experience in the world. Similarly, in the case of our syllogism on human mortality, our learning of people dying in the past is an experience that leads us to believe in human mortality. Only as we accept as a premise that all humans are mortal—because we cannot know from past experience that all people (past, present, and future) die—can we conclude that any one person, Socrates, is mortal. Therefore, although our knowledge begins with sense perception, the capacity of reason to grasp or apprehend universals in our experience of particulars enables us to form premises on which deductive reasoning depends. Inductive or scientific thought provides the foundation for demonstrative thought. Throughout the whole process, the autonomy of reason is presupposed by Aristotle as the means by which man discovers truth and knowledge.

Conclusion

Plato and Aristotle effectively answered the skepticism of the Sophists. Sophists doubted that people could achieve true knowledge because of their shifting, relativistic experiences of the empirical, physical world. Plato and Aristotle, by contrast, believed that reliable knowledge is possible because it rests upon unchanging and universal forms discovered by human reason. Knowledge is absolute insofar as it is based upon the eternal forms.

Plato and Aristotle built an epistemology on the assumption that human reason is autonomous, self-sufficient, and essentially good. Through reason human beings obtain knowledge and salvation. The Greek philosophers, unlike the biblical writers, recognize no need for God or for revelation from on high. Rational man can achieve the good life on earth by his own efforts.

In the years that followed, most Greeks rejected the teachings of Socrates, Plato, and Aristotle and returned to the Sophistic reliance on sense experience as the best path to knowledge. This approach again led to relativism, and, consequently, skepticism and cynicism revived. These three great Greek thinkers, however, lifted philosophy to new heights, which have seldom been equalled.

Classical Greek thinkers never succeeded in relating eternal, invisible, universals or forms to particular objects. They did, however, impress upon Western culture an awareness that the basis for knowledge is eternal and is beyond physical objects. Despite Socrates', Plato's, and Aristotle's failure to recognize the limitations and deficiencies of reason, they initiated a long tradition based on reason's ability to discover truth and to establish knowledge. The classical Greeks tended to deify humanity and reason and thus laid a foundation for centuries of naturalistic humanism. But their emphasis on human potential lifted man above bondage to nature. It is not surprising that in every age people have turned back to reexamine the philosophies of the Greeks. The problems with which they wrestled are ageless. Even in the twentieth century thoughtful persons still struggle with the questions they raised, and some rationalists and humanists still rely upon the answers they proposed.

For Further Reading

Amadio, Anselm H. "Aristotle," *The Encyclopedia Britannica*. 15th ed. Chicago: Britannica, 1974.

Burnet, John. *Greek Philosophy: Thales to Plato*. London: Macmillan, 1914.

Cherniss, H. F. *Aristotle's Criticism of Plato and the Academy*. Baltimore, 1944.

Clark, Gordon H. *Thales to Dewey*. Boston: Houghton Mifflin, 1957.

Copleston, Frederick C. *A History of Philosophy*, vol. 1. Garden City, N.Y.: Doubleday, 1962.

Cornford, F. M. *Before and After Socrates*. New York: Cambridge University Press, 1960.

———. *Plato's Theory of Knowledge*. New York: Liberal Arts Press, 1935.

Hamlyn, D. W. "Epistemology, History of," *The Encyclopedia of Philosophy*, vol. 3. New York: Macmillan, 1967.

Kerford, G. B. "Aristotle," *The Encyclopedia of Philosophy*, vol. 6. New York: Macmillan, 1967.

———. *The Sophistic Movement.* New York: Cambridge University Press, 1981.

Randall, John H. *Aristotle.* New York: Columbia University Press, 1960.

Ross, W. D. *Plato's Theory of Ideas.* Oxford: Clarendon Press, 1951.

Runciman, W. G. *Plato's Later Epistemology.* Cambridge: Cambridge University Press, 1962.

Stewart, J. A. *Plato's Doctrine of Ideas.* New York: Oxford, 1909.

II.
MEDIEVAL AND
REFORMATIONAL
EPISTEMOLOGIES

12
Augustine, Aquinas, and the Reformers

W. Andrew Hoffecker

Introduction

Today we tend to assume that all people living during the Middle Ages thought alike, that they all embraced the same system of thought, namely Christianity. Some scholars speak of a "medieval mind" as if we could select any two thinkers at random from the fifth to the fourteenth centuries and find that their thought was identical. While there was much theological agreement during the Middle Ages, alternatives to Christianity did exist. Not only did Judaism have able philosophers and theologians during these years, but in the seventh century the world's third monotheistic religion burst onto the scene. In less than one hundred years Islamic civilization became such a threatening force to the Christian West that crusades were mounted against the "infidel" from the eleventh to the thirteenth centuries. The ideas of outstanding Muslim philosophers such as Averroes and Avicenna were read widely by Jewish and Christian thinkers alike.

Despite this diversity of belief, two Christian theologians dominated the epistemology of the Middle Ages: Augustine, Bishop of Hippo, and Thomas Aquinas, the great Dominican scholar. While both appealed to biblical revelation, they used the ideas of Greek philosophers to interpret this revelation. Augustine drew from Plato's thought; Aquinas leaned heavily on Aristotle. Their epistemologies, therefore, combined biblical and Greek principles, though toward the end of his career, Augustine espoused a more thoroughly biblical view. Thomas, however, unabashedly employed Aristotelian rationalism as an apologetic tool to fashion a distinctive natural theology.

As the Reformation dawned, disagreement with medieval Catholics over epistemology figured as prominently in Luther's and Calvin's thought as their views on indulgences, merit, and justification by faith. One of their themes, *sola Scriptura*, affirmed the Bible as their only authority for Christian doctrine. The Reformers' efforts to recover a biblical epistemology reflected their desire for a church reformed according to the Word of God.

Augustine's Epistemology

During his stormy career Augustine passed through several schools of thought prior to his conversion to Christianity. First a teacher of rhetoric, he then turned to skepticism. For a time he dabbled in Manichaeism, but he gave it up because its dualism failed to answer sufficiently the problem of evil. He adopted Neoplatonism for a time and continued to be influenced by that school, especially its epistemology, even after his conversion. His whole life was a search for truth, and after becoming a Christian, he wrote strong critiques against the schools of thought he had once espoused.

In *Concerning the Beautiful Life* Augustine sharply attacked the first group he had joined, the skeptics. Skepticism had its roots in pre-Socratic Greece. Its subsequent leaders rejected Plato's metaphysical position. As their name implies, the skeptics denied that man can achieve certainty regarding anything. Despite this assertion, they purported to make their pupils wise. Obviously "wisdom" here must mean something different from the usual understanding of the term. In their view, a person is wise not because he knows something but because he refuses to assent to anything for fear of falling into error. Wisdom, therefore, results from denying certainty and substituting in its place mere probability. Happiness is found in the pursuit rather than the attainment and possession of the truth. To suspend judgment is the mark of the wise man. The skeptic who is true to his position does not even claim that he is certain he cannot know.

Augustine retorted that it is absurd to attribute wisdom to people who by their own admission have no knowledge of the truth. No one is truly wise if he does not know anything. Not only is truth attainable, said Augustine, but it is impossible not to know some things. In *Against the Academics*[1] Augustine proposed that when some kinds of disjunctive statements are made, ("either . . . or" statements) even skeptics must agree that certainty is possible. For example, they are sure that there is *either* only one world *or* more than one. If more than one world exists, its number must be *either* finite *or* infinite. Of these pairs of assertions one statement must be true and the other false. Both cannot be true.

If the objection is raised that such statements are misleading because they presuppose a knowledge of the world based on the senses, which can deceive the knower, Augustine had a ready answer that he considered to be the fatal blow for skepticism. Even if the knower is deceived in his knowledge, he is at least *certain* of his subjective impression. No sophistry can deprive him of the knowledge that he thinks his impressions are correct. Augustine concluded: "If I am deceived, I exist! For one who does not exist cannot be deceived. Consequently I exist if I am deceived." Therefore, even in the very act of deception itself some *certainty* is possible.

Augustine's statement preceded Descartes's famous "I think, therefore I am" (*cogito ergo sum*)[2] by hundreds of years. The important difference between Augustine and Descartes was how each used his respective idea. Descartes made his *cogito* the all-important premise from which the rest of his philosophy was rationally deduced. He considered self-existence the first premise of all thinking. Augustine by contrast used such an idea as only *one* of several basic presuppositions or premises. Knowledge of God's existence and knowledge of the created order are other certainties in his view of reality. Man cannot abstract one of these and isolate it from the others. Self-existence especially cannot replace the existence of God as the basis of thought. Our basic ideas must be *correlative*. In the act of knowing ourselves, we are

1. The skeptics were members of the New Academy in Athens in the third century b.c.
2. Descartes's ideas are discussed in chapter 13.

aware of God on whom we are dependent. In knowing God, we are also aware of ourselves, and the world around us.

The point of Augustine's discussion is the primacy of immediate intellectual cognition, the awareness of self, and the awareness of God. He begins not with sense experience but with an intellectual awareness of one's own existence. In the same act of knowledge he also knows the existence of God. Such a dual act of knowledge is due to the unique constitution of our minds. We do not know our own existence or God's existence by inference. While both may be explained by inference, something is prior to inference: our intuitive awareness of ourselves and of our Creator. To any form of empiricism—whether that of the skeptics, who said we can know only our impressions, which are probable, or that of Aristotle, who said that knowledge begins with sense experience—Augustine gave the same response: knowledge begins with neither sensation nor abstract speculation, but in immediate awareness of our own and God's existence.

Augustine's epistemology, therefore, has faith as its foundation. His faith was not some nebulous cognitive act by which he hoped God exists, but an activity of the whole man, heart, mind, and soul. The object of his faith was his all-important epistemological foundation. In his commentary on the Gospel of John he wrote: "Understanding is the reward of faith. Therefore seek not to understand in order that you may believe, but believe in order that you may understand." He shortened this into a succinct motto that captures his epistemology: *credo ut intelligam*—"I believe in order that I might understand." Augustine took his motto from the Old Testament prophet Isaiah (7:9): "Unless you believe, you shall not understand." He noted that Jesus Himself invited men first to believe in Him: "He [Jesus] did not say 'This is life eternal so that they may believe.' Instead he said, 'This is life eternal that they may know thee. . . . ' Then to those who believed He said, 'Seek and you shall find' " (*On the Freedom of the Will* 2. 2). People believe first what they come to understand afterwards. In fact the task of reason is to seek deeper understanding of what a person already believes by faith.

No Greek philosopher would ever have contemplated making

revealed truth (faith) the necessary starting point for rational knowledge. Augustine's epistemology stands Greek thought on its head. Man's knowledge is rooted in what he believes by faith; unless we believe first, we shall not understand by reason.

Augustine did not relegate reason to the ash heap. Far from it. He did not opt for a simple fideism, a system resting on blind faith incapable of being rationally interpreted. Augustine simply subordinated reason to revelation. Divine revelation is the precondition for all that we know. The existence of a sovereign God who created the world, made man in His own image, and redeemed him by His grace serves as the epistemological starting point for all thinking. We cannot think about anything, therefore, without presupposing God and His revelation: "From God we derive the beginning of existence, the principles of knowledge, the law of affection" (*Contra Faustum* 20. 7).

Once God and His Word are accepted as the starting point for all predication, then believers seek to understand all truth in light of God. All truth that is to be known by means of reason is founded not in our use of reason, but in God Himself. Augustine viewed all knowledge, whether rational or sensible, in the larger context of God's existence and creative activity. God is the source not only of all existence but also of its meaning and therefore of man's knowledge of both being and meaning.

Augustine's epistemology sprang from his biblical theism. The God of Christianity as revealed in the Bible has shown Himself to mankind, whom He has made with a mind that can think God's thoughts after Him. That does not mean our minds are merely an aspect of God's thought. B. B. Warfield rightly captured Augustine's thinking on this crucial point: Augustine "preserves the distinctness of the human soul at the same time that he discovers in the intelligible world open to the soul a point of contact with God" (*Studies in Tertullian and Augustine*, p. 148). Thus in his soul man perceives the existence of God with the same force and clarity that he perceives his own existence; and because the two are correlative, man perceives both to be true simultaneously.

Augustine's View of Illumination

Augustine elaborated a view of innate ideas or wisdom that is consonant with the perspective of general revelation discussed in the chapter on biblical epistemology. *All* of man's knowledge is based on God's illuminating truth to the mind. His view of innate ideas is not to be confused with seventeenth century deism. In that rationalist tradition innate ideas are impressed on the mind to give human beings autonomy in their thinking with the result that God has no relation to the truth that people know in exercising their rational capacities.

In *On Freedom of the Will* Augustine elaborates this view of ideas. He begins with an exhortation that illustrates his motto: "Lean upon piety and follow the paths of reason. There is nothing so hard and difficult that it cannot be made clear and obvious by God's help. Let us take up our investigations, then, depending on Him and praying for His help" (1. 6). The rational quest for Augustine begins with an acknowledgment of our dependence upon God in the search itself.

We know truth because it is illuminated to our minds by God. Truth is real, objective, and unchanging. "It is God Himself who has empowered your reason to think so clearly and devoutly about Him." But reason is not itself the starting point of intellectual pursuit. As a human faculty it is prone to human weaknesses. Reason is clearly proved to be "mutable [changeable] now struggling to arrive at the truth, now ceasing to struggle, sometimes reaching and sometimes not." Reason has its limitations and is therefore inferior to God's revelation. As revelation's inferior, its task is to *submit* to the truth rather than judge it. "If reason . . . catches sight of something eternal and immutable, ought it not at the same time recognize its own inferiority and proclaim this something to be God?" Insight, therefore, stems not from our autonomous epistemological search, but from God's gracious disclosure. Augustine thereby deftly affirmed that Christianity is rational (capable of rational explanation) but not rationalistic (under the dominance of an impersonal, abstract reason, which usurps the place of God).

Augustine's view of illumination has some affinities with Plato's.

Augustine claims that wisdom is impressed on our minds. It is objective in that it is based on something external to the mind, yet simultaneously it is present within the mind. He illustrates this in two ways. Man knows numbers not by means of the senses but by means of reason: " . . . the order and truth of number have nothing to do with the bodily senses, but are unchangeable and true and common to all beings" (2. 8). Second, he points out that the rules of wisdom are the same for all people. We know that wisdom exists and that we ought to seek it. For example, we know that we ought to live justly and that we ought to prefer the better rather than the worse. These norms and "guiding lights" are "true and unchangeable, and whether taken singly or all together, are there in common sight for each who with his own mind and reason can perceive them" (2. 10).

When we recognize truths such as these, Augustine contended, we are aware that our minds do not control truth, but that truth controls our minds. That is why he used the terms *norm* and *guiding light* to refer to wisdom or truth. Recognizing that truth is superior to the mind is crucial. Our minds are incapable of judging these norms because we use them to think. The laws of the mind serve to reveal God's truth to us. For example, our minds do not make two plus two equal four. They simply recognize that it is so. Our minds cannot make the sum any different because our thinking is under the authority of the truth.

Using striking similes Augustine sings the praises of truth. Just as men are enthralled when they embrace their wives, so are they happy in the arms of truth. Just as water quenches one's thirst, so truth satisfies the seeking mind. In the same way that people are enchanted with the perfume of flowers and ointments, so they love to inhale the "bouquet of truth." As much as an individual person can appreciate truth, it is not the private possession of one alone.

> It abides in no place yet is absent from none. It admonishes us from without, it teaches us from within. All who hold it are changed for the better; by no one is it changed for the worse. No one passes judgment upon it or judges rightly without it. That is why it is clear beyond the shadow of a

doubt that it is superior to our minds, none of which dares judge it, yet each of which becomes wise and a judge of all other things by means of it (2. 14).

But what is this that is superior to the mind of man? Only God Himself, who reveals Himself to be Truth.[3] Whenever anyone knows truth, therefore, his knowledge is due to God's illuminating it to his mind. Any man who knows truth knows it because "the true Light that enlightens every man" has revealed it (John 1:6).

While Augustine's view of illumination is superficially similar to Plato's explanation, it breaks sharply with Plato's contention that knowledge by illumination consists in mere recollection. Augustine argued that knowledge by illumination is connected to natural revelation and God's providential activity in history. Divine illumination as God's gift to the entire human race enabling them to attain knowledge is similar to God's order of the universe and control of events in history, which reveal God's power and wisdom to all people. Such a view underscores Augustine's strong reliance on the biblical world view, which teaches that we are constantly dependent on God as Creator and sustainer of life.

Another element of Augustine's epistemology also departs sharply from Plato's: his view of the relation between sin and knowledge. Because of original sin the human will is a slave to sin, making people powerless to save themselves from their sins. But original sin affects more than our wills. Sin renders the mind blind to the truth and ignorant of God. Even though people know their Creator exists, they refuse to worship Him, and they rebel against Him. Sin, therefore, impedes human knowledge, and this obstacle grows worse with the passing of time. The *a priori* knowledge of God given in our immediate relationship with God is held in disobedience, or suppressed. We know God innately but refuse to worship Him and instead use our knowledge to rebel against God and His kingdom. Augustine reiterated the biblical teaching that no thinking is ethically or spiritually neutral. All

3. Cf. Jesus' words in John 14:6, "I am . . . the truth."

knowledge carries with it a moral or spiritual obligation to act in keeping with the moral character of its source, God Himself.

This means that God's special revelation, His saving grace, is an absolute necessity. Viewing man holistically, Augustine stressed that people's willful disobedience not only cripples their wills and their affections, but clouds their knowledge as well. God's illumination of truth to the mind and His communication of Himself in the incarnation are the twin foci of His revelatory activity. The first prepares us for the latter but is insufficient without it. Human sinfulness necessitates both that God reveal Himself in history so that people can know Him as Savior and Lord and that He actually release sinners from their lost condition.

In the Platonic tradition, by contrast, no individual sins intentionally. No such serious obstacle stands between knowing the Good and pursuing it. As long as a person avoids the error of trying to use his senses to know the truth and instead uses clear rational insight, he can ascend to, apprehend, and follow the Good. But according to Augustine, we first need God's grace in order to know and accomplish the Good.

Augustine's understanding of illumination differs from Plato's as well. Plato's Good is an impersonal, abstract being, a "sun" that enlightens the mind. In Plato's famous allegory of the cave, man works his way from the "shadows" of ignorance into the "light" of day, which is knowledge. For Augustine, as we have seen, the Light that illuminates our thinking is none other than the transcendent, personal Triune God of the Bible.

Summary of Augustine's Epistemology

In his epistemology Augustine brought out the implications of ideas that dominated his theology and anthropology. Because God's sovereignty is paramount, knowledge is wholly dependent on His revelation. God requires people to submit to His sovereign self-disclosure. Because human beings use reason to understand truth they received by faith, belief is the prerequisite for further understanding. The Triune God teaches individuals all facts of true knowledge. In the external world known by the senses we are prone to error, and our finiteness and sinfulness limit our understanding. Augustine concluded, therefore, that just as man needs God's grace to be saved from the peril of sin and death, he also needs God's illumination to regenerate or renew his knowledge. Mankind is not self-sufficient and autonomous but is dependent upon the sovereign grace of God. In our thinking, as in all other faculties, we display both our finite limitations and our sinfulness. The grace of God, however, can transform the mind into an instrument that moves from faith to understanding.

Thomistic Epistemology

Thomas Aquinas lived almost eight hundred years after Augustine during the high point of the Middle Ages. An earlier chapter described Aquinas's preoccupation with Aristotelian philosophy and his break with the predominant medieval synthesis of Platonic and Christian elements. Christian, Jewish, and Moslem philosophers were all confronted with a novel epistemological method in the Aristotelian world view. It placed the same reliance on human rationality as Plato's did, yet with a totally different emphasis. Knowledge, instead of originating in the human mind through recollection and illumination, was regarded as beginning with the senses. As noted in the chapter on Greek epistemology, Aristotle attributed to our minds the power to organize sense data and to demonstrate truth through deductive reasoning. Aristotle used his empirical method to prove the existence of his "God," the unmoved mover.

Thomas found Aristotle's method very appealing. With its emphasis on rational demonstration using evidences from everyday experience, it promised him an apologetic method that could, with a few minor alterations, establish the existence of the Christian God and the truth of the Christian faith.

Thomas reaffirmed Aristotle's teaching that the mind at birth is like a blank wax tablet, in need of sense perception to supply the materials for natural knowledge. "The first thing which is known by us in the state of our present life is the material thing, which is the object of the intellect" (*Summa Theologica* 1a. 88. 3). Since human beings are a unity of body and soul, our minds are affected by the senses in the acquisition of ideas and knowledge. This reveals the empiricist cast of Thomas's epistemology and underscores his basic assertion that the Aristotelian method provides a proper foundation for natural knowledge.

But Thomas was not a pure empiricist, and he did not believe that the mind is merely a passive receiver of sense impressions. Man's mind is active as well. It synthesizes sense data and interprets the information the senses provide. In Aquinas's view the mind contributes certain self-evident principles to the knowing process. Aquinas could well have endorsed the dictum of the eighteenth-century philosopher Immanuel Kant that "though all our knowledge begins with experience, it by no means follows that all arises out of experience" (*Critique of Pure Reason*, Intro. 1). This is evident when Thomas explains the role of what he called the imagination: "For the mind actually to understand something there is required an act of the imagination and of the other sensitive faculties not only in receiving fresh knowledge, but also in using knowledge already acquired. . . . " (*Summa Theologica* 1a. 84. 3). The mind's activity is apparent in its reflective capacity: "Truth is known by the mind according as the mind reflects on its act" (*De Veritate* 1. 9).

Thomas's method represents a distinct break from Augustine's. Following Plato, Augustine questioned sense experience and began instead with purely intellectual intuition. Thomas, however, boldly accepted sensation as the legitimate starting point of knowledge. To Aquinas material things are the primary objects of the human mind. If we are to get beyond them to a being who transcends the physical world, we must accept as valid the data of sense experience and reflect systematically on their significance. Knowledge by inference rather than immediate intuition is at the heart of Thomas's epistemological method.

Thus Thomas sought to show the feasibility of a natural metaphysic, that is, a rational investigation of what lies beyond physical reality. Using the senses to analyze the physical world enables man to know something of the reality that transcends this realm. Reason equips the Christian and the non-Christian alike to (1) begin with the immediate data of sense experience, (2) reflect on that experience, and (3) come to a mutual conclusion that a God exists who transcends the physical reality known by the senses. Knowledge of God comes primarily through inferences drawn from the physical world rather than through personal experience felt in the heart. Specifically, Thomas believed that the world is so structured and the mind of man so constituted that systematic reflection will lead all who reflected rationally on the data of sense experience to believe in God's existence.

Therefore, the point of departure for Aquinas is what all people already know and understand. When we utilize what we know without any doubt, reason is sufficient to lead us to a conviction that God exists. Thomas's epistemological motto is the converse of Augustine's. Whereas Augustine had said "I believe in order that I may understand," (faith is the presupposition that leads to rational understanding), Thomas's motto was *intelligo ut credam*: "I understand in order that I may believe." Systematically reflecting on the data of experience leads to the conclusion that these data are not self-sufficient. Because these data are not self-explanatory, humans must assume or postulate that there is a transcendent being on which these data depend for their very existence.

Building on these views Thomas attempted to construct rational arguments to prove God's existence. We call his attempt a *natural theology* because he sought to demonstrate the existence of God not from revelation (the Bible) but from rational arguments based on empirical evidences verified by any impartial observer. Each argument begins with a common observation about the physical world. Thomas attempted to demonstrate that these data do not possess of themselves a sufficient explanation for their being and are therefore dependent upon some higher explanation—God. Thomas claimed that if the agnostic would give his unbiased attention to some readily verifiable facts about the world, he could be convinced that God exists. Thomas's proofs for the existence of God are so significant in the history of Christian thought that we will examine them in some detail. Because of their number they have been called "the Five Ways."

Thomas adopted Aristotle's argument from motion as his first proof. We observe through sense perception that objects in the physical world move or change in the sense that an object's potentiality becomes actual. A piece of wood, he said, can be heated and burned if fire is applied to it. Thus anything in the process of change or motion is being changed by something else, which in turn is moved by still another thing. Since an infinite regress of movers is impossible, there must be a first, unmoved mover, "and all understand that this is God."

The second "way" is similar to the first, but it focuses on efficient cause rather than motion. We commonly experience in nature series of causes. For example, in billiards a cue ball striking another ball causes it to move. Since nothing can cause itself, and we experience causes in succession—x (the billiard player hits the cue ball) causes y (the cue ball rolls across the table and strikes the eight ball), which causes z (the eight ball rolls into the corner pocket)—and since, as in the first proof, an infinite series (in this instance a series of causes) is impossible, therefore, there must be a first cause "which all call 'God.' "

Thomas's third proof is from contingency. A careful examination of physical reality reveals that natural objects are contingent. Because they come into being and finally perish, they are not necessary beings. Animals are born and die, plants bloom in the spring and perish in the fall, and man-made objects are created and can be destroyed. Contingent beings can be and not be; there is no necessity to their being. If they were necessary, they would always be. Thomas argued that a necessary being must exist to explain the existence of contingent beings. For if everything is contingent, once there was nothing, which would leave us with no basis for reality since something cannot come from nothing.

That everyone makes judgments of good, better, and best is the basis for Thomas's fourth proof. Using Aristotle's *Metaphysics* Thomas argued that everyone discerns degrees of perfection, goodness, and truth in everyday experiences. We make judgments such as "Tom plays tennis better than Robert, but Drew is best on the team." Our recognition of comparatives implies that not only is there in actuality a most perfect, a best, or an ultimate truth, but such a perfect being is the source of perfections we observe. "And this we call 'God.' "

Thomas's final "way" is the well-known argument from design. In inorganic nature we frequently discern patterns exhibited by things that, lacking the power of intention, cannot direct themselves. Changes of the tides, the seasons, and even day and night result from the orderly movement of planets. Thomas's example is that an arrow flying through the air and into the bull's eye moves not by chance but as aimed by an archer. Thus everything in nature is moved toward its goal by someone with intelligence, "and this one we call 'God.' "

The Five Ways illustrate how people can use unaided, autonomous reason to prove the existence of God. Thomas began with the assumption that God is known indirectly or by inference. Augustine had maintained that knowledge of God was directly or immediately given to the mind simultaneously with the awareness of one's own experience. Only thus could knowledge of God and self be so clearly related. This knowledge, for Augustine, is not merely intellectual in nature but also preeminently personal, or what we might call in contemporary terms "existential." Knowing that God exists cannot be separated from being personally related to Him.

Thomas adopted a different view. We know God by means of a two-step sequence. We can separate knowing that God exists from actually knowing Him existentially. We first come to an intellectual conviction that God exists, an assent of the mind to the proposition that there is a God. Only then do we take the second step, the deeply personal act of placing our confidence or trust in God. What Augustine joined together in one act of intellectual and personal awareness, Aquinas separated into two parts. Thomas's view is open to the charge that, at one level, knowledge of God is merely an interesting philosophical problem to be solved by the activity of the mind.

All of the Five Ways are devoted exclusively to producing rational assent to the proposition that a first mover, first cause, necessary being, most perfect being, and designer exists. The arguments focus our attention on motion, cause, contingent being, etc., in order that we might see their dependence on transcendent being.

Philosophers and theologians after Aquinas have debated the cogency of the Five Ways. Since Immanuel Kant's refutation of them in the eighteenth century, most thinkers have recognized them to be invalid as proofs. At most, they establish the probability that God exists rather than actually demonstrating the necessity of God's existence. All of the arguments assume a real relation between finite thought (the arguments) and the supersensible reality the arguments represent (God). But, as has so often been pointed out, we must not confuse argument with being (ideas with the actual existence of what they represent). Therefore, the arguments do not constitute *proof* in the strictest sense.

Another major criticism of Thomas's approach is that although each argument concludes with words to the effect that "all call this 'God,' " only the fifth argument in any way necessitates that God be personal in nature. The remaining arguments at best establish the existence of the impersonal, abstract, aloof, philosophically speculative construction of Aristotle—his unmoved mover. They do not present the sovereignly transcendent, personal God of the Christian faith.

Thomas regarded God's existence as the last or highest proof of philosophy. As such it is adequate only to demonstrate *that* a superior being really exists. But in order to know more about that being, philosophy must be supplemented with sacred doctrine. Man requires a knowledge superior to that provided by philosophy.

> Sacred doctrine is a science. We must bear in mind that there are two kinds of science. There are some which proceed from principles known by the natural light of the intellect, such as arithmetic and geometry. . . . There are also some which proceed from principles known by the light of a higher science. . . . Sacred doctrine is a science because it proceeds from principles made known by the light of a higher science, namely, the science of God (*Summa Theologica* 1. 2).

Theology is a science of sacred doctrine. It provides the higher knowledge man needs. Whereas God's existence is the *last* or highest proof of philosophy, it is the *first* truth of theology. Theology continues where philosophy and human reason end. We need to know more than the mere fact that God exists. Without theology we would not know that God is triune, that He is love, that He saves man from sin, that there is a future judgment, etc. In order to find out what God is like and what He requires of man, the natural knowledge of philosophy must be supplemented with the superior knowledge provided by revelation.

> It was necessary for man's salvation that there should also be a knowledge revealed by God besides the philosophical sciences investigated by human reason. First because man is directed to God as to an end that surpasses the grasp of his reason (*Summa Theologica* 1. 1).

Revelation confirms the truth about God achieved through rational argument but goes on to elaborate what we need in order to be saved. Aquinas, therefore, recognized the inadequacy of Aristotle's epistemology. It does not equip us to know all that we need to know. Revelation is especially necessary because not all people are able or take the effort to engage in rational argumentation.

> Instruction by the divine revelation was necessary even about truths concerning God which are accessible to the human reason. For otherwise they would have been found only by a few men and after a long time, and then, mixed with many errors. And the whole salvation of man, which is to be found in God, depends on the knowledge of this truth (*Summa Theologica* 1a. 1. 1).

Once again, this time in Thomas's epistemology, we find a sharp distinction between the natural and the supernatural. In separating reason and revelation, philosophy and theology, Aquinas allowed considerable autonomy to human rationality. In distinguishing theology from philosophy and claiming that we are capable of demonstrating God's existence apart from revelation, Aquinas exalted our rational capacity and implicitly affirmed that sin has virtually no effect on one important area of man's life, his knowledge. The Thomistic method denies any noetic effect of sin.

In Thomas's epistemology, theology is "queen of the sciences," over all other academic disciplines. It is distinct from and superior to the rest of man's rational pursuits. Theologians are to study revealed truth, and the visible church as instructor in the Christian faith is entrusted with the task of interpreting it to Christians. In order to instruct believers and combat heresy, the church is to use two sources: Scripture and sacred tradition—the writings of the church fathers and decisions of the ecumenical councils (such as Nicaea). The church also stands under the authoritative leadership of the pope, the Bishop of Rome. Even though papal infallibility was not officially declared the dogma of the Catholic Church until 1870, Thomas was one of its strongest advocates in the Middle Ages.

Summary of Aquinas's Epistemology

The idea we have found to be central to the theology and anthropology of Thomas—the dichotomy between nature and grace—reappears in his epistemology. Seen in the distinctions between soul and body, clergy and laity, the church and the world, philosophy and theology, and reason and revelation, it is clearly the dominating theme of his world view.

Thomas intended to show that the Christian faith rests on rational foundations and that philosophy need not lead to a rejection of the Christian faith. Reason and revelation are correlated, not antithetical. While revelation might reveal something that transcends reason, it will not contradict it. To say otherwise would be to suggest that God gave man a rational faculty that actually leads to a denial of the Christian faith rather than its defense. Thomas considered it inconceivable that God would give man a gift of reason that would make him an atheist. Thomas's emphasis on the rational foundations of faith, however, amounted to the humanistic epistemology of Aristotle dressed up in Christian garb. In his epistemology as in his theology and anthropology, Thomas adopted a synthetic mixture of Greek and Christian ideas.

Luther's and Calvin's Recovery of Biblical and Augustinian Thought

The debate between Augustinian and Thomistic thinkers over epistemological issues did not cease with the Middle Ages. The struggle came to a head as Martin Luther grew dissatisfied with the Thomistic medieval tradition. An opening skirmish of the Reformation was Luther's dramatic debate with John Eck, a staunch defender of the medieval church and all it represented, at Leipzig in 1519. Prior to their confrontation Luther rejected papal infallibility and final authority. During the actual debate Eck pressed the Wittenberg professor until he also denied the authority of church councils in favor of trusting the Bible alone for what he believed.

Thus Luther began publicly to reject medieval epistemologies. Finally in his own inimitable fashion, Luther waged a frontal assault on Aristotelian reason by declaring that unregenerate reason is "the Devil's whore!" He denounced Thomistic rational- ism and condemned universities where Aristotle's ideas were held in higher esteem than Christ's teachings. Christians should reject as authorities in natural or spiritual matters Aristotle's *Physics*, *Metaphysics*, *On the Soul*, and *Ethics*. Luther's attack on Aristotle was not an anti-intellectual tirade. He was simply protesting Christians' uncritical acceptance of a pagan perspective on mat- ters where the Scriptures spoke very clearly.

Instead he called for the reintroduction of the Scriptures as the primary source of Christian thought. For even though they were written by men, they are not "of men nor from men, but from God." Furthermore, Christians should read and understand the Bible in the simplest way possible: " . . . the words of God . . . are to be retained in their simplest meaning wherever possible, and to be understood in their grammatical and literal sense unless the context clearly forbids" (*The Babylonian Captivity of the Church*). Thus Luther not only reaffirmed biblical authority but also rejected the much used allegorical interpretation of Scripture. By this method theologians try to find "spiritual" or figurative, rather than historical and literal, interpretations of all passages. Luther returned to the Scripture, arguing that Aristotle exalted human reason to a position of autonomy in its quest for knowledge. Not that Luther believed that rational knowledge was useless. He thought, rather, that it was unable to give man in his fallen condition knowledge of spiritual things. Only scriptural revelation could provide this. Like other human faculties, reason was marred by the fall. Thus people could not apprehend even such rudimentary spiritual concepts as the existence of God by reason alone:

> The knowledge of how one may stand before God and attain to eternal life . . . is truly not to be achieved by our work or power, nor to originate in our brain. . . . In spiritual matters, human reasoning is not in order; other intelligence, other skill and power are requisite here—something to be granted by God himself and revealed through his Word (Epistle Sermon, Twelfth Sunday after Trinity).

Luther translated into action his belief in the Bible's authority. When Frederick the Wise, his political benefactor, hid Luther in Wartburg Castle after Luther was declared an outlaw at Worms, Luther used Erasmus's Greek text to translate the Bible into German. His writing was so idiomatic and eminently readable that his Bible left an indelible mark not only on the Protestant world view, but on the German language as well. Thus in his epistemology, as in his theology and anthropology, Luther broke radically with medieval Catholicism. As long as the church of his day continued to hold to the theology of Aquinas, harmonious relations were impossible.

Calvin also carefully integrated his theological and anthropological themes into his epistemological views. In fact, the *Institutes* begin by discussing our knowledge of God. Calvin saw it not as an abstract subject unrelated to our knowledge in other areas, but rather as the very integrating basis of all our knowing. Medieval philosophers had tended to discuss the knowledge of God as knowing truths about God. As we have seen, Calvin, by contrast, stressed how knowing God is indispensably experiential or, in contemporary terms, personal and intimate. To know God as omnipotent, omniscient Creator and Redeemer was, to Calvin, no mere cognitive, intellectual experience. To know God is to worship Him. Christians do not hold abstract speculations in their minds; they commune with a living, personal Reality. Theoretical knowledge about God is far different from knowing God existentially in humble adoration and praise.

Calvin also believed that it is impossible for a person to know God without knowing himself and to know himself without knowing God.

> No one can look upon himself without immediately turning his thoughts to the contemplation of God. . . . Again, it is certain that man never achieves a clear knowledge of himself unless he has first looked upon God's face, and then descends from contemplating him to scrutinize himself (*Institutes* 1. 1. 1, 2).

Some theologians agree that the term "existential" best describes Calvin's view of the knowledge of God. It reflects the dynamic and personal character of human knowledge. Calvin maintained a balance between the objectivity of our knowledge and the subjective nature of the knowing act itself.

In addition, Calvin stressed that every person intuitively possesses some sense of deity. This is not a speculative knowledge; God has so made us that we have an innate sense of His deity. "All have by nature an innate persuasion of the Divine existence, a persuasion inseparable from their very constitution" (*Institutes* 1. 3. 1). Such knowledge is not learned in the universities "but one of which each of us is master from his mother's womb and which nature itself permits no one to forget . . . " (*Institutes* 1. 3. 3).

Even though God has implanted knowledge of Himself in every person, sinful men ignore and even deny this "seed of religion." Rather than benefiting from it, they suppress and distort it so that they fail to do what knowledge of God demands—worship Him. Under the blinding influence of sin, all people turn from God. But the evidence of His existence is so clear that we are responsible for turning from Him. Because of our sinfulness our unaided rational powers and natural will cannot enable us to know God. We need the gift of God's Word, the Bible. Calvin compared the Bible to a pair of spectacles given so that people can see God, themselves, and the whole creation more clearly.

For Calvin, as for Luther, the true source of the knowledge of God is not Aristotelian reason or the tradition of the church, but the Scriptures alone. As God's revelation it is "self-authenticated," which means that the Bible is dependent for its authority not on external "proof and reasoning," but on the inner testimony of the Holy Spirit. God's Holy Spirit produces a conviction "that requires no reasons" (*Institutes* 1. 7. 5). While others might dwell on rational proofs, Christians receive their conviction that the Bible is the Word of God from the inner witness of God's Spirit, who is also author of the Word. Calvin's perspective is clearly analogous to Augustine's view in which we are dependent on God's illumination for all knowledge, and especially for our knowledge of God. Believers know God because God's Spirit opens their eyes in the reading of Scripture so that, in Calvin's words,

> the undoubted power of his [God's] divine majesty lives and breathes there. By this power we are drawn and inflamed, knowingly and willingly, to obey him, yet also more vitally and more effectively than by mere human willing or knowing! (*Institutes* 1. 8. 5).

Calvin regarded the knowing process as the most profound human experience. He did not stress man's cognitive powers to know facts about God. Rather, Calvin emphasized personal experience whereby people are moved to adore God. Calvin thereby achieved a balance between objectivity and subjectivity. It is this balance that distinguishes Reformed thinking from the rationalism and empiricism that became the hallmarks of the period immediately following the Reformation (see the next chapter) in which human autonomy is not only revived but flaunted.

This balance also distinguishes Reformed theology from the views of medieval mystics and some radical Reformers. Stressing the subjectivity of knowledge, they either sought deep mystical experiences by which to immerse themselves into the very being of God, or purported to receive additional special revelations through visions, which supplemented the Bible. Both Luther and Calvin emphasized that God's revelation is complete in the

Scriptures and sufficient for our knowledge of God. Christians are to seek neither inexpressible mystical experiences nor additional revelations. For Calvin especially, the Spirit always works in conjunction with His Word to give men truth. They do not function independently.

Augustinianism and Thomism Today

In their epistemology as in their theology and anthropology Luther and Calvin acknowledged Augustine's ideas as the medieval world view most in keeping with the Bible. Reformation thought, therefore, in large measure was a revival of Augustinianism. But contemporary Christians still debate the virtues of Augustine's and Aquinas's epistemologies. Heirs of both traditions champion their respective methods today most conspicuously in discussions over the nature of apologetics—the defense of Christianity. Is the proper starting point for defending Christianity faith in God, or is it rational certainty in the finite world? Is human reason so corrupted by sin that our only sure method in knowing is faith in God's self-revelation in Scripture; or is reason unscathed by the fall so that in following reason faithfully we can demonstrate God's existence?

Those who follow Thomas warn Augustinians that a presuppositional approach to knowledge places our knowledge in the throes of subjectivism. They reject Augustine's claim that God reveals the presuppositions that lead to knowledge. If there is no appeal to evidence and empirical verification, Thomists argue, one person's presuppositions are supposedly as good as another's, and Christianity stands to lose the apologetic battle with all forms of unbelief almost before it begins. Presuppositionalism, they contend, posits no means by which the superiority of Christianity can be validated rationally. Thomists affirm on the contrary that God has given us reason in order to construct a viable natural theology. They claim that Christians can exploit undeniable evidences to demonstrate God's existence to anyone willing to examine the evidence in a sympathetic and unbiased manner.

Those in the Augustinian tradition reply that only a presuppositional view of knowledge honors God as sovereign and transcendent, for it makes the God who reveals Himself, not man and his environment, the ultimate reference point for knowledge. The Thomistic way, Augustinians argue, is a rationalistic, speculative method yielding an intellectualistic Christianity with its undue reliance on our rational powers. Such a view contrasts sharply with the biblical view of God and man. In the Bible there are no such proofs for God. The Thomist view posits a being that can be reduced to a piece of speculative data, far less than the dynamic personal God of Scripture. Likewise, the Thomist view has far too optimistic a view of human rational capabilities. What we end up knowing is a speculative system, not the personal God of grace.

The presuppositionalism of Augustine denies the basic Thomist premise that nonbelievers maintain *intellectual* and *moral* neutrality and can approach the existence of God in a "sympathetic and unbiased manner." All people either believe and worship God or rebel against Him. No one takes a neutral stance regarding God. Such neutrality is a myth. It is the ultimate affront to God that people consider His existence a matter of debate while they put faith in reason without question. The Augustinian position challenges the non-Christian view of reality at every point and asserts that our only true method of knowledge is to submit our thinking in obedience to God. Paul posed the issue succinctly in II Corinthians 10:5, when he stated that man is commanded to "take every thought captive to obey Christ." Only on such a basis is man enabled to know correctly. The intellect cannot be surgically separated from the will. Since we know that human beings have willfully turned from God, their rebellion has not only moral and spiritual but epistemological consequences. The Augustinian view attempts to do justice to both God's sovereignty and human responsibility. Augustinians stress God's sovereign revelation of truth. Man's responsibility receives due emphasis in the challenge man faces of understanding what he believes by faith through the obedient use of reason to understand the Bible.

For Further Reading

Clark, Gordon H. *Thales to Dewey*. Boston: Houghton Mifflin, 1957.

Copleston, Frederick C. *A History of Philosophy*, vol. 2. Garden City, N.Y.: Doubleday, 1962.

———. *Aquinas*. Baltimore: Penguin, 1955.

Gilson, Etienne. *Reason and Revelation in the Middle Ages*. New York: Charles Scribner's Sons, 1938.

———. *The Philosophy of St. Thomas Aquinas*. Cambridge, 1937.

Henry, Carl F. H. *God, Revelation and Authority*, vol. 1. Waco, Tex.: Word, 1976.

Holmes, Arthur. *Faith Seeks Understanding*. Grand Rapids: Eerdmans, 1971.

Maritain, Jacques. *A Monument to St. Augustine*. London: Sheed and Ward, 1930.

Murray, John. *Calvin on Scripture and Divine Sovereignty*. Grand Rapids: Baker, 1960.

Nash, Ronald H. *The Light of the Mind: St. Augustine's Theory of Knowledge*. Lexington, Ky.: University of Kentucky, 1969.

———. *The Word of God and the Mind of Man*. Grand Rapids: Zondervan, 1982.

Polman, A. D. R. *The Word of God According to St. Augustine*. Grand Rapids: Eerdmans, 1955.

Van Til, Cornelius. *A Christian Theory of Knowledge*. Phillipsburg, N.J.: Presbyterian and Reformed, 1969.

Walvoord, John, ed. *Inspiration and Interpretation*. Grand Rapids: Eerdmans, 1957.

Warfield, B. B. *Calvin and Augustine*. Phillipsburg, N.J.: Presbyterian and Reformed, 1956.

III.
ENLIGHTENMENT
EPISTEMOLOGIES

13
Rationalism and Empiricism
V. James Mannoia

Introduction

As we have seen, to study epistemology is to be concerned with knowledge. It is to ask, How does a person come to know what he thinks he knows? Epistemology involves at least two distinct but interrelated questions.

First, what is the nature of *real* knowledge? What kind of knowledge is *certain* and not simply belief, or opinion, or probability?

But to answer this first question, we must answer a second one. Where does this knowledge come from? How can we find certainty? Do we look to God or to self, to mathematics or to science, to logic or to intuition?

Taken together, these two questions constitute the essential concern of epistemology. It is the search for the "source" (question 2) of knowledge (question 1). Or to make the relationship more obvious, epistemology is the quest for the source of certainty.

The study of epistemology became particularly important during the seventeenth, eighteenth, and nineteenth centuries of European history. Until the 1600s, philosophy—which still included inquiry that today is classified as science—was concerned primarily with the nature of God and of all that exists, especially with the nature of "existence" itself. But the concern of philosophy changed drastically and suddenly in the seventeenth century. Philosophers and indeed much of the entire intellectual community became obsessed with epistemology.

Why this obsession? Two major intellectual movements arising at the end of the Middle Ages—the Reformation and the Renaissance—focused attention on epistemology. Neither can be separated entirely from the other, for they both sprang from cultural forces affecting Europe from A.D. 1200 to 1600. Leaders from both movements expressed anthropological presuppositions that, though differing sharply from each other, stood in opposition to those of the medieval period.

The Renaissance was literally the "rebirth" of culture and confidence in humanity. Renaissance philosophers revived Greek and Roman notions of human dignity and autonomy. They repudiated the Christian understanding of human sinfulness and dependence upon God, stemming primarily from Augustine, which had prevailed for centuries. Augustine held a lower estimate of human ability than the classical view of the Greeks and Romans. Increased international trade, cultural development, and intellectual achievement brought a renewed appreciation for human capabilities. And in the late Middle Ages Thomas Aquinas incorporated newly rediscovered classical Aristotelian thinking into his views of God and man, thereby making reason much more important in theology. This new confidence in human ability, coupled with renewed interest in the physical world, helped to make science a distinct discipline, separate from theology.

Most residents of the medieval world, accustomed to accepting as certain only those things decreed by the authority of the church, thought that the new science required justification. To their minds, the teachings of the church and even the testimony of ancient philosophers and church fathers required no further justification. But observations obtained through the physical senses were generally not considered trustworthy. Some church leaders protested that Galileo's use of the telescope was a "black magic" that caused viewers to see nonexistent heavenly bodies (moons of Jupiter). Some priests even preached sermons against the use of such satanic, scientific tools. One sermon was entitled punningly, "Ye men of Galilei, why stand ye gazing up into heaven?!"

Such attitudes are very hard to understand from a twentieth-century perspective, where the certainty of science is deeply ingrained, while individual and institutional authority are often questioned. This development underscores today's obviously different epistemological perspective and testifies to how well the obsession with epistemology has succeeded in justifying the efforts of science. We are the products of that shift in epistemological perspective.

The Reformation broke with the Catholic Church and gave birth to Protestantism. Reformation ideas were for the most part a reaction to precisely those elements of the Renaissance that had overestimated human ability. Much of the corruption in the church to which the Reformers objected stemmed from attributing too much ability to human reason and ability to function without God's aid. The Reformers rejected this exalted view of humanity, evident in both the church's semi-Pelagian theology and Renaissance humanism, and returned to Augustine's biblical perspective.

And yet, like the Renaissance, the Reformation explicitly rejected the authority of the medieval church and its leaders to determine what is certain in religious matters. The Reformers agreed with Catholic theologians that certainty rests upon authority. But for Protestants Scripture alone, not the church, is authoritative. Their principle of *sola Scriptura* implies the corollary principle that each individual should read and interpret the Bible himself ("universal priesthood"). This shift from the longstanding Catholic tradition of ecclesiastical authority to the Protestant focus on scriptural authority produced a great uncertainty about what to believe and what not to believe. It promoted interest in epistemology just as much as had the humanistic forces of the Renaissance. Thus, both the Renaissance and the Reformation—the one primarily cultural, the other principally religious—helped focus attention on the sources and certainty of knowledge during the seventeenth through the nineteenth centuries.

In brief, the concern for epistemology was directed toward finding a new source of certainty. Protestant and Renaissance rejection of church authority, the consequent religious uncertainty, the birth of modern science, and its need for justification all shook the foundations of medieval faith. Though, as a result, many people turned to the biblical theism of the Reformation, many more opted for Renaissance humanism, thus tending to make self rather than God the epistemological starting point.

Seventeenth-century epistemologists explored two basic man-centered alternatives: (1) that certainty arises primarily from human reason; or (2) that it arises principally from human sense experience. The first alternative is called "rationalism," and the second "empiricism." These two perspectives describe one of the classic distinctions in epistemology.

Rationalism

Among the important contributions of Sicilian scientist Archimedes (best known for his cry "Eureka" as he emerged from his bath) is his original work with levers. His investigation led to his famous statement, "If you give me a lever long enough, and a place to stand, I will move the world." Most of us know enough about levers to appreciate how very useful they are in accomplishing many tasks. Usually, the longer they are, the better. But we also know that a lever is useless without a fulcrum (or pivot). One cannot very well seesaw with just a board on level ground, or cut paper with two scissor blades without the screw holding them together, or sweep the floor one-handed.

This analogy can help us to understand the goal of rationalism. We could change Archimedes' phrase to read, "If you give me a lever long enough and a place to stand, I will give you certainty." What then is the "lever" and what is the "place to stand" by which rationalism promised to deliver certainty?

The "levers" for rationalism are the "rules of logic" by means of which human reason operates. Logic, like a lever, is a very powerful device for achieving certainty. The rules of logic are the keys to proofs, and proof is what people demand in seeking certainty. But the rules of logic are not enough for a proof. Proofs need premises just as walls need foundations and levers need fulcrums.

The "fulcrum" for rationalism—its "place to stand"—is the solid, permanent truth said to be built into each and every human mind. Rationalists often call these the "innate ideas," and people can know them by reason or intuition alone. These ideas can be compared to the numeral *IV* stamped in steel by a sweaty fist and sledgehammer at the conclusion of the television series "Dragnet" and other "Mark IV Productions." The innate ideas are stamped in the mind from its beginning. They are certain—Knowledge with a capital *K*—and they serve as the solid "place to stand," the fulcrum upon which the lever of logic is able to build still other knowledge.

The key tenet of rationalism, therefore, is that certainty begins with truths of reason inside the mind, independent of the five senses. The following diagram illustrates rationalism. The pentagon represents the human mind, with each side one of our senses; and the letter *K* stands for the innate ("built-in") ideas, which serve as the foundation of knowledge.

Plato is an excellent example of a rationalist. For Plato, real knowledge (*episteme*) is quite different from mere opinion or belief (*doxa*). It arises not from sense experience of the shadow-like physical world, but by using the tool of reason to examine the "ideas" ("forms") imprinted in the human soul (mind) before birth. In Plato's case this rationalistic assumption about innate ideas, coupled with his views about never-ending reincarnation, led to an interesting theory of education. He believed that we can never learn anything new, but that with the aid of sense experience and teachers, we merely "recollect" innate knowledge our mind has always known. The teacher becomes merely the "midwife of knowledge," not the "father of knowledge."

The figure who perhaps best exemplifies modern rationalism is Rene Descartes (1596-1650). Descartes, above all, sought to know what is certain. He lived in a rapidly changing world in which long-held foundational principles were being challenged. Both France, where Descartes was born, and the Netherlands, where he lived most of his adult life, were caught in a religious struggle between Catholics and Protestants over the question of what constitutes religious truth. The new scientific world was also in turmoil, and its picture of the physical world was rapidly changing. Galileo, Kepler, and Newton revolutionized physics and astronomy with theories of inertia and planetary motion. Harvey's theory of blood circulation transformed physiology.

Amid this intellectual change skepticism flourished. This was the belief that nothing could be known for sure; there was no knowledge. But Descartes was not a skeptic. He was a devout Catholic who contended that human beings are capable of attaining indubitable knowledge. Yet he realized that many in his generation would not accept the old sources and bases for certainty, even though they were (and still are) acceptable to many theists. As a rationalist, he sought to find a basis or fulcrum for certainty in human reason. Before people can obtain certainty, however, they must first become aware of how dubious or uncertain most of their accepted beliefs are. Descartes's now famous six *Meditations on First Philosophy* recount the story of his epistemological odyssey from uncertainty to certainty.

He began his first *Meditation* with what he called "methodic doubt," showing how the sources of everything we think we know are not as reliable as we think.

> Everything which I have thus far accepted as entirely true has been acquired from the senses or by means of the senses. But I have learned by experience that these senses sometimes mislead me, and it is prudent never to trust wholly those things which have once deceived me.

Furthermore, Descartes admitted that "there are no conclusive indications by which waking life can be distinguished from sleep." Yet if that is so, then all of what sense experience indicates to be real might just as easily be illusion, nothing more than a long dream.

But even if sense experience cannot be trusted, Descartes reassured, perhaps the truths of mathematics might still be known.

> For whether I am awake or asleep, two and three together will always make the number five . . . and it does not seem possible that truths so apparent can ever be suspected of any falsity or uncertainty.

And yet Descartes cautioned that if a God exists who is a deceiver, He might cause a person always to be mistaken when he adds two and three. Although we can believe God exists and believe He does not deceive us, neither assertion can be known for certain.

Descartes concluded, "I am constrained to admit that there is nothing in what I formerly believed to be true which I cannot somehow doubt. . . . " He thus put himself entirely in the shoes of his contemporaries who were skeptical about knowledge.

But in the second *Meditation,* his rationalism lead him to discover what is perhaps history's most famous "place to stand." It was apparent to Descartes that whatever doubt there might be about anything he thought he knew, the fact remained that his own mind must exist in order to think the doubting thoughts at all. Even if sense experience is untrustworthy, even if we are actually asleep, and finally, even if all the truths of mathematics are the malicious prank of some evil genie or deceitful God, his mind had to exist to be deceived.[1] Because he *did* doubt, he knew with certainty he must himself exist, not necessarily as a body, but at least as a thinking self. This discovery he took to be an innate idea, clear and distinct to reason. It is summarized by the Latin phrase *Cogito ergo sum,* which means literally, "I think, therefore, I exist."

Upon this presumably unshakeable fulcrum of certainty, Descartes built successive bits of knowledge using the "lever" of logic in the third through sixth *Meditations,* just as we would expect a rationalist to do. Among these secondary bits of knowledge built upon his first premise were the certainty of God's

---

1. Contrast Descartes's discussion of deception with Augustine's in our previous chapter.

existence and His lack of deceit, the trustworthiness of sense experience, and finally the existence of a physical world (including one's own physical body) outside of the self. The important thing to notice is that knowledge in every case begins with knowledge of self. Self is the starting point, not God. In particular, the innate idea of the certainty of self-existence is the rationalistic "place to stand." Justification for knowledge is reason, not God, and the autonomy of man apart from God is again affirmed.

Empiricism

A second basic alternative was available to the seventeenth-century epistemologist who sought to ground certainty in self rather than God. This alternative is empiricism, the view that knowledge arises primarily from human sense experience and not from reason. It is often summarized in what is called "the empiricist dogma": "There is nothing in the intellect not found first in the senses."

Empiricism repudiates the rationalistic notion of a mind "prestamped" with knowledge and closed to the effect of the senses in its search for certainty. On the contrary, empiricism supposes that whatever knowledge is to be found in the mind ("Intellect") must have originated first in one or more of the five senses. This view can be diagrammed as follows:

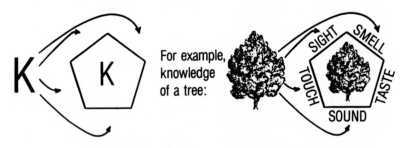

John Locke (1632–1704) was an excellent example of empiricist thinking. This British philosopher developed an early interest in experimental science, which helps to explain his inclination to base knowledge on sense experience.

The same practical orientation is also clearly evident in Locke's preoccupation with politics. In fact, he is much better known, at least outside philosophical circles, for his important contributions to the politics of liberalism and his defense of the inalienable rights of the individual. Locke believed that tyranny is repugnant, whether at the hand of the king (absolutism) or at the hand of the majority (democracy). Not only was he influential in the Glorious Revolution in England in 1688, but his thinking helped shape the American and French constitutions nearly one hundred years later. His emphasis upon the value of the individual reflects the burgeoning exaltation of human autonomy that characterized the age of the Enlightenment (1660–1800).

His major work on epistemology, *An Essay Concerning Human Understanding,* was published when Locke was fifty-seven years of age. It emerged out of a discussion with five or six friends one evening about the nature of the knowledge our minds are capable of attaining.

> I thought all I should have to say on this matter would have been contained in one sheet of paper; but the further I went, the larger prospect I had . . . and so it grew insensibly to the bulk it now appears in [several *hundred* pages].

In the first book of the *Essay,* Locke refuted the rationalist position that the origins of knowledge are innate ideas, stamped in the minds of men. At least part of his evidence was the obvious disagreement among men as to which ideas are innate and which are not, and that neither idiots nor children share with other individuals an acceptance of these universal truths.

In the second book of the *Essay,* Locke presented his alternative to rationalism: an empiricist concept of the mind and the source of knowledge. He described the mind as a blank tablet (*tabula rasa*) upon which the five senses write whatever knowledge is to be found there, much as five fingers or sticks might leave impressions on the smooth surface of sand as waves retreat from the beach. The tracings created on the mind are the ideas (either simple or complex) we call knowledge. These ideas are the representations of qualities (either primary or secondary)[2] to be found in the objects outside our minds. The mind itself is passive as the senses draw the representative ideas upon it. Of course these ideas—as the word *representation* suggests—are just copies of the object itself, a stage play in the mind. When we know a tree in the mind, we do not have actual trees growing in our brains. We possess only the idea (representation) of one traced there by sight, sound, touch, smell, and (in the case of fruit-bearing trees) taste.

Thus the key to empiricism is that certainty in knowledge is strictly dependent upon experiences of the five senses. This empiricist perspective became the spirit and hallmark of the newborn modern science. From Bacon and Newton to the present day, the typical attitude has been, "I'll believe it when I see it!" Even rational argumentation is usually perceived as pointless; the senses alone are to be trusted.

It is apparent here, just as it was for rationalism, that self—and our senses in particular—not God, or any authority, is the ultimate authenticator of knowledge. The individual is autonomous.

Because so many of us are unconsciously steeped in the empiricist epistemology, we unjustifiably tend to apply this criterion of certainty to other beliefs—such as a religious faith—that presuppose an entirely different epistemology. For example, Yuri Gagarin, the Russian cosmonaut who was first to orbit the earth, is said to have reported, apparently with some seriousness, that he could not see God. He seemed to be saying that since "seeing is believing," and we cannot see God, then belief in Him is unjustified. But is it fair to referee a game of football by the rules of baseball? Or can you see the wind?

Before moving to a brief criticism of both rationalism and empiricism, we may note how these two epistemologies lead to contrasting theories of education. (Of course, there are other

2. Examples of primary qualities are number, motion, size, shape, and solidity, while secondary qualities are color, smell, taste, sound, and warmth. In primary qualities a true correspondence exists between objects and our perceptions, while secondary qualities are not intrinsic to objects but are present in that they cause certain experiences in the senses.

implications and contrasts of equal significance, some of which will be treated later in this and successive chapters.) If, as rationalists suggest, knowledge begins in the mind, education should consist primarily of instruction on how to think logically. Students might be taught to probe their own minds for awareness of "clear and distinct" truths. The emphasis would be on concepts and techniques of reasoning. Such was in fact the emphasis in Plato's system of education in his utopian "Republic."

Believing that knowledge originates in the senses, an empiricist by contrast would emphasize techniques of observation and discovery of facts. A student would perhaps be expected to cram his "blank tablet" with as many facts as possible and to develop a keen awareness of the sensory world around him. Laboratory and life experience would become the raw material for learning.

Criticism of Rationalism

Locke's argument against the rationalist doctrine of innate ideas was perhaps misguided. He appealed to the lack of universal consensus regarding what is knowledge. But this confuses the psychological question of whether everyone recognizes certain universal (innate) truths with the epistemological question of whether there are such truths and in particular whether they are the exclusive source of certainty.

Perhaps a more significant criticism is his objection that even generally accepted universal truths seem useless in advancing our knowledge of the world. Though they may be certain, statements such as "What is is" and "It is impossible for the same thing to be and not to be" or "All bachelors are single" do very little to extend our knowledge into new areas. (And perhaps they do nothing at all!) Rationalism seems to provide knowledge of philosophical abstractions, but not of the physical world.

Descartes is often criticized along these very lines. It may well be that the statement, "I think, therefore I exist" is unequivocally true. But so too is "All bachelors are single," which, like Descartes's statement, sounds like it tells us something about what exists in the world, in this case bachelors. Yet once we accept and understand the meaning of the word *bachelor*, the last part of the sentence adds nothing more. It is little more than a definition. Some critics say Descartes's statement is of the same sort, merely a definition of what *I* means. Just as the statement "All bachelors are single" can be true without there being any bachelors, so too Descartes's statement could be true but empty of reference to things in the world. Furthermore, does Descartes's statement imply that I exist as a body, or only as a nonphysical entity? It would appear that the rationalists' certainty is impotent to give us knowledge of the physical world, thus leaving us quite skeptical about the cosmos. It is nice to know for certain that two plus two equal four, but unless we can be sure that two oranges plus two oranges make four oranges, we have no knowledge of the world.

Of course, Descartes did attempt in his *Meditations*—as described above—to avoid this egocentric predicament by moving from the certainty of self-existence to the knowledge of God's existence and finally to knowledge of the existence of the physical world. Unfortunately Descartes made God merely the link between certainty of self-existence and certainty of the physical world. Thus, God was only a convenient tool for Descartes—one link in the chain of knowledge—instead of its anchoring presupposition. Such a low view of God was tolerable to the rationalist. What was *not* acceptable to other rationalists was the weak link between knowledge of self and knowledge of God (forcing the proof of God's existence to stand on its own). Also problematic was the unjustifiably extensive knowledge of the nature of God required to support the link from knowledge of His existence to that of the physical world. Knowledge that the self exists is insufficient to show that God exists, and Descartes's argument from the one to the other is very dubious at best. Even had he successfully shown that God exists, we would also need to know that He is not a deceiver before Descartes's justification of knowledge of the physical world would be valid.

In short, rationalists are criticized for failing to give us knowledge of the world at all. Their philosophy results in skepticism.

Criticism of Empiricism

The typical criticism of empiricism—at least of the empiricism of John Locke—is straightforward yet devastating. If, as Locke held, all knowledge consists of ideas "drawn" in the mind by our sense experiences of objects outside the mind, how can we know if the idea in the mind resembles the object outside? How can we be sure that our senses do not introduce a "copy error" much as colored glasses might distort our perception of a colored object? This problem of correspondence or representation must ultimately leave the empiricist (the Lockean Representational Realist) utterly ignorant of the true nature of the world outside his mind. He can never be certain of (i.e., have knowledge of) the nature of the objects (if they exist at all) that presumably affect his senses to produce his ideas. Knowing only his own sensations, he can never be sure he is not locked forever in the dark room of his mind watching fictitious movies of a world he assumes exists outside. Like the rationalist, the empiricist too is left with only skepticism about knowledge of the world.

Though himself a second generation empiricist, David Hume (1711–76) provided a still more devastating blow to the hope that certainty could be grounded in experience. So thoroughgoing and biting was Hume's skepticism—he is sometimes called "the Father of Modern Skepticism"—that when Boswell, Samuel Johnson's biographer, called on Hume during the last weeks of his life, and queried whether Hume thought that there might perhaps be an afterlife, Hume responded "Yes, it is *possible* that a piece of coal put upon the fire would not burn." Despite his thoroughgoing and biting skepticism and his pessimism regarding man's ability to know, Hume was, above all, utterly consistent in his empiricism and unafraid of its consequences.

His position rests upon three major assumptions. First, Hume accepted completely the empiricist dogma that knowledge always originates with sense experience. Second, he assumed—as most everyone must do—that knowledge is by its very definition structured in its nature; it consists of definite objects in definite relationships, more like a brick wall than a pile of bricks. Finally, Hume assumed what is called "sensory atomism." When he

examined the sense experience from which all knowledge originates, he observed that those sensations come in discrete bits and
pieces, or sensory "atoms." Patches of color here and there in our
visual field, bursts of sound, whiffs of odor, and tingles of vibra-
tion are the only experiences we may legitimately claim to have.
When we experience a "tree," we experience only "greeness
here," "browness there," "roughness here," "smoothness there,"
and perhaps "pungency now." Our sensations come in unstructured pieces or atoms, not connected in wholes except by force of
habits in our mind. The world of experience is—as William James
would say—"a buzzing blooming confusion."

From these three assumptions it appears that little if any
knowledge of the world is possible. The nature of experience
(unstructured), of knowledge (structured), and the empiricist
position, which always bases knowledge on experience, makes
actual knowledge impossible to obtain. Hume's argument produces a very strong skepticism, the logical consequence of the
classic empiricist epistemology.

Summary and Conclusion

In summary, seventeenth-century philosophers used their rejection of all authority, especially divine and ecclesiastical authority,
to base their search for the source of certainty on man instead of
God. They elevated human autonomy to the status of dogmatic
belief. The two basic alternatives, rationalism and empiricism,
took human reason and human sense experience respectively to
be the ultimate source and authenticator of knowledge.

Our discussion, though simplified, has shown that neither of
these two alternatives was successful. The criticisms of both
rationalism and empiricism offered above demonstrate that each
attempt, rather than leading to certainty, led instead to skepticism. It remained for Immanuel Kant (1724–1804) to draw
together elements of both rationalism and empiricism in a revolutionary synthesis that turned the epistemological world upside
down in its search for knowledge.

Kant's "Copernican Revolution" in epistemology gave the
mind of man the active role of creating knowledge rather than

the passive role of just discovering it—by either reason or experience. His radical approach clearly reaffirmed the centrality of self as the source of knowledge and the autonomy of the individual. But as will become evident in the chapters that follow, Kant set the stage for such modern self-centered, subjectivist movements as positivism, existentialism, and emotivist ethics. The last reverberations of Kant's epistemological revolution have yet to be felt.

Kant's revolution was in part also a synthesis. From empiricism Kant accepted the need for sense experience as the raw material for knowledge. He rejected, however, the empiricist belief—so aptly captured in Locke's *tabula rasa*—that this experience "writes" upon a passive mind. Knowledge, like cookies, must be made from something—the cookie dough of experience. There are no prepackaged (innate) "cookies of knowledge" just waiting to be found.

From rationalism Kant accepted the need for innate characteristics of the mind. Although there are no ready-made "cookies," there must be innate "cookie-cutters"—categories and intuitions of the mind—for use in shaping that "dough" of experience into the "cookies" of knowledge. But, of course, Kant rejected the rationalists' notion that knowledge is independent of experience. Just as cookie dough (experience) without cookie-cutters (innate categories of the mind) cannot be called cookies (knowledge), so too cookie-cutters without dough satisfy no one's palate. To paraphrase Kant: if experience without categories is *blind*, then categories without experience are *empty*. Knowledge is the product of the synthesis of these empiricist and rationalist elements.

Changes in epistemology during the seventeenth and eighteenth centuries led to exalted views of human capability, rationality, and autonomy. By the beginning of the Enlightenment in the seventeenth century, most people had rejected Augustine's and the Reformers' appraisal of unregenerate humanity. The appeal to human reason or experience as the source of knowledge is only one illustration of the growing optimism regarding humanity's inherent and autonomous capabilities. Beginning with Aquinas's limited acceptance of reason and extending through the Renaissance, the epistemologies of Descartes, Locke, and Kant, Alexander Pope's rationalism, and on to what may be its self-destructive conclusion in modern materialistic behaviorism, there is a steady growth of confidence in human self-sufficiency.

The theological conclusion of this discussion follows quite clearly from the comments on humanity above. As persons are understood to play a greater and greater role in shaping knowledge and society for themselves, God is relegated to an inferior position. Until the seventeenth century, God and His authority were considered more or less foundational to all knowledge. Many rationalists, however, reduced God to a convenient device, often invoked arbitrarily, to hold the pieces of a man-centered system together. As empiricism became progressively more consistent, God was regarded, at best, as nonessential and a matter of empty faith. Hume's own attitude was typical. He professed to believe in God and Jesus Christ on the basis of faith, but he termed his belief "unreasonable." Positivism, which emerged in the twentieth century, reached the ultimate theological conclusion of empiricism. For positivists, nothing is meaningful unless it can be verified by sense experience. Since God cannot be seen, heard, touched, or tasted, the very concept is meaningless; it is not even a proper subject for belief. The autonomy of self, it appears, was purchased at the cost of the death of God.

For Further Reading

Clark, Gordon H. *Thales to Dewey.* Boston: Houghton Mifflin, 1957.

Collins, James. *God in Modern Philosophy.* Chicago: Henry Regnery, 1959.

———. *A History of Modern European Philosophy.* Milwaukee: Bruce, 1954.

Copleston, Frederick C. *A History of Philosophy,* vols. 4, 5. Garden City, N.Y.: Doubleday, 1963, 1964.

Descartes, Rene. *A Discourse on Method.* Translated by John Vertch. London: Dent, 1969.

Henry, Carl F. H. *God, Revelation and Authority*, vol. 1. Waco, Tex.: Word, 1976.

Hume, David. *An Enquiry Concerning Human Understanding.* LaSalle, Ill.: Open Court, 1958.

Jones, W. T. *A History of Western Philosophy.* New York: Harcourt Brace Jovanovich, 1952.

Keeling, S. V. *Descartes.* London: Oxford University, 1934.

Locke, John. *An Essay Concerning Human Understanding.* Chicago: Henry Regnery, 1956.

Maritain, Jacques. *Three Reformers: Luther, Descartes, Rousseau.* New York: Charles Scribner's Sons, 1950.

Nash, Ronald H. *The Word of God and the Mind of Man.* Grand Rapids: Zondervan, 1982.

Schaeffer, Francis A. *Escape From Reason.* Downers Grove, Ill.: Inter-Varsity), 1968.

Smith, Norman Kemp. *The Philosophy of David Hume.* New York: Macmillan, 1960.

Spinka, Matthew. *Christian Thought From Erasmus to Berdyaev.* Englewood Cliffs, N.J.: Prentice-Hall, 1962.

14
Kant's Copernican Revolution

Charles S. MacKenzie

Kant and His Enlightenment Predecessors

The long shadow of German philosopher Immanuel Kant (1724–1804) is cast over millions of our contemporaries. In highlighting human autonomy, Kant built upon many previous thinkers, especially those who had praised reason as the last judge and guide in all things. The enthusiasm for and confidence in reason on the part of Kant and other Enlightenment philosophers was virtually boundless. They often displayed hymnodic rapture before reason as they tried to outdo each other in their praise of this great human faculty. Addison in "The Spacious Firmament" wrote:

> In reason's ear they all rejoice
> And utter forth a glorious voice;
> Forever singing, as they shine,
> "The hand that made us is divine."

Kant very self-consciously advanced the Enlightenment belief that people should reject previously held views of reason as a servant of Christian philosophy. Kant even defined the Enlightenment in terms of liberating man:

> Enlightenment is man's exodus from his self-incurred tutelage. Tutelage is the inability to use one's understanding without the guidance of another person. This tutelage is self-incurred if its cause lies not in any weakness of the understanding, but in indecision and lack of courage to use the mind without the guidance of another. "Dare to know!"

Have the courage to use your own understanding; this is the motto of the Enlightenment.

Kant's words are as much a challenge as they are a statement. While criticizing all authorities and traditions of the past, Kant and other leaders of the Enlightenment substituted a virtually unbounded faith in human reason. Even though rationalists and empiricists differed substantially over how to attain knowledge and what its limits are, they formed a united front in their demand that new world views were necessary. Central to their efforts to restructure philosophy was their insistence on framing new views of knowledge. Previous dependence on the Bible or the church's teaching must give way to rational inquiry. Interest in transcendent values, saving souls, and life after death were repudiated in favor of this-worldly efforts to verify human values rationally and to reorder our individual and collective lives accordingly. Kant's contribution to this movement was so influential that we can hardly overestimate his importance.

Immanuel Kant lived his eighty years in the small East Prussian town of Konigsberg. His family's pietism had an enduring religious impact on his life, and Kant fondly recalled his mother's showing him the starlit heavens, declaring them to be the handiwork of God. Subsequent experience with the daily regimen of required Bible study and prayer in a Lutheran pietist school, however, had such a negative influence on the young Kant that in his adult life he virtually denied any value of prayer and worship.

Kant studied at the University of Konigsberg where a young professor introduced him to the rationalism of Christian Wolff (1679-1754) and G. W. Leibniz (1646-1716) and the physics of Isaac Newton (1642-1717). After completing his studies at the university, Kant spent eight years there as a tutor, and then fifteen years as a lecturer during which time he enjoyed great success as a stimulating teacher. In 1770 he was appointed Professor of Philosophy at the University.

A warm conversationalist and a gracious host, Kant was a lifelong bachelor. His personal self-discipline became legendary as illustrated by the fact that his neighbors could set their clocks when he stepped from his house each afternoon precisely at 4:30 to walk up and down the street exactly eight times. Such discipline reflected a methodical, orderly mind, which enabled him to be an extremely productive teacher and scholar.

A heavy teaching schedule ranging from sixteen to twenty-eight hours a week kept Kant from producing any books until he was fifty-seven years of age. But beginning with his famous *Critique of Pure Reason* in 1781, he published a series of earth-shaking books that included *The Critique of Practical Reason* (1788) and the *Critique of Judgment* (1790).

His most lasting contribution to the history of philosophy was his revolutionary synthesis in epistemology, which served as a watershed in Western thinking. The major scholarly traditions of his day were Continental rationalism, British empiricism, and Newtonian physics. Continental rationalism, which influenced Kant's early thought, emphasized the relation of ideas to each other but ignored their connection to physical reality. For this reason, the later Kant, having been influenced by Newtonian science, was inclined to favor science as the chief means of increasing knowledge. He recognized, though, that a mechanical, Newtonian universe left little room for moral values, God, and freedom. In his mature years, he came to question rationalist metaphysics, which had produced disparate conclusions by Descartes, Spinoza, and Leibniz.

Kant's dissatisfaction with rationalism was encouraged by the attack by the British empiricist David Hume upon its metaphysics. Hume argued that we cannot know causality because all our knowledge comes from experience, and causality is not *in* events. One cannot empirically verify in a game of billiards, for example, that when one ball hits another, which then moves, there is a force named "causality" operating between the balls. Rather than existing "out there" between the billiard balls, causality actually exists inside the mind of the observer, who has developed the habit of reading a cause-effect relationship into events that are experienced together. Therefore, we cannot be said to know cause.

Thus Hume attacked rationalist metaphysics by denying that we have any certainty that ideas in our minds actually correspond to what exists outside our minds. He also refuted scientific induction, which is based on the principle that causality is something outside the mind to be apprehended by the scientist in his controlled experiments. Hume's viewpoint, therefore, led to total philosophic skepticism. Consequently, Kant and his contemporaries confronted a developing philosophical tradition that declared that only a person's own sense impressions are useful in the quest for knowledge. And even they are suspect when they report that anything is true about reality external to the mind! Knowledge of all that had been important in Western philosophy—the physical universe and its order, moral values, human nature, God and His purposes in the world—was being called into question. Kant confessed that Hume's skepticism about human knowledge awoke Kant from his "dogmatic slumbers." Hume's criticism stimulated the brilliant German professor to analyze and articulate the capacities of the human mind in his monumental work *Critique of Pure Reason.*

Critique of Pure Reason
In this weighty and ponderous volume Kant accomplished his famous "Copernican Revolution" in philosophy. Just as Copernicus had demonstrated that the sun, not planet earth, is the center of the solar system, so Kant hoped to show that man, not God, is the center and source of all valid knowledge. Kant's "critical" philosophy sought to save and build upon elements of both rationalism and empiricism. He agreed in part with Hume that knowledge is acquired through sense experience. But, he also concurred with the rationalists in his determination to justify a knowledge of things beyond sense experience (i.e., God, the soul, moral values, and freedom).

Kant began his investigation of human thought in *Critique of Pure Reason* by analyzing the various types of judgments the mind makes. The question he wished to answer was, "Are synthetic a priori judgments possible?" These are judgments that are true neither because of rational definition nor because of sense experience. He began by distinguishing between analytic and synthetic judgments. A judgment connects a subject and predicate. For example, in the simple statement "The man is short," the predicate ("short") describes the subject ("man"). In an analytic judgment the predicate is already contained in the idea of the subject, and thus the mind acquires no new knowledge as a result of its having made the judgment. Thus, in the statement "The man thinks," thought is implicitly contained in the idea of man for every man is capable of thought. However, a synthetic judgment is quite different, for if we were to say "The rose is red," we would be adding something new to our understanding of the rose. Roses come in a variety of colors, and thus a judgment that tells us the flower's color is a synthetic judgment. As can clearly be seen from this illustration, a synthetic judgment usually is based upon experience.

Kant also distinguished between "a priori" and "a posteriori" judgments. "A priori" judgments are made prior to experience, and "a posteriori" judgments are made after (post) experience. All analytic judgments are a priori because they depend exclusively on our apprehending the definitions of words and not on experience. "All triangles have three angles" is an example of an analytic, a priori judgment independent of sense experience. Synthetic judgments, in contrast, usually are a posteriori, depending to some degree upon our experience, on our apprehending the characteristic in question. "The apple is sweet" is a synthetic, a posteriori judgment because the predicate adds to our knowledge of the subject and is dependent upon our experience of tasting the apple.

Having explained the meaning of these terms, Kant could now decide whether a synthetic a priori judgment is possible. Such a judgment would be true without depending on sense experience, thus a priori. It also would be true since no sense experience can refute it. And yet it would be synthetic in that it adds to our rational knowledge. Kant showed that such judgments are possible in mathematics. For example, the statement that "five plus three equals eight" is a priori because it is true regardless of our experience. At the same time, it is synthetic since eight cannot be determined by simply analyzing the number five or the number three. Eight is not implicitly contained in either five or three. Thus Kant showed that synthetic a priori judgments are possible in mathematics and physics. He went on to show that they also are possible in metaphysics. For example, the judgment that "all men are free" is synthetic, for the predicate ("are free") adds new knowledge not necessarily implied in the subject ("all men"). "All men are free" is also a priori since we are unable to experience freedom for all men. Having pointed out that synthetic a priori judgments exist in philosophy, Kant went on to analyze how such judgments are made.

Kant's Copernican Revolution

The basic principle of his "Copernican Revolution" is that objects and events we know in our experience conform to the operation of our minds and not our minds to the objects. The movement is from the mind toward the world not from the world toward the mind. Kant stated his view as follows:

> Hitherto it has been assumed that all our knowledge must conform to objects. But all our attempts to extend our knowledge of objects by establishing something in regard to them a priori by means of concepts, have on this assumption ended in failure. We must, therefore, make trial whether we may not have more success in the tasks of metaphysics, if we suppose that objects must conform to our knowledge.

In effect, he was saying that the mind brings something to the objects it experiences. As an active agent, the mind organizes our experiences by projecting onto objects its way of knowing. No wonder it has been said that Kant viewed the mind as a pseudocreator rather than a knower! Knowledge is the result of cooperation between the knower and the thing known. Kant's fundamental premise is that although all knowledge begins with sense experience, not all knowledge arises from experience. The mind receives simple sensations from the world, but then it imposes organization and structure upon those impressions to create knowledge.

Since knowledge begins with our perception of the phenomenal world (physical reality), our senses passively receive sensory data. Our minds, however, sift these experiences through two intuitions (time and space) and twelve categories (grouped as quantity, quality, relation, and modality). These a priori intuitions and categories are built-in *structures* of the mind through which sense data are filtered, organized, and synthesized. Kant therefore accepted the empiricist argument that knowledge begins with sense experience. But his explanation of these categories of under-standing showed his agreement with the rationalists that our minds contribute to what we know. (Remember the rationalist belief that the mind is not a *tabula rasa* but rather has innate ideas.) The categories of understanding are our mind's "spectacles" through which we see everything we know.

For example, "quantity," as a structure of the mind, determines that we know things in terms of number. We cannot think of things apart from a numerical attribute. You could not read these words without thinking in terms of number. In the same way, another important category of our minds determines that we think in terms of cause and effect. Kant believed that his synthesis of empiricist and rationalist ideas answered Hume's radical skep-ticism. Whereas Hume said that we cannot know cause because we are in the habit of reading cause into events, Kant said that cause is built into our mind's very structure and we cannot think *except* in terms of causality. It is a mental category that orders all of our thought.

Kant thus believed that his Copernican Revolution adopted the best insights from both rationalism and empiricism, while eliminating their errors. He assumed that his analysis of the human mind was universally valid, for all men, in all places, and in all ages. On this point he has been severely criticized.

If in knowing an object the human mind virtually creates knowledge, the question has been raised then, What is the exter-nal world when it is not being perceived? Kant replied that we cannot know a thing-in-itself (*ding an sich*). The world, as it exists apart from our experience of it, is unknowable. Kant called these unknowable realities or things-in-themselves (such as Plato's forms or ideals, which underlie the external world) the *noumenal* realm. It is a realm beyond our knowing. When we study a man biologically or scientifically we deal with the *phenomenal* and the experiential. When we examine the freedom of the human soul, however, we discuss the noumenal realm, which is beyond sensory experience.

Thus Kant radically redefined knowledge by assuming a sharp dualism between phenomenal reality (the world of physical, sensate objects) and noumenal reality (the realm of supernatural, nonsensate entities). Thinkers before him such as Plato assumed both realms could be known, although people arrive at knowledge of each by different methods. Kant's radical dualism, however, declared knowledge to be limited only to the phenomenal realm of Newtonian physics.

To this point Kant was saying that we can only know empirical objects as perceived through the intuitions and categories of the finite human mind. Yet because people constantly seek to unify their experiences, he argued that pure reason inclines us to accept (not necessarily to experience) three transcendent, regulative ideas, which do not correspond to any object of experience but which unify our knowledge. Without the unity these ideas give to knowledge, Kant noted, scientific knowledge would be impossible.

The transcendent ideas, forced upon us by pure reason, are the self, the cosmos, and God. The self harmonizes all our thought and knowledge. The idea of cosmos describes a systematic order to all reality. And the idea of God unifies all things. He said of the idea of God:

> It becomes evident that the idea of such a being, like all speculative ideas, seems only to formulate the command or reason, that all connection in the world be viewed in accordance with the principles of a systematic unity—as if all such connection had its source in one single all-embracing being as the supreme and sufficient cause.

Thus Kant believed he had reconciled empiricism and rationalism. Agreeing with the empiricists, Kant declared that all knowledge comes from experiences that have been filtered through the structures of the mind. With the rationalists, Kant argued there were transcendent ideas that regulate other ideas. But Kant reminded rationalists that they erred by assuming that these transcendent ideas are actual realities. He maintained that these transcendent ideas are *only* ideas. Cogent arguments could be put forth both for and against the existence of the self, the cosmos, and God as actual realities. Reason is deadlocked because it is unable to resolve the debate over whether these ideas are real or not. So Kant taught that the self, the cosmos, and God are useful, but their actual existence cannot be verified or known. By urging people to accept these purely rational ideas in order to unify their thinking about reality, Kant gave these ideas a major role in facilitating the interaction of mind and experience.

Kant and his immediate followers saw two benefits to his epistemology. First, as we have seen, it was a revolutionary synthesis that effectively ended the stalemate between rationalists and empiricists. Second, Kant claimed that his view of knowledge was capable of settling the growing quarrel between science and religion. He invited Newtonian scientists to explore the phenomenal world using a scientific method and to publish their findings as knowledge. And he declared noumenal reality the domain of philosophers and theologians, thereby relegating religious beliefs to mere speculation. Kant believed that his system saved both science and religion, but in fact, they were preserved only at the great cost of dividing reality into a rigid dualism. In effect he constructed an impregnable wall between science and religion. And he said that "knowledge" belongs only to the phenomenal world of scientific study, not to the noumenal world of ideas. For example, people are allowed to have faith in, express opinions on, and argue about God. But philosophers and theologians must never confuse their beliefs or opinions with scientific knowledge of phenomena. By the same token, scientists must stick to their study of the physical world and not presume they can use their methods to settle philosophical or theological debates. Science and religion can be at peace only as long as their spokesmen recognize and function within their respective realms.

Kant's epistemological solution continues to draw widespread acceptance in the twentieth century. Whenever we hear, for example, that science produces "facts" while theology deals only with matters of "faith," we are listening to the disciples of Kant. Modern world views in which knowledge rests predominantly on empirical findings are due in large measure to Kant's wall. How different from the apostle Paul, on the other hand, who professed in one of his Epistles, "I know whom I have believed and am persuaded that he is able to keep that which I have committed unto him against that day" (II Tim. 1:12).

Critique of Practical Reason

To many it seemed that Kant had demolished any knowledge of the actual existence of God. Since an infinite God could not be squeezed through the finite intuitions and categories of the mind, God could not be experienced or known. The best that man could do was *to use* the unifying idea of a God who may or may not exist. The story is told that Kant returned home one day and found his servant in tears. When Kant inquired why the servant was weeping, he replied, "You have taken away my God." In order to explain the importance of these transcendent ideas Kant undertook a second major analysis of human reason. This critique probed reason not in its cognitive function as it affirms what *is*, but in its moral task as it legislates our duty—what *ought to be*.

In the *Critique of Practical Reason* Kant proposed that there is in the realm of practical, moral behavior partially justified belief in the reality of an invisible, noumenal realm toward which "pure reason" is agnostic. Kant focused his discussion on reason in its practical role. The will is pure reason in operation. In his second critique, Kant, therefore, sought to explore the principles of practical reason. He alleged that all men possess a "categorical imperative," a sense of duty or "oughtness." The categorical imperative is, "Act as if the maxim of thy action were to become a universal law in nature." Thus, practical reason expresses an inner sense of "oughtness." It is called *categorical* because like the categories of pure reason, which organize our knowledge of phenomena, it exerts an a priori influence and applies to all rational beings. And it is *imperative* because it has the force of an obligation.

Kant then proceeded to show that human experience of the moral law proposes three postulates: freedom, immortality, and God. Experience of the categorical imperative leads people to believe that man is free to obey or to disobey an inward sense of "oughtness." "Because I must, I can." A free will is such because it is under the moral law and not under an external law or authority. Human freedom, therefore, is assumed or postulated though it cannot be empirically demonstrated.

Because the moral law implies a soul that makes indefinite progress toward perfect goodness, Kant also postulated the existence of immortality. "This endless progress is possible only on the supposition of the unending duration of the existence and personality of the same rational being, which is called the immortality of the soul." Freedom implies an immortal soul that is free.

To Kant, belief in freedom and immortality also requires belief in God. If our moral knowledge is correct, reason demands that virtue be connected with happiness, that virtue be rewarded with happiness. But we do not see such a connection in everyday experience, as evil acts often remain unpunished while virtuous acts are not rewarded. Therefore, we must postulate not only an afterlife, but a moral being, omnipotent and omniscient, who upholds moral principles specifically by rewarding virtuous acts with the happiness they deserve. Kant went on to say:

> Through the idea of the supreme good as object and final end of the pure practical reason the moral law leads to religion, that is to the recognition of all duties as divine commands . . . which, however, must be looked on as commands of the supreme Being, because it is only from a morally perfect and at the same time all-powerful will . . . that we hope to attain the highest good.

In his *Critique of Pure Reason* Kant had tried to demolish any knowledge of the actual existence of the transcendent because it could not be experienced by our senses and subsequently ordered by the categories of the mind. In his *Critique of Practical Reason* he declared, however, that practical morality demands that we "postulate" the *existence* of freedom, immortality, and God. They cannot be "proved" rationally, but they can be assumed, and in fact they must be postulated if our moral experience is to be possible. Without these postulates, he argued, morality and virtue are destroyed. Kant called the affirmation of his postulates an act of "pure rational faith." In the *Critique of Pure Reason* he said, "I have found it necessary to deny knowledge (of the supersensible) in order to make room for faith." In the *Critique of Practical Reason* Kant defined faith as purely rational. In the *Critique of Judgment* he declared that faith (as "habitus" or disposition) is the moral attitude inclining toward belief in something beyond theoretical knowledge.

Future generations of thinkers followed Kant's lead arguing that the *only* basis for knowledge of the existence of God lies in human experience, that is, in ethics and morality. Many accepted his view that the only way to discover any knowledge about God is through ethical action based on faith in ideas that cannot be demonstrably known. In spite of his pietistic upbringing, Immanuel Kant became the father of theological liberalism, which denies that God has revealed sure and certain knowledge of Himself in the Bible and in Jesus Christ. Such liberalism asserts instead that God may be assumed to exist on the basis of the needs of subjective human moral consciousness. Kant's dualism between noumenal and phenomenal reality led to a modern skepticism that limits knowledge to what can be apprehended by means of our senses and denies that spiritual reality can be known at all. For Kant and his modern disciples, Plato's forms are unknowable because they cannot be apprehended by the senses. Moreover, people can discuss God, the nature of the soul, salvation, etc., only by making an intellectual "leap of faith" out of space-time reality to the noumenal realm where no verification is possible. We can *believe* in such things, but we cannot *know* them. Thus "the philosopher of Protestantism" pushed generations of seekers after knowledge into the abyss of subjectivism.

Critics charge that Kant's idea of the thing-in-itself is unnecessary, that his classification of the categories of the mind is arbitrary and artificial, and that his morality is hopelessly subjective. Yet many applaud his effort to relate conceptual thought (rationalism) to perceptual content (empiricism).

Summary

What were the basic presuppositions of Immanuel Kant? They may be summarized as follows:

1. He viewed man as essentially good, rational, and autonomous. Kant postulated an invisible, noumenal world in which man is free and immortal. In the concrete, empirical, phenomenal world, man's mind is capable of a limited knowledge of objects. Seen from either the noumenal or the phenomenal perspective, man is noble, good, and capable of knowledge. Reason is the essence of man. In one of his last writings, *Religion Within the Limits of Reason Alone*, Kant admitted that there is a radical evil in man. In practice, however, he implicitly ignored this conviction in order to save man's ability to know and perform the moral law. Human beings are autonomous, free to choose between good and evil, and capable of virtue. Because reason is innate to all people, we are under no other authority than our own rationality. We know what is and what ought to be, and therefore we have no need of repentance or forgiveness or a Savior.

2. Kant believed that the human mind creates knowledge as it interacts with sense experience. Unless something is empirically objectifiable and capable of being "squeezed" through intuitions and categories of the mind, it has no existence. Pure reason, according to Kant, only leads to hopeless contradictions called antinomies. Kant never acknowledged that since the fall human reason has been limited and deficient. In his insistence that reason cannot demonstrate the existence of God, Kant exemplified the biblical teaching that "the natural man receives not the things of the Spirit of God: for they are foolishness to him, neither can he know them" (I Cor. 2:14). Kant seems to have confused noetic statements (how we know) with ontic statements (what we know), making the former determinative for the latter. Our knowledge of objects is ultimately the work of our minds because we are basically rational. Kant pictured the postulates

not as revelation but as creations of the human mind, which, in turn, regulates human thought. He nowhere acknowledged that God participates in the knowledge process or that man's mind has been corrupted by sin. In stark contrast to the biblical teaching that knowledge comes from God, Kant presented the mind of man as the creator and sustainer of knowledge.

3. Kant rejected the notion of the revealing, Triune God of the Judeo-Christian revelation. Experience gives us no valid knowledge about God. By faith and in conformity with reason, Kant assumed God exists because the moral life demands a being who could connect virtue and happiness. But God is of relatively little importance to Kant's philosophy. As an abstract, logical principle created by reason, God was brought into his philosophy merely to provide support for his moral system. Man's mind is the final judge of morality. In fact, because human reason was Kant's starting point, the real ultimate for him was man himself. Autonomous man actually replaced the God whose existence he had postulated.

Kant's attempt to reconcile rationalism and empiricism gave birth in the nineteenth century to subjective existentialism, positivistic scientism, and religious moralism. His long shadow has stretched across the years to our own day.

What is the Christian response to Kant? Some Christians maintain that Kant should have acknowledged as his basic presupposition that the biblical God of revelation exists and that He has revealed His truth both in the phenomenal and the noumenal worlds. Such a position reconciles the rational and empirical worlds in God. It explains that God's revelation of the noumenal world took place in the phenomenal world of nature and history (especially of Old Testament Israel and the Christian church) and in the processes of human thought. Accepting this presupposition of the revealing God of the Bible allows us to see God at work, permeating and uniting the noumenal and phenomenal realms. This view, moreover, asserts that God cleanses, heals, and enables human minds to perceive and experience both noumenal and phenomenal realities. It also explains the limitations of human reason as resulting from the fall.

A significant task awaiting Christian thinkers in the late twentieth century is to rethink Kant's philosophy upon the foundations of biblical teaching.

For Further Reading

Adler, Mortimer J. *Ten Philosophical Mistakes*. New York: Macmillan, 1985.

Brown, Colin. *Philosophy and the Christian Faith*. Downer's Grove, Ill.: Inter-Varsity, 1968.

Clark, Gordon H. *Thales to Dewey*. Boston: Houghton Mifflin, 1957.

Collins, James. *God in Modern Philosophy*. Chicago: Henry Regnery, 1959.

———. *A History of Modern European Philosophy*. Milwaukee: Bruce, 1954.

Copleston, Frederick C. *A History of Philosophy*, vol. 6. Garden City, N.Y.: Doubleday, 1985.

Davis, John Jefferson. "Kant and the Problem of Religious Knowledge." Chap. 17 in *Perspectives on Evangelical Theology*. Grand Rapids: Baker, 1979.

Henry, Carl F. H., *God, Revelation and Authority*, vol. 1. Waco, Tex.: Word, 1976.

Jones, W. T. *Kant and the Nineteenth Century*. New York: Harcourt Brace Jovanovich, 1952.

Kant, Immanuel. *Critique of Pure Reason*. Translated by Norman Kemp Smith. New York: St. Martin's, 1965.

———. *Religion Within the Limits of Reason Alone*. Translated by T. M. Greene. Chicago: Open Court, 1934.

Korner, S. *Kant*. Baltimore: Penguin, 1955.

Nash, Ronald H. *The Word of God and the Mind of Man*. Grand Rapids: Zondervan, 1982.

Walsh, W. H. "Kant," *Encyclopedia of Philosophy*, vol. 4. New York: Macmillan, 1967.

IV.
CONTEMPORARY
EPISTEMOLOGIES

15
Positivism, Existentialism, and Pragmatism

Charles S. MacKenzie

Kant's Influence on Contemporary Thought

Dispute over epistemological issues lies at the heart of the contemporary cultural crisis. In earlier periods of history most members of Western societies agreed on a certain core of convictions. Those beliefs rested upon a widely accepted world view or epistemological outlook. But in the modern period no such central core of beliefs unifies people because they now disagree about basic epistemological presuppositions.

In reaction to Immanuel Kant, epistemology has moved in at least three different directions. Kant's teaching that the phenomenal world feeds raw data into the mind eventually inspired the rise of positivism. His emphasis on the inner, subjective workings of the human mind stimulated the development of modern existentialism. A third epistemology, pragmatism, arose as an alternative to positivism (objectivism), on the one hand, and existentialism (subjectivism), on the other.

Positivism

What is positivism? It is an attitude or an approach to life that assumes first that human beings can only have knowledge of physical phenomena and second that our knowledge of phenomena is relative, not absolute. Positivists argue that nature has no underlying purpose or inner essence to shape its development or direction.

French philosopher Auguste Comte (1798–1857) formulated the basic assumptions of positivism. In his efforts to reshape society he developed a positivistic science of society, which he called sociology. He taught that the history of ideas has moved progressively through three stages. The earliest societies were *theological*; their people explained what is meant by the idea of the divine. Later, societies advanced to a *metaphysical* stage, which used abstract philosophical ideas to explain the world and life. In the highest stage, the *positivistic*, or scientific, interest in relations among phenomena came to dominate. Comte argued that human society was evolving toward this third stage. In Comte's positivistic religion humanity became the new deity struggling to create a new society based solely on its own empirical experiences.

Positivism has assumed varying forms in the twentieth century. It has emerged as *scientism*, which repudiates all that cannot be reduced to the physical and studied by means of scientific method. Positivism has also taken the form of *logical positivism*. In the 1920s a group of philosophers, scientists, and mathematicians who met in Vienna became known as the "Vienna Circle." They developed the logical positivism espoused by Rudolph Carnap, Ludwig Wittgenstein, and others who rejected traditional metaphysics, declaring its language to be meaningless. Instead, they advocated an empiricism relying exclusively upon man's sense experiences. According to their dominant idea, the "verification principle," the "meaning" of a statement is its method of verification. Only utterances that can be verified by the senses have any meaning. Thus the logical positivists assumed that (1) verification rests upon empirical observation alone, and (2) an utterance that cannot be verified in this manner is meaningless and therefore not worthy of attention. They focused not so much on what is true or false as on what is meaningful or meaningless.

Like Kant, positivists distinguished analytic from synthetic statements. In analytic statements the subject already contains the predicate, and therefore the statement adds no new knowledge about the subject. The significance of such statements does *not* depend upon experience. Analytic statements simply allow positivists to analyze the meaning of words and their consistent or inconsistent usage. In synthetic statements, however, the predicate provides new knowledge about the subject, information that is verifiable by sense experience. Positivists focused their attention primarily on the *meaningfulness* of these synthetic propositions. In this way, they rejected all metaphysical, theological, or value statements as "meaningless." Such statements are not worth investigating because they cannot pass the stringent verification principle.

Thus positivism discards talk of "God's existence" as nonsensical and describes man as a totally materialistic being. It leads either to a skepticism or to complete philosophical relativism, which rejects all traditional absolutes.

From the beginning positivism was fraught with serious problems. *First*, the verification principle upon which this philosophy was based is itself incapable of verification. The positivist cannot rightly say that "no proposition is meaningful unless it can be empirically verified" until he has examined every statement ever uttered or written. If somewhere there is one statement that is meaningful apart from verification by the senses, positivism is demolished. Until the positivist has examined all statements, he cannot verify his own verification principle. Such a task, however, is impossible. And, in fact, the positivist cannot properly make any universal, negative statement. He is inconsistent to say "there is no God." Unless the positivist can be everywhere at the same moment, he is unable to verify his atheism empirically because God may be dwelling somewhere, waiting to be discovered.

Second, the positivists' frequent use of the word *meaning* is nonsensical. Apart from some ultimate value or being, "meaning" is relative to each person's experience and has no objective existence.

Third, the positivists' exclusive preoccupation with the physical is lopsided. It utterly ignores the invisible, spiritual dimensions of life, which humanity has both affirmed and experienced through the centuries. Positivists also fail to appreciate those grand human emotions aroused by praying, being in love, hearing a symphony, or viewing a magnificent work of art since positivism reduces these emotions to physical or chemical reactions.

Yet in our technological society, positivism increasingly attracts adherents even as its rejection of transcendence and of ultimate meaning inevitably dehumanizes and destroys man. Societies that regard man as a mere body, a mass of physical reactions, will come to regard him as simply a cog in a giant machine and will treat him accordingly. Objective values will sink into the quicksand of relativism. People eventually will be considered animals to be manipulated and controlled.

Existentialism

Like positivism, existentialism draws inspiration from Immanuel Kant. Modern existentialists build upon his teaching on the subjective inner workings of the mind. Some see roots of existentialism in Augustine's stress on the internal state of the Christian as he relates to God.

In modern times existentialism has achieved worldwide popularity in such diverse cultural fields as literature, drama, poetry, art, and theology. Its main themes were developed by Soren Kierkegaard in the mid-nineteenth century. Variations of existentialist themes also appear in the works of Schelling, Marx, and Nietzsche. In the twentieth century Jaspers, Heidegger, Marcel, Sartre, and Camus are among those who have advocated existentialism. It has flourished in the West since World War II. Spreading from the left bank of Paris to Greenwich Village in New York City, and then across America, it has been popularized by such diverse sources as neoorthodox theology, beatniks, hippies, the Theater of the Absurd, the films of Ingmar Bergman, and Zen Buddhism.

With its emphasis on individual existence, existentialism is in part a reaction against the dehumanizing tendencies of mass society. The social sciences, which stress collective behavior, philosophical systems that deny individual freedom, oppressive dictators who violate human rights, and industrialism and technology, which make workers into anonymous, interchangeable units of production, all push the individual with his feelings and aspirations into the background.

What then is existentialism? It is not a philosophy, an attitude, or a system, but a way of life that grows out of concrete existence in the midst of the sweat and tears of experience rather than out of theoretical contemplation in a philosopher's ivory tower. Existentialists hold that only those who are self-consciously immersed in living amidst the concrete situations of life will encounter reality. Man *is* his existence. Existentialism is concerned more with what a person does than with what he thinks, though thought is not abandoned. Existence and one's thoughts about existence interact and feed on each other.

At its heart, existentialism is subjective. It concentrates on the moods of man—fear and dread, anxiety and guilt. These moods, to the existentialist, reflect reality and reveal in part the nature of existence.

Common to all existential thinking is the concept that "existence precedes essence."[1] This phrase simply means that you *are* before you discover *who* you are. At first a person has only an awareness of being in one time and place: a situation. He is aware only of the fact that he exists. Awareness of one's existence provokes a compelling need to determine *who* one is in that time and place, to discover personal identity or essence. Only by committing his life to something can a person discover this essence. Presupposing that there is no God, atheistic existentialism declares every person to be "free" to make of himself precisely what he chooses. People act in "bad faith" any time they allow the wishes of society, religion, or politics to interfere with what they want to be. Theistic existentialists such as Kierkegaard, Dostoevsky, and Berdyaev disagree. Believing God to be the ultimate source of reality in the universe, they argue that one discovers real essence by a commitment to God. Biblical Christianity asserts, contrary to both groups of existentialists, that "essence precedes existence." In His divine omniscience, God knows who and what man is before he is ever born; God gives to man both existence and essence.

Comparing man to the first automobile can help us understand this crucial concept that "existence precedes essence." The inventor of the first automobile sought to design a vehicle to fulfill a

1. The following four paragraphs were contributed by Dr. John Timmerman, Professor of English, Calvin College.

function, to transport people under its own power from one point to another, to be a mobile auto. Thus the inventor asked himself how best to accomplish this task. The auto must have wheels, a motor to power the wheels from point A to point B, and a place for passengers to sit. With this picture in mind, the inventor built a car. Therefore, the essence of the automobile—all the things it was designed to do or that warranted its existence—preceded its existence.

A Christian anthropology asserts similar things about man. In His divine plan God had an idea of who man would be and what he would do. Jean Paul Sartre said that Christians tend to think of God as the "supernal craftsman," implying that when God created He knew exactly what He was creating, that God had in mind a conception of people just as the inventor had of the automobile.

For Sartre, an atheist, the situation is quite different. He argued that there is no *given* human nature because there is no God to have a conception of it. Man merely exists and only later becomes his essential self. At first man simply is. Man becomes what he makes of himself.

Existentialists, whether atheists or theists, make the existing individual their starting point or basic presupposition rather than God. The existing individual is central to their method. For that reason, existentialism has been called humanism (Sartre) or philosophic anthropology (Berdyaev).

Soren Kierkegaard described the human situation in this way: People are thrown into a dangerous sea, where their lives are at stake. They thrash about in an effort to stay afloat. As they do, they discover that they are barely able to support themselves. Thus they conclude that human beings are self-dependent, autonomous, and alone in the universe. Atheistic existentialism developed out of this analysis of the human situation. But Christian existentialists, while thrashing about in the sea, discover a source of help outside themselves. In such a struggle to find meaning, Kierkegaard encountered the crucified one. When their whole existence is at stake, some meet God, while others discover nothingness, leading to two forms of existentialism: Christian and atheist.

The Christian Existentialism of Kierkegaard

Chief among Christian existentialists was Soren Kierkegaard (1813–1855), the "melancholy Dane." His major works include *Fear and Trembling, The Concept of Dread,* and *The Sickness Unto Death.* These titles indicate his preoccupation with the subjective. Born in Copenhagen, he attended the University of Copenhagen where he studied the philosophy of German idealist G. W. F. Hegel (1770–1831). Hegel's comprehensive philosophy purported to explain rationally all of reality, but it practically ignored the actual existence of the individual. Kierkegaard reacted strongly to the abstractness of Hegel's system, which taught individuals to *think* rather than to *be.* Kierkegaard distinguished between the uninvolved spectator in the audience and the involved actor on the stage and argued that only the actor is authentically involved in existence.

Kierkegaard described "three stages on life's way." Each of these stages, he believed, provides valuable insight into human existence. The first stage is the *aesthetic,* where a person is ruled by his senses. He has no specific beliefs and lives only for his own pleasures. Since his only choices are between what pleasures he wants to indulge in, he makes no long-term commitments. He merely exists and finds little authenticity (quality). While it might appear attractive on the surface, the aesthetic life leads ultimately to boredom and despair. At this stage, man lives in the cellar; he does not develop his authentic self and does not truly experience existence. Having arrived at despair, however, man finally has a true choice, an either-or. *Either* he can stay in this inauthentic existence *or* he can commit himself to something.

Choice impels a person to the second stage of existence, the *ethical,* where he is aware of the rules of conduct that reason formulates. Socrates typified the ethical man who thinks himself to be responsible and self-sufficient and thus commits himself to living morally. He recognizes his need to make personal commitments and attempts to fulfill the demands of the moral law. While boredom eventually brings the aesthetic man to despair, his inability to fulfill the moral law inevitably causes the ethical man to feel guilty. Thus ethical men eventually confront another radical either-or decision. They respond to their awareness of guilt and estrangement from God *either* by remaining at this stage and struggling to fulfill the moral law *or* by advancing to a higher stage. Individuals can reach this next stage, Kierkegaard explained, only by an act of commitment, by an existential leap of faith.

In this third stage, the *religious*, suffering man (suffering is the most intense subjectivity) is confronted with a paradox that defies reason. Truth for Kierkegaard is subjectivity. He mercilessly attacked objective conceptions of truth in which a serenely detached thinker philosophizes on what is true. Truth that ultimately matters is seized by a passionate leap from all that is objectively safe to what appears absurd to our reason. The paradox is that the *infinite* (God) is revealed in the *finite* (Christ). When ethical man risks his life by making a commitment and taking a leap of faith in which his whole existence is at stake, he discovers his authentic self, and he spans the chasm between man and God.

Kierkegaard's central theme is that each person has an essential self, which he ought to actualize. Individuals may live to some degree at each stage along life's way. But each stage is separated from the others by qualitative differences of authenticity. Movement from one stage to another involves passing through the "moment" when one leaves error and is "in the truth" (has faith). Moving from one stage to another demands choices (either-or) that involve one's total existence.

Kierkegaard's epistemology reveals certain theological and anthropological presuppositions.

1. As thinking man is Descartes's starting point (*cogito ergo sum*), so existing man is Kierkegaard's starting point. Man's estrangement from God as a result of the fall produces his *existential*, alienated condition. Sin violates the person of God. Only by trusting God can man's essential self become actualized. Fallen man's focus has been on essence, and he is estranged from

his essential being. Until he finds his essential self by having faith in God, his life is filled with anxiety because his existential self is alienated from his essential self.

Though Kierkegaard recognized man's estrangement from God and his consequent guilt, anxiety, and despair, he did not believe man is "dead in trespasses and sin" (cf. Eph. 2:1). Critics charge that Kierkegaard's view of the human condition is semi-Pelagian because he seemed to argue that the will of man is capable of doing its part in achieving salvation (that is, actualizing his essential self). That human beings retain power to choose whether or not they will take the leap of faith indicates they possess some degree of autonomy. Admittedly, Kierkegaard taught that man should live according to the will of God and should follow Jesus' teaching. Yet by emphasizing human choice and initiative in self-actualization, Kierkegaard seems to have made man at least semi-autonomous.

2. Kierkegaard's view of God is orthodox, though some have argued that it is not fully biblical. He believed in the Trinity. He regarded Christianity as the ultimate paradox. Even though he considered Christ to be God and Savior, Jesus appears to have been most important to Kierkegaard as a *teacher*. Therefore, he did not seem aware of the full scope of the grace of God—His unmerited love and favor. This is illustrated by Kierkegaard's use of the metaphor that God is like a woman who keeps her lover guessing whether she loves him so as to stir up passion within him. The personal sense of anguish and guilt that haunted the "melancholy Dane" for most of his life also suggests that his conception of God's free gift of grace was inadequate and incomplete. This undoubtedly led him to believe that people could play a major role in achieving their own salvation. His understanding of redemption therefore minimized the sovereignty of God's grace and attributed too much ability to human power of choice.

Moreover, to Kierkegaard, man, not God, was the starting point. It is not God who seeks a relationship with man, but man who discovers God as he struggles to survive in the sea of existence. Although Kierkegaard viewed God as the *subject* who encounters man the *object*, God seems to be standing offstage, waiting for semi-autonomous man to make the first move out of despair and leap in faith toward Him.

3. Epistemologically, Kierkegaard was a romantic subjectivist. For Kierkegaard, truth is subjectivity—not something cold and objective, a system of ideas that can be grasped by intellectual cognition. Truth is subjectively appropriated, as individuals passionately hold it with great inward emotion. The *strength* of ones beliefs is much more important than the *content* of one's beliefs. Whatever an individual believes intensely is true *for him*. Truth must be lived, and an individual discovers truth by listening and responding to his own moods and feelings. Since thought needs to be rooted in existence and action, reason is less important than emotions. Those feelings which are experienced in the moment of existential decision and action reveal reality and are the basis for any true knowledge. Knowledge becomes possible only through the experience of action, involvement, decision, and encounter with existence. Knowledge of God comes only through a leap of faith, which is the ultimate involvement.

Thus Kierkegaard's conception of knowledge and how we apprehend it broke sharply from traditional views of special revelation. According to traditional views, God reveals truth in His written Word, and Christians use the Scriptures to write creeds and statements of doctrine. To be a Christian is to believe Christian teachings. By depreciating the content of truth Kierkegaard severely undercut Christianity's claim that God's revelation is objectively true.

But even Kierkegaard's opponents acknowledge that his emphasis on subjectivity effectively challenges Christians not to reduce faith to intellectual cognition alone. Faith that is genuine is not merely a calculated assent to dogmatic statements. Vital Christian faith is an affair of the heart, as well as the intellect, and thus includes one's emotions and will.

The existentialist emphases on individual existence, subjectivity and inwardness, and commitment and existential involvement all spring from Kierkegaard. In the final analysis, his epistemology stressed man more than God.

The Religious Existentialism of Jaspers and Marcel

Karl Jaspers and Gabriel Marcel are twentieth-century advocates of religious existentialism. Jaspers, deeply influenced by Kierkegaard, also saw three stages in life. In the first, man has a knowledge only of objects. Those who reach the second stage realize that they themselves are the foundation stones of existence. Some individuals move on to a third stage where they recognize their finitude as they face limiting situations, like death, and become conscious that they are reaching toward their real selves. As people recognize their own finitude, they also become aware of the transcendent, which theology describes as God. Concurrently, individuals realize that they are free to choose a relationship with the transcendent. Choosing that relationship gives them authentic existence. The self and the subjective are part of existence. The subject matter of existence is the immediate personal experience of the individual. An individual's own experience enables him to grasp the meaning of existence. Those who understand their own existence have a new basis for thinking and acting and achieve union with the depths of reality (the transcendent).

Gabriel Marcel, a Roman Catholic thinker, also espouses religious existentialism. He considers fidelity to be the key to one's existence. He is preoccupied with the mystery of "What am I?" Because the "I" is not an "it," the question remains a mystery that man lives with, not a problem he analyzes by reason. For Marcel, individuals always exist in situations. Human beings are unique because they make promises with others. Through being faithful a person discovers clues concerning his existence, shapes his life, expresses his faith in that which is beyond himself, and achieves authenticity. Fidelity gives life meaning and thereby affirms man's own existence. However, Marcel seems to regard fidelity as a human accomplishment. All three religious existentialists, Marcel, Jaspers, and Kierkegaard, seem to view human beings as semi-autonomous and to some degree self-perfectible.

The Atheistic Existentialism of Sartre

The twentieth century has also produced powerful proponents of nonreligious (or atheistic) existentialism. After service in the French army and Resistance movement during World War II, Jean Paul Sartre began to write about existentialism. His major works are *Being and Nothingness* (1943) and *Existentialism Is a Humanism* (1946). Sartre followed after Kant in limiting knowledge to experience, although he criticized Kant for appealing to a "thing-in-itself" (noumenon) behind phenomena. Deeply influenced by Martin Heidegger, who was concerned chiefly with being and with the existence of the individual as a means for understanding being, Sartre also became preoccupied almost exclusively with the individual's existence. As with Descartes and religious existentialists, man is his starting point. But for Sartre there is no God. Apart from the existing individual there is nothingness. Our awareness of nothingness leads us to an awareness of freedom, which, in turn, produces anxiety. For Sartre, man is free in his condition in life. In the spirit of Descartes's methodical doubt, Sartre's freedom is a freedom to say no. Freedom becomes the basis of action.

What gives man dignity is his inner, subjective life. Sartre distinguished being that rests in-itself (*en soi*), such as a rock, from being that is aware of itself (*pour soi*), such as a man. To have inner consciousness is to have a future, and to have a future is to put the full responsibility for each individual's existence upon his own shoulder. All men must ask whether they would be willing to have others choose the same road they choose. Since man has no given essence or being, there are no values or guidelines. Man must choose—or invent—his future.

Sartre's basic presuppositions are the following:

1. Autonomous man is everything. "Man is the being who wants to be God." The human situation is one of absurdity and tragic abandonment. Man is not basically either good or evil because to Sartre there are no values that man does not create. Only by expressing their own individual humanity in behavior can people become authentic. Those who do not act, who do not

make choices and commitments, are guilty of inauthenticity, of playing a role. Man is basically free, though his freedom is limited by the "facticity" (conditions or facts) of the situation in which he is abandoned. Man *is* the sum total of *his actions*, and he must accept responsibility for what he makes of himself. Thus Sartre saw man as completely autonomous and self-sufficient.

2. Sartre further highlighted human existence as the sole value in reality by saying that there is nothingness apart from the existing individual. All beings are framed by nothingness, and to exist is but a brief interlude in nonbeing; therefore, there is no God. Using another striking image Sartre wrote, "Nothingness lies coiled in the heart of being, like a worm."

3. Reality is only experienced by action. There is no meaning or purpose or knowledge in life apart from choices of the will that result in action. Each person puts sense into his own life. Existing man creates whatever knowledge he has.

An Evaluation of Existentialism

How should we evaluate existentialism? Since every person has moments when his entire individual existence seems at stake—his inner feelings speak loudly and clearly—and since everyone experiences new insights into reality when he makes difficult decisions, it must be admitted that existentialism has many valid insights.

One major weakness of existentialism, however, is its almost total preoccupation with the subjectivity of the existing individual. Are feelings, moods, and inner self-analysis all there is to reality? Does the objective world have any validity? Existentialism's neglect of reason, science, and the objective world leaves it open to the charge that it fails to deal adequately with the vast areas of the human experience including the objective world. Sartre's classic work *Nausea* pictures the objective world as a vague, ephemeral, almost unknowable dream world. Is this reality? Is subjectivity everything, or do stable, objective realities exist? Existentialists need to reconsider their position and balance subjective and objective elements by affirming the primacy of existence while preserving the importance of essences. Existence without essence and subjectivity without objectivity is inadequate as a comprehensive world view. Existentialists correctly criticize rationalists and pseudoscientists who claim exhaustive knowledge of human beings and their values through rational or scientific methods, or both. But they fail to provide an alternative epistemology that takes into account the complexity of existence provided by the biblical world view.

A second weakness in existentialism is the relativism that results when each person does his own thing. Because actions rest on feelings instead of values, they may change from day to day. Consistency is not important. So Sartre could espouse freedom and yet join the communist party. And Kierkegaard could espouse the "teleological suspension of the ethical" (suspending the requirement to obey the moral law in order to obey some "higher" call from God, as if God would contradict His law by requiring a person to suspend it) and yet profess Christianity. Consistency is meaningless to those who focus on the shifting subjective states of the existing individual. But society would collapse if there were no universal laws to which people are responsible. Atheistic existentialism, if practiced by everyone, would tend to produce anarchy, which would destroy society. By its extreme emphasis on individuality, even Christian existentialism threatens the well-being of both society and the church.

A third weakness of existentialism is its fragmentation of reality. According to this philosophy, each individual experiences existence uniquely and differently. Without an unchanging essence or an immutable God to give unity and universality, however, reality becomes hopelessly fragmented since one individual's experience is as valid as another's. Thus existence becomes a tangled, kaleidoscopic melange of millions of experiences of existence. Reality becomes quicksand where no one can tread or act. Yet people *do* act. And individuals *do* achieve. The facts of life refute existentialism.

While existentialism has weaknesses, it also has great strength inasmuch as it draws attention to crucial human concerns. By appealing to man's inner feelings and affirming the importance of the individual, it strikes a responsive chord in the human heart. It expresses the desires of autonomous man to be free of dehumanizing systems. Existentialism, with both its ennobling and its destructive emphases, will influence civilization for many years to come.

Pragmatism

Into contemporary culture, saturated with positivist and existentialist presuppositions, has come a third new epistemology: pragmatism. Pragmatism shares similarities with the views of Heraclitus ("All is change"), the Greek Sophists (knowledge is based on sense experience) and Francis Bacon (the experimental study of nature). It is, however, a peculiarly American philosophy that was defined by Charles S. Peirce, popularized by William James, and infused into American social structures by John Dewey.

Pragmatists sought to mediate between scientific positivism and the philosophical idealism developed by Kant, Hegel, and the neo-Hegelians. Both rationalists and idealists continued Kant's emphasis on the power of the mind in shaping how reality is understood. Pragmatists agree with empiricism that people must adopt a pluralistic approach to knowledge. Pragmatism rejects universals and absolutes and focuses instead on man's experience of the shifting, changing environment. To the pragmatist, the environment is critically important because the world is constantly changing, and it affects each person differently from moment to moment. With the rationalists, pragmatists regard values as highly important, though they considered them transitory and not ultimate. Pragmatism combines the positivist emphasis on the observation of facts with its own stress on human belief and volition. Its proponents profess to link facts and values, science and philosophy. They argue that their epistemology accounts for both knowledge and value. It produces knowledge to the limited degree that insight and meaning emerge from experience. Knowledge, however, is incidental and secondary to action. Only as people are engaged in active experience with situations does "knowing" occur. Experience is like a stream in which people and things meet and interact. Pragmatism supposedly yields value by prompting action that brings about results suited to specific situations. Values which emerge in the interaction of people and things, are always changing, never absolute.

Charles Sanders Peirce (1839–1914), an American philosopher, physicist, and mathematician, was more of a realist than a pragmatist. Because he coined the term "pragmatism," however, and used it to determine the meaning of ideas, and because of his influence upon William James, he has been considered the founder of pragmatism. He said, "to determine the meaning of any idea, put it into practice . . . and whatever its consequences prove to be, these constitute the meaning of the idea." His criterion was better suited to determining the content rather than the truth of an idea.

The "function of philosophy," declared Harvard professor William James (1842–1910), "ought to be to find out what definite difference it will make to you and me . . . if this world-formula or that world-formula be the true one." He practically reduced the pragmatic method to the words "does it work." Yet his pragmatism stood for no particular results. "Truth happens to an idea." Ideas become true as they help us to connect and explain the various parts of human experience. An idea is significant if it can be carried out in a successful, self-fulfilling way. James regarded truth, once it was verified by the pragmatic method, as having some permanence. Thus his was not the naturalistic pragmatism of John Dewey.

Believing that thought is instrumental in solving problems, John Dewey (1859–1952) gave his mature theories the name "instrumentalism." His philosophy also is known as "experimentalism" because he insisted that thinking tested by experimentation is most likely to result in knowledge. Consistent with the vast majority of modern and contemporary philosophers, Dewey repudiated classical epistemologies. He disparaged contemplation of eternal forms or essences as mere "spectator theory." He also rejected any absolute truth. There are no norms, or givens, or self-evident principles that are indubitable or absolutely certain. Rather, knowledge is an ongoing, self-corrective quest of a community of scholars who constantly revise what we know based on critical research. No knowledge can claim exemption from experimental testing that helps philosophers sharpen and refine their ideas. "There is but one sure road of access to truth—the road of patient, cooperative inquiry operating by means of observation, experiment, record and controlled reflection." Man's mind relates him as an organism to his environment. Man is a concrete social phenomenon whose deeds result from social interaction, not individual volition. Man is simply a part of nature. Thinking enables people to adjust to their environment, not to find eternal truth. Man can interact with the world, but he is not an acting, free cause of change. Philosophies ought to be evaluated by whether or not they make life situations "more significant, more luminous to us and make our dealings with them more fruitful."

Dewey also taught that human nature has certain inherited capacities that work differently under different social conditions. Evil is in the environment, not in human nature. Alter the environment and human conduct can be improved. Dewey's presuppositions were borrowed from secular science. There are no absolute values that we can use to structure the social environment. Rather, people must use those techniques which emerge when the scientific method is applied to human experience.

James and Dewey differed sharply over whether a spiritual reality exists. James argued that simply because the empirical world is dynamic and changing does not mean that a spiritual world of unchanging essences could not exist. Dewey's later thought was totally naturalistic, denying the possibility of unchanging, transcendent realities. James tended to be a polytheist, believing in several finite "gods." "It need not be infinite," he wrote, "it need not be solitary. It might conceivably even be only a larger and more godlike self . . . and the universe might conceivably be a collection of such selves . . . with no absolute unity realized in it at all." Neither James nor Dewey believed, however, in the biblical God who reveals Himself to humanity. Dewey called God an ideal that does not exist in the present but that becomes a part of man's life as the future becomes present. His "God" was not personal but was the relation uniting the ideal and the actual in the experience of man.

A Common Faith

"God" was seen as the highest ideal that man could conceptualize. "Suppose for a moment," Dewey theorized, "that the word 'God' means the ideal ends that . . . one acknowledges as having authority over his volition and emotions, the values to which one is supremely devoted. . . . " Dewey's goal was to destroy belief in a personal God and "the sacred ark of absolute permanency" in order to transform "the treatment of morals, politics and religion." He succeeded in spreading the use and influence of pragmatic principles in American politics, education, and ethics.

Appointed as head of the department of philosophy, psychology, and pedagogy at the University of Chicago in 1894, Dewey and his associates achieved national and international fame for revising American educational philosophy. Dewey adapted pragmatist principles to reject teaching that imposed a formal, rigid curriculum upon predominantly passive children. He proposed instead a "progressive education" in which children experimentally interact with their environment. Education became a continuous reconstructive experience cultivating the students' creativity and autonomy as children learned "by doing." Dewey and his followers taught morality, for example, not by telling the pupil what is right and wrong—for no absolute knowledge of moral principles is possible—but by encouraging students to remain open minded so that they could change their views as experience and circumstances warranted. Acceptance of Dewey's pragmatic philosophy has produced belief that public education is to be morally neutral and that values are merely reflections of radically shifting opinions in the public order.

Pragmatists hold that statements are meaningful if they have favorable consequences. But the question they never adequately answer is Who determines what consequences are meaningful or favorable? By what standard can one determine whether a proposition "works?" What "works" for one person may not "work" for another. Inevitably, pragmatism leads to relativism and fragmentation because it rejects or ignores an ultimate (God), it requires each individual to determine what works for him, and it bases its knowledge exclusively on the created order. Most pragmatists stress the connection between one's ideas and one's purposes rather than the actual truth or falsity of ideas.

Pragmatism is helpful insofar as it tends to keep people in touch with the real world. But it overemphasizes the experimental method. Are there not situations such as being in love or praying to God in which other epistemological methods may be more appropriate? In addition, it exalts individual experiences and depreciates experiences that are common to all people. Consequently, it lacks an overarching unity that can bring together all experience into interrelatedness and meaning. Even the original pragmatic idea is subject to question. Do the consequences following from an idea or an act actually constitute its meaning or essence? Or are the consequences of an idea or act merely evidences of a more important and even ultimate essence or meaning?

Conclusion

Following Kant, each of these contemporary epistemologies makes man or nature the center of reality and knowledge. All of them reject the God who has revealed Himself through Christ and the Bible as the source of knowledge. They all make knowledge earthbound and steadily abandon that transcendence without which no culture can survive. As man separates himself from God, knowledge becomes increasingly fragmented and relative. The crisis of our times is in large measure an epistemological one. Contemporary epistemologies leave society bewildered and alienated as people grope for some essential truth that can unite their minds and ethical perspectives. But this crisis may also serve to highlight the inadequacies of naturalistic philosophy and to encourage human beings to look toward the living God, who alone is the source of truth and knowledge.

For Further Reading

Bretall, Robert. *A Kierkegaard Anthology*. New York: Random, 1936.

Brown, Colin. *Philosophy and the Christian Faith*. Downers Grove, Ill: Inter-Varsity, 1968.

Burtt, Edwin A. *Types of Religious Philosophy*. New York: Harper, 1938.

Clark, Gordon H. *Thales to Dewey*. Boston: Houghton Mifflin, 1957.

Collins, James. *The Existentialists: A Critical Study*. Chicago: Henry Regnery, 1952.

———.*The Mind of Kierkegaard*. Chicago: Henry Regnery, 1953.

Copleston, Frederick C. *A History of Philosophy*, vols. 8, 9. Garden City, N.Y.: Doubleday, 1966, 1975.

———.*Contemporary Philosophy*. London: Burns and Oates, 1956.

Dewey, John. *A Common Faith*. New Haven: Yale University Press, 1934.

Henry, Carl F. H. *God, Revelation and Authority*, vol. 1. Waco, Tex.: Word, 1976.

Holmes, Arthur. *Christianity and Philosophy*. Chicago: Inter-Varsity, 1960.

James, William. *Pragmatism*. New York: Meridian, 1955.

Jones, W. T. *Kant and the Nineteenth Century*. New York: Harcourt Brace Jovanovich, 1952.

Kallen, Horace M. *The Philosophy of William James*. New York: Random, n.d.

Mackintosh, H. R. *Types of Modern Theology*. New York: Charles Scribner's Sons, 1937.

Schaeffer, Francis A. *The God Who Is There*. Downers Grove, Ill.: Inter-Varsity, 1968.

Tillich, Paul. *Perspectives on 19th and 20th Century Theology*, ed. Carl Braaten. New York: Harper and Row, 1967.

Wells, David F. *The Search for Salvation*. Downers Grove, Ill.: Inter-Varsity, 1978.

Epilogue:
A Challenge to Our Generation
W. Andrew Hoffecker

Our historical survey and biblical evaluation of Western world views has traced the development of both Christian and non-Christian thought. Biblical and naturalistic perspectives have vied for dominance in the history of philosophy and religion. In earlier times Christian ideas frequently held sway only to be eclipsed by naturalistic philosophies in subsequent generations. Then Christianity reemerged at some later time to win renewed allegiance. Since humanists by and large have taken the mantle of cultural leadership at the end of the twentieth century, we should recall that Christians have been more influential for longer periods of time than any other group in Western history. Christians recognize that numbers of adherents and length of dominance do not determine the validity of a philosophy. Their hope that the biblical world view will prevail rests upon their belief in God's providence in history. The Bible urges its readers to be faithful caretakers of its ideas and to implement its principles in all areas of life. Nevertheless, the success or failure of Christianity in any era is ultimately determined not by the faithfulness of believers but by God's will, which directs not only the times and seasons of nature, but also the reign of ideas.

Christian and non-Christian leaders alike acknowledge that their fundamental ideas directly or indirectly shape their thoughts, choices, and actions. World views thus are not only total in scope but also totalitarian in their daily, even hourly, impingement on life. Like the incessant ticking of a clock, our basic ideas continually intrude into our living. When we think, choose, and act (or fail to act), we portray for all to see what is most uniquely and intimately our own. Ideas have consequences; we act as we think. The apostle Paul said that our daily lives are like letters of recommendation "known and read by all men" (II Cor. 3:2). If our lives are really an open book, they are far less private than we may have ever realized. Our public and private behavior and conversation inevitably and distinctively reflect our ultimate commitments.

Thus we must not draw back from the conclusion that all of life is religion—that all people are religious. Religion is not reducible to private and public prayer, worship in church buildings, serving on boards and committees of religious groups, or giving money to missionaries. We should not draw a sharp line between the sacred and the mundane, the Reverend and Mr. or Mrs., the evangelist and the accountant, or so-called "full time Christian service" and ordinary jobs.

Our study of Western thinkers should confirm that all world views are religions, not just those expressed by theologians. Every philosopher we have studied intended, consciously or unconsciously, that his ideas be foundations for life. Plato, for example, was religiously devoted to a transcendent world of forms. His system was not simply an intellectual game but an all-encompassing perspective, which he proposed to replace the woefully inadequate and immoral Homeric deities. He envisioned his ideas transforming every area of Greek life.

Similarly, the Enlightenment debate between rationalists and empiricists was not a frivolous quarrel over the primacy of innate ideas or sense experience in knowledge. Both groups struggled to fill the void created by their rejection of the Christian world view and to recapture the hearts and minds of Europeans for their own world views. Kant meant his Copernican Revolution to turn the world of thought upside down. Schleiermacher refashioned Christianity to suit a romantic world in order to win people to his version of biblical faith. Darwin's theory of evolution fundamentally altered many people's perspective of themselves. As a result of his work, many saw themselves not as unique creations of God, but simply as part of the changing world of nature. Twentieth-century humanists' belief in the scientific method, existential choice, and pragmatic experimentation is no less religious than other views, even though their proponents deny belief in God.

Our survey of the cultural expressions resulting from these world views testifies to their religious foundations and the religious nature of all life. For world views are not merely a private matter; they are expressed by social groups in political and economic programs, artistic and literary works, and institutions such as the family and education. People pattern their governments, print and distribute money, regulate marriage and divorce, and send their children to college on the basis of their world views. We will examine social structures in greater detail in the second volume of our study, which focuses on cosmology, society, and ethics. At this point we simply point out that ultimate commitments, which are religious in nature, directly determine social as well as individual life. What we say, think, and do collectively— as members of familial, economic, and political groups and institutions—springs from our shared religious convictions.

Our review of the intellectual legacy of Western civilization has shown that people have espoused many different views of God, humanity, and knowledge. During those periods when a developed concept of the ultimate was expressed compellingly enough to influence large numbers of people, culture tended to be unified (e.g., biblical culture, Plato's Greece, the Middle Ages, and the Reformation). Conversely, when the ultimate has been viewed as weak and impersonal, or no one conception has held sway, culture has splintered into contradictory and diverse elements (e.g., Homer's Greece and the Enlightenment through the contemporary periods). It seems reasonable to conclude that an era's understanding of the ultimate strongly shapes for good or ill the culture of the period. Therefore, in every period of time individuals must wrestle with ultimate questions if their society is to be strong and healthy. In the late twentieth century, when society is immersed in temporal concerns, men and women must seek satisfactory answers to these questions with a renewed sense of urgency. Otherwise society will continue to fragment and disintegrate.

We have attempted to demonstrate that a correlation exists between a person's views of God, humanity, and knowledge. In the process of examining world views, we have strongly advocated the Christian perspective as unified, as coherent, and as offering true (though not exhaustive) answers to mankind's basic questions. If a person believes and accepts the biblical view that God is absolutely sovereign holy love, he will consider people to be dependent creatures who can only find their destinies and perfectibility in God. Meaning in life and salvation from sin are grounded not in human potentiality but in God's sovereign grace. In addition, if God is absolutely sovereign holy love, knowledge becomes dependent upon His gracious revelation and assistance.

The Reformational themes of *sola gratia*, *sola fide*, and *sola Scriptura* establish our theology, anthropology, and epistemology in a God-centered pattern. Certainty about our ultimate destiny and about our everyday knowledge cannot be achieved through our own human power, no matter what method we use. Our knowledge is not abstract and impersonal like a syllogism, but stems from an intimate relationship with our Creator. Certainty in the biblical perspective is similar to happiness. We obtain both not by directly seeking them, but as by-products of knowing God, which occurs through His sovereign grace. Therefore, biblical revelation is neither a record of Jewish and Christian attempts to reach God nor a compilation of their responses to His revelation. Both of these views are relativistic portrayals of God's Word. While the Scriptures contain history, poetry, and letters, they are uniquely and authoritatively God's Word written. In knowing God and His world, living according to His commandments, and experiencing salvation from our sins we must honor and glorify Him alone. Biblical views of God, humanity, and truth are not meant to discourage our efforts to gain knowledge by various scientific and experimental methods. Nor does recognition of the insights and achievements of Western thinkers detract from our belief that all knowledge is ultimately given by God. God has so constituted us that our knowledge should honor Him. Because of our limitations and the many sinful uses of knowledge, we must diligently hold what we know in obedience to His will.

Our study has demonstrated certain facts. When the ultimate is conceived as impersonal transcendence (cf. the forms and Demiurge of Plato), man will be considered autonomous, independent, and perfectible by virtue of his inherent rationality. In such a perspective knowledge becomes a self-directed ascent from the cave of ignorance to the fullness of rational enlightenment. Views like Plato's, however, fail to reconcile real, personal human beings to abstract, impersonal ideals. An impersonal, aloof, and impassive ultimate cannot supply the unique qualities such as love, personhood, and our capacity for spiritual relationships upon which Christians argue that human dignity rests. To whom or what do we pray? How do we control our passions when human strength falters?

Those who reject God and believe the world of nature is ultimate are left with two logically possible views of man. Either human beings are nature's autonomous masters, working their will upon a passive and conquerable natural world (the view of contemporary humanists and most scientists); or people are nature's pitiful servants, subject to impersonal forces or fates, the objects upon which it acts (the view of biological evolutionists such as Charles Darwin and literary naturalists such as Stephen Crane). For both groups man discovers or "creates" knowledge primarily through sensory investigation of the world. In their radical materialism, contemporary naturalists far outstrip Plato and Aristotle. For humanists nature is inert and mechanical, parts that we can disassemble and reassemble at will. Not only do they deny a personal, transcendent God; they disavow any transcendent beings and forces. And they repudiate the idea that absolute values exist.

For rationalists, empiricists, behaviorists, existentialists, positivists, and pragmatists, the ultimate is man himself, and therefore human beings are considered autonomous, self-sufficient, and self-perfectible. As we have already argued and will demonstrate in greater detail in our second volume, belief that human nature and social institutions can be perfected becomes the premise for the dehumanizing social plans instituted by Marxists, behaviorists, and others. For these groups knowledge is derived from some combination of autonomous reason, free choice, the scientific method, and behavioral engineering.

Essentially, there are two basic perspectives and two correlations we may use to summarize the options presented above. First, the view that man is independent, self-sufficient, and perfectible is logically related to the view that autonomous individuals create knowledge, and both of these convictions derive from a limited view of the ultimate. When humans consider the ultimate to be either being or becoming, they declare themselves to be either autonomous or semi-autonomous in all of life. According to a second perspective, the ultimate encompasses and transcends both being and becoming without losing its identity in either. In this view man and knowledge become dependent upon the ultimate and are not self-sufficient, autonomous, or self-perfectible.

Many contemporary thinkers favor the former viewpoint, while Christians and Jews adopt the latter. As we pointed out in our study of the medieval and modern eras, some Christians have attempted to devise a mediating position between these two extremes. While not rejecting the Christian faith, they have judged it inadequate to stand on its own and have searched elsewhere for pillars of support. Aquinas used Aristotelian reason to defend the Christian faith and constructed rational arguments from cause, motion, and design to convince skeptics of God's existence. Descartes believed the one essential thing was certainty, which he considered achievable only through geometric proofs. Kant chose conscience as his foundation for a fully rational faith, and Schleiermacher rejected both reason and conscience while claiming that another human faculty—intuition, with its awareness of the infinite—provided the indispensable and indisputable basis for Christian faith. Many twentieth-century Christians have succumbed to the claim that scientific methods alone provide a stable and secure platform for Christian truth.

Trying to erect Christian ideas on some aspect of creation, however, is like building on sand instead of solid rock. Constructing a biblical world view while affirming human autonomy means dividing a loyalty that belongs to God alone. Just as winds and tides inevitably change the contour of a shoreline, so Christians who base their faith on human categories and faculties rather than the Word of God etch new and alien patterns in our understanding of the faith.

Even though human beings have the capacity to think rationally (Aquinas and Descartes), sense right from wrong (Kant), experience God intuitively (Schleiermacher), and study the world using scientific method (post-Darwinians), we believe it is fundamentally wrong to *base* the Christian world view on human abilities or to exalt human categories above God's authoritative Word. God indeed enables us to use reason, the senses, and conscience. But they are usable only as servants who bow in worship to Him. Human intellect, empirical sensibilities, moral awareness, and intuition can be engaged and equipped to serve God. Where would we be without them? But such human abilities are given to us by God to perform their proper functions, not as lords but as obedient servants. Through them we can be filled with the mystery that is God, but none of our faculties can contain the totality of God's greatness, power, and love. God overwhelms our rationality by the excess of His being, yet without destroying our rationality. While human conscience can contemplate God's moral perfection, it can never duplicate it. The intuitive awareness that enables us to experience God should help us reverently to worship Him rather than vainly to boast that our feelings reduce the infinite to human size. Science helps us to study the cosmos and to increase our knowledge, but its primary function is to prepare us to worship the world's Creator. No human faculty can supply the crucial starting point for comprehending God and His world. Only by grounding our abilities in God alone can they be used properly.

The Bible teaches that because of our sinful nature we inevitably attempt to dethrone what is truly ultimate, to commit treason against God, by substituting something creaturely in His place (Rom. 1:16–25). People use God's good gifts to affirm their own autonomy. In sharp contrast, the biblical writers require us to submit our intellectual, moral, intuitive, and empirical faculties to God. Paul states that we are to bring our ideas into captivity to Christ (II Cor. 10:5f.). Christian thinkers must labor to render other world views captive to the Word of God. We are commanded to use reason, conscience, intuition, and science in service to the Lord. The synthesis perspective, however, repudiates the view that Christianity is all-sufficient. History shows that previous syntheses have seriously undercut the unity and ultimately the integrity of Christianity as a world view. This should compel us to reject all synthetic approaches that make something other than God the center or fulcrum of all thought.

Above all else, the challenge remains for Christians at the end of the twentieth century to think through their faith and carefully evaluate various historical and contemporary alternatives. This introductory exploration of Western ideas has attempted to enable readers to move from being spectators on the sidelines to becoming active participants in the drama of life. Since we are no longer at the mercy of others' ideas, we are responsible to defend our faith and point out naturalism in whatever form we find it, for naturalism will work itself into our very bones and undermine our faith if we allow it. Only a clear understanding and presentation of the gospel by members of this generation will ensure that our children will embrace and embody the biblical world view.

Scripture Index

General Index

Abraham, 22, 25-26, 28, 66, 132
Adam, 19-20, 49, 65f., 92f., 105, 123, 130f.
   as federal representative, 65f., 69
   two Adams, 65, 92
   rejection of historical, 148
Agnosticism, 163, 164, 246, 287
   Descartes's methodic doubt, 266f.
Ambrose, 83f.
American Humanist Association, 163, 178
Anaximander, 35, 139
Anaximenes, 35, 139
Anthropology
   anthropocentric world view, 3, 5, 7, 138, 142, 148, 264, 305f., 308, 315, 325
   creation of man, 20-22, 89
   fall of man, 24-25, 90f., 105 (see Fall)
   homo mensura, 7, 116, 132,169f.
   human goodness, 41, 43, 44, 93, 167, 170, 176
   human perfectibility, 43, 44, 47, 91, 149, 165, 167
   human progress, 165f., 170
   image of God, xv, 4, 18-21, 90f., 123, 130, 170, 198, 202, 204
   original sin (*see* Original sin; Sin)
   relation of man to gods, 34-35, 42, 45
   relationship to epistemology, 185-89, 214f., 253f.
   relationship to theology, 3, 185-89, 214f., 253f., 262f.
   soul (*see* Soul)
   views of
      Aquinas, 97-112
      Aristotle, 41-44
      Augustine, 89-94, 148
      the Bible, 14-17, 49-69, 94, 122f., 130-35, 302f.
      Calvin, 127-34
      Darwin, 153-55
      deism, 15, 141, 144, 150, 159, 166
      Dewey, 313
      Epicurus, 139f.
      Feuerbach, 151f.
      the Greeks
         Dionysian, 34
         Homer, 31-35
      Hobbes, 141
      humanists, 169-71
         critique of, 173-74
      Kierkegaard, 305-6
      Luther, 122-27
      Marx, 158
      naturalists, 150-58
      Pelagius, 92-94, 170
      Plato, 38-41
      romantics, 145f., 150
      Sartre, 302, 308-9
      Schleiermacher, 146-49
Anthropomorphism, 17

331

medieval, 119–21, 263
Common grace, 178–79
Comte, Auguste, 166, 297f.
Conscience, 199f., 324f.
Constantine, 85, 169
Conversion, 69
  examples of
    Augustine, 83–84
    Calvin, 127
    Luther, 119f.
Corporeal monism, 139, 152
Councils, ecumenical, 74, 251f.
  Ephesus, 93
  Nicaea (see Nicaea)
Covenant, 4, 11, 22–28, 66
  of creation, 22–25, 49f.
  of redemption, 25–28, 49f., 66–69
  law, 25–26
  promise, 25
  suzerain-vassal treaty, 25–26
  sanctions, 26, 64f.
Crane, Stephen, 155–56, 323
Creation, 17–18, 85, 103, 199
  Sartre on, 302
  ex nihilo, 85
  denial of, 167
Creeds 75, 77f., 80, 149, 306
Cynicism, 44f.
Darwin, Charles, 153–55, 157, 166,
  179, 320, 323
David, 22, 142–43
Death. See also Christ, resurrection of
  views of
    Aristotle, 41–42
    the Bible, 60–69
    Epicurus, 46
    Pelagius, 93
    Plato, 39
Deism, 15, 141, 144, 150, 159, 166
Demiurge, 5, 15, 40, 43, 85, 323
Democritus, 139f., 164
Depravity, total, 5, 65f., 90, 105, 124,
  127, 130f., 133
  Enlightenment rejection of, 148

Descartes, Rene, 141, 144, 166, 237,
  280, 324f.
  on epistemology, 265–69, 271f., 276
Dewey, John, 163, 312–14
Dionysian religion, 34f., 47
Dualism, 22
  biblical denial of, 20f.
  Greek, 45
  Kantian, 297, 285–87, 289
  Manichaean, 82–83, 85, 236
  Neoplatonic, 37–38, 236
  Platonic, 21, 37–39, 89, 111
  Thomistic, 106, 109–11, 250f.
Ecumenical councils. See Councils,
  ecumenical
Election, 89, 131–35
  and human accountability, 133f.
  biblical teaching of, 131f.
  Calvinist defense of, 133f.
    Arminian response, 134f.
Elijah, 14f.
Engels, Friedrich, 157–58
Enlightenment, 111f., 143–45, 165–67,
  278f., 320f.
Epicurus, 46f., 139–40
Epistemology, 185–89
  certainty, 47, 212, 237, 256, 312f.
  biblical view, 212–14
  rationalist claim, 143, 263–68,
    272, 324
  dialectic, 219f., 223, 228
  empiricism, 188, 255, 264, 279, 320,
    322f.
  critique of, 273f.
  views of
    Aquinas, 244–46
    Hume, 273f.
    Kant, 283–86
    Locke, 268–71
  eristic, 223, 228
  existentialism, xii, 291, 300–311, 323
  critique of, 309–11
  views of
    Jaspers, 307

Schleiermacher, 146–49
Socrates, 217–20
Sophists, 217–19
Erasmus, Desideramus, 123, 253
Evil. *See* Augustine, problem of evil;
  Original sin; Sin
Evolution, 170–72
  Darwinian, 153–55, 166, 320, 323
  naturalism, 170, 196, 320
  macro-, 154
  micro-, 153–54
Existentialism. *See* Epistemology,
  existentialism
Exodus/passover, 12, 27
Faith
  nature of, 87, 131
  sola fide, 122, 322
  views of
    Aquinas, 105, 108
    the Bible, 66, 100, 122, 131
    Calvin, 130f.
    Kierkegaard, 304f.
    Luther, 122, 126
  and works, 66, 68, 122, 126, 131
Fall. *See also* Original sin; Sin
  New Testament, 65f.
  Old Testament, 24f., 64
  views of
    Aquinas, 105f.
    Augustine, 89–90, 92–94
    the Bible, 131
    Calvin, 130
    Luther, 123, 253
    Kierkegaard, 304
    Schleiermacher, 148
Farel, William, 127
Feuerbach, Ludwig, 151–53, 157–58,
  168
Foreknowledge and predestination,
  134
Forgiveness, 27f., 60
Forms, ideas, 37–39, 41–43, 220f., 225,
  265, 284f., 289, 323
Freedom, 174, 177

of God's will, 129
of man's will, 313
views of
  Aquinas, 105f.
  Augustine, 105f., 124
  Calvin, 131–33
  existentialists, 305, 307f.
  Kant, 280, 285, 287–89
  Luther, 123f.
  Pelagius, 92–95
  and original sin (*see* Original sin)
French Revolution, 145
God. *See* Theology
Grace. *See also* Redemption
  Imputation, 27, 67, 108, 122,
    126, 131f.
  Infusion, 107–9
  operative, cooperative, 94, 107f.,
    124, 322
  views of
    Aquinas, 106–9
    Augustine, 91–95
    the Bible, 67, 92, 122
    Calvin, 132, 134f.
    Kierkegaard, 305
    Luther, 108, 122, 124, 126
    Pelagius, 92–94, 110
    semi-Pelagians, 94
Heaven, 33, 171
Hegel, Georg W. F., 151, 303, 311
Heidegger, Martin, 300, 308
Heraclitus, 35f., 37–38, 45, 111
Hesiod, 33f.
History
  chronology, xiii–xvi, 11
  Comte on, 298
  cyclical view, 13, 88
  Enlightenment view, 166
  general revelation, 4, 200, 242, 291
  historical power, xv
  linear, 13, 88
  meaning of, xi, xivf., 174, 197, 200
  revelatory, 11, 26, 200, 242, 291
  understanding of, xiii–xvi, 12f., 88,

Morality, 40, 44, 314, 325
and humanism, 174-77
Kant on, 287-89, 290f.
Kierkegaard on, 303f., 310
Moses, 12, 16, 22, 132
Mystics, 47, 224, 255
Natural law, 139, 144
Aquinas on, 106f., 111
and supernatural law, 109
Natural selection, 154
Natural theology, 235, 245-49, 256
Naturalism, 7
ancient roots of, 139-40
modern, 150-58, 161, 170, 175,
179, 312f., 315, 326
Nature, 13, 60, 167, 169, 291, 323
as closed system, 142, 144, 151, 153,
194
laws of, 165-66
and natural rights, 165-66
Neoplatonism, 83, 85, 124f.
Newton, Isaac, 165, 266, 270, 279f.
Nicaea, 74, 76-80, 251
Nicene creed, 149
Original sin, 65
views of
Aquinas, 105-8
Arminius, 135
Augustine, 89f., 92f., 148, 242
the Bible, 94
Calvin, 130f., 134
Pelagius, 92-93
Schleiermacher, 148
Pantheism, 15f.
Papacy, 118, 251
Parables. See Christ, parables of
Parmenides, 36, 37, 38
Peirce, C. S., 312
Pelagianism, 6, 90-94, 132
Pelagius, 90-94, 104f., 105, 110, 127,
131, 134f., 170, 257
Perfectibility, 322-24
views of
Aristotle, 43f., 229

Augustine, 90-94
the Greeks, 40, 47
humanism, 164f., 171
naturalism, 143
Pelagius, 90-94
Plato, 40, 43f., 225f., 229
Schleiermacher, 148f.
Plato, x, 12, 15, 50, 74, 105, 111, 187,
217, 265, 271, 285, 320-23
on anthropology, theology, 37-45,
144
on epistemology, 221-26
Positivism. See Epistemology,
positivism
Pragmatism. See Epistemology,
pragmatism
Predestination, 89, 91, 94-95
biblical basis of, 131-34
and human accountability, 103f.,
133f.
views of
Aquinas, 103, 131f.
Augustine, 89, 91, 94f.
Calvin, 131-35
Presuppositionalism, 256-58
Presuppositions, ix, 69, 186, 193-98,
212, 256-58, 272, 276, 297, 313
evaluating, x, xi, 256
Priesthood of all believers, 122, 124
Propitiation, 67f.
Protagoras, 164, 217f., 220
Pythagoreans, 37, 144
Rationalism. See Epistemology,
rationalism
Reason. See Epistemology, reason
Redemption, 7, 82, 94-95, 172. See
also Sacrifice; Original sin; Sin
views of
Aquinas, 105-10
Arius, 76f.
Athanasius, 77
Augustine, 91-95
the Bible, 27-29, 56, 66-69
Calvin, 131-35

CPSIA information can be obtained at www.ICGtesting.com
Printed in the USA
BVOW070325250112

281330BV00001B/66/A